Letters from Prison

Jennifer Furio

Letters from Prison

—

Voices of Women Murderers

Algora Publishing
New York

Algora Publishing, New York
© 2001 by Algora Publishing
All rights reserved. Published 2001.
Printed in the United States of America
ISBN: 1-892941-59-7
Editors@algora.com

Library of Congress Cataloging-in-Publication Data 00-012989

Furio, Jennifer.
  Letters from prison : voices of women murderers / by Jennifer Furio.
    p. cm.
Includes bibliographical references.
  ISBN 1-892941-59-7 (alk. paper)
  1. Women murderers—United States—Correspondence. 2. Women murderers—
United States—Biography. I. Title.
  HV6046.F87 2001
  364.15'23'082092273—dc21
                              00-012989

Front Cover: *Guardian of the Lost* by Veronica Compton
Back Cover: *From top left clockwise: Carol Bundy, Pamela Smart, Kristine Bunch, Diane Bowerman, Betty Broderick (center), Terri Rachals, Toni Lawrence*

New York
www.algora.com

Table of Contents

Foreword   5

A Message to the Reader   7

The Women and Their Letters

    "Laney": The Making of a Murderer   15
    Terri Rachals   21
    Kristine Bunch   45
    Pamela Smart   67
    Diane Bowerman   85
    Hope Rippey and Toni Lawrence   97
    Brenda Spencer   121
    Christina Riggs   139
    Betty Broderick   151
    Carol Bundy   161
    Shirley Curry   177
    Suzan Carson   193
    Veronica Compton   211

Epilogue   229

Acknowledgements   233

About the Author   235

Cameron Hooker

"It wasn't as hard as you think. Before long, Colleen would put herself in the box. I didn't have to beat her or rape her. She just learned her place. I was her master and she was my slave. People make it out like it's strange that she chose to stay with me for ten years. A lot of people say she was a hostage. I think she just learned her place. Slavery is misunderstood. In the end, I could let her out, she rode her bike and went to church or whatever she wanted. But if I told her to strip down, she did it. If I told her it was time for sex, we did it. It was just this understanding."

—Convicted kidnapper and rapist, serving a life sentence at Folsom Prison, California

Foreword

Letters from Prison: Voices of Women Murderers is not an exercise in voyeuristic curiosity but a journey to understand women who have been the
victims of violence that has generated further violence. This journey en-
courages us to understand that evil is not innate, and these stories may
serve as "windows of enlightenment" to encourage societal change. The
reader is not asked to forgive, accept or condone these women and their
actions, but to attempt to understand the root causes of their behaviors.

Jennifer Furio has once again skillfully procured graphic word-of-
mouth personal descriptive material from the main characters, words that
resonate with our desire to understand the "why" of murder while illumi-
nating what we already sense — that violence begets violence. This book's
contribution lies not only in its highly charged material, which would not
be readily available to even the most seasoned and serious of researchers,
but in its non-judgmental and non-exploitative presentation. It is this ele-
ment of sincerity and depth of purpose that has elicited the trust and confidence of the subjects of this book, some of whom are on death row. Ms.
Furio has been able to delve into the recesses of the lives of the perpetrators, when others have been denied.

The author has been able to humanize the seemingly "un-
humanizable" perpetrators of society's most abominable crimes. For instance, we learn that even in the darkness of infanticide women remain
nurturers. . . and they, too, suffer. Their destructive behaviors are a product

of distorted drives for survival and a repetition of early life traumatic experiences, such as abandonment by maternal figures, sexual molestation and rape, and repetitive physical and psychological abuse. The circumstances of these desperate women are left for the reader to ponder and to integrate into a conceptual scheme based on a sense of justice and morality.

Unlike their male counterparts — including serial killers — these women murderers are non-predatory. Their behavior represents a "soul death" at an early age and their words tell the story. Their crimes are crimes of survival — psychologically, physically and spiritually. These women are not born murderers. Depth psychology teaches us that the internalization of stable nurturing parental images is crucial in the formation of a healthy personality. Interference in this process results in a malignant transformation of the self. The result is a projection of deeply repressed rage onto others, usually victimizers who have recapitulated the early traumatic experiences of these women. Thus, these perpetrators engage in a "repetition compulsion" of self-destruction, rage and acting out.

Hope lies in the prevention of early abuse by addressing the needs of children early on. The solution lies with the legal system — judges and lawyers. Only with an educated understanding of these experiences and influences can laws be changed, allowing societal intervention in the lives of children to thwart this malignant transformation.

Letters from Prison: Voices of Women Murderers is an important contribution to the science of forensic psychology. It opens the doors to a sense of humanity and hope for victims and victimizers alike.

Ronald Turco M.D.
Trustee, American Academy of Psychoanalysis
Reserve Homicide Detective, Beaverton Police Department
Author of *Closely Watched Shadows: A Profile of The Hunted and The Hunter*, *The Architecture of Creativity: Profiles Behind The Mask*, and *Walk East on Burnside*.

My first published title, a compilation of letters from male serial killers, created more controversy than I had anticipated. Why would a woman choose to correspond with killers? Readers were left to wonder how I "pulled" information from the men who were being profiled, and many readers reported that they were left with a feeling of something missing.

There is a distinct value in listening solely to the voice of a killer. When the author's perspective is withheld, an intimacy with the perpetrator evolves. I believe this to be an unsettling but enlightening journey, and a unique opportunity for readers to "become" the person at the other end of the dialogue. But with new books come new ideas and new ways to relate to the subject — and to the reader.

The questions that were asked most frequently (aside from those regarding the murderers, themselves) were, What about the author — what did she say to the convicted, and what was her stance? To address those concerns, I decided to offer a few of my own letters as part of this book. After all, if the women were so candid as to reveal their darkest moments and their greatest tragedies, I should reciprocate by sharing, myself. Asking a person to reveal an intimate story is asking for a great deal of faith. The women first had to trust and, indeed, respect me, before truly opening up; a woman would certainly be less inclined to tell me why she shot her husband if she thought I would respond with a vivid description of my garden in spring! As a friend and a writer, I offered parts of myself, and stories from my own life, to women whose lives and selves have been perpetually exploited and controlled.

I am the mother of two, and married. There is no great mystery in the dichotomy between my own tranquil life and my ability to communicate with the subjects in this book. The "housewife-meets-killer" tabloid slant is not the great intrigue behind my work. In truth, this writing derives from a simple belief that we all have both an inner greatness and beauty, and an inner capacity to commit even the most evil and despised acts. Of course, we are not all murderers, and most of us will never go further than fantasizing about such an act (if that!), but we have all known moments of darkness.

Why did these women write to me? Because of my willingness to relive their tragedies with them, and to offer places where we could tap into shared commonalities. I didn't have to be a killer to understand rage. I didn't have to know rape to understand violation. I learned to speak to the women about their experiences by addressing any shred of similarity and by exposing any connection that provided the women with a belief that I could find a way to relate to them. These women needed to offer their thoughts about their crimes to someone who would listen without shock or disdain. Because I offered the women empathy, understanding, and the space to share without judgment, I succeeded in forging relationships with them.

I spoke candidly about some of my own less-than-memorable experiences, at times with shame, and at times with an insight gained only in hindsight. Sometimes, I allowed for conversation about my family, but this was kept to a minimum.

When a woman was sharing thoughts about children, possibly having killed her own, she might ask me: "How does a 'regular' person deal with frustration when her children can't be quieted?" Answering such a question, I would perhaps discuss my own family life in comparison and open up my own experiences to inquiry. While I might be empathetic to feelings of confusion and emotional despair, I could only write that I understood from afar. My openness should not be mistaken as affiliation with murderous thoughts, but rather as an intention to look more closely and more honestly.

While I was willing to disclose parts of my own life (if I felt it would help the women in their process of correspondence), I was less than eager to share specifics when it meant giving up my own privacy or that of my family. If my letters appear trite at times, it may simply be that I have chosen to edit myself in those paragraphs or pages, interrupting the dialogue for reasons of anonymity. At other times, I may seem to ramble on too long, but this may be what I sensed the woman on the other end of the correspondence needed in order to allow trust to develop. I have included only a few of my letters, since the focus of this work is the words of those women imprisoned for murder, and my role is, at heart, secondary.

My letters to the different women are as unique and individual as the women themselves. I learned how to speak on many levels and to different ages and mentalities, with the purpose of coming to understand why these women murdered — or to argue that they did not. I addressed the women in a variety of ways, not to manipulate them or to con information from them, but rather, to listen carefully to their individual needs, and to write accordingly. The book is pure, honest, and infinitely personal.

At the core of the book lies an understanding of the women whose lives have been filled with tragedy, and who have themselves created horrific tragedy; it is also the story of the woman who was interested in knowing why.

*

The letters that follow offer intimate details from the lives of women who were driven to kill. They also provide honest explorations of the emotional scars born from these women's childhood, familial, and adult experiences of violence, abuse, and neglect. Abuse and molestation weave through the lives of these female killers like road maps of pain. Their letters volunteer a recognition of the damage done to their souls, the death and decay of their spirits as women, and the overwhelming darkness that finally led them to murder.

It is not my intention to devalue the lost lives of the victims by corresponding with murderers, but until somebody listens to these women's stories, such atrocious crimes *will* continue. Evil begets evil; violence perpetuates itself; and victims of violence do what they must to survive.

In order to identify the origins underlying the violent path these women have taken and how to circumvent this in the future, each woman must be examined and understood in her entirety. For the women themselves, and for us as readers, investigating their childhoods and their own victimization is a difficult but necessary endeavor.

Why should we care to understand these killers? Because their stories and their experiences resonate with our own lives in powerful and frightening ways. Because we are all in some way connected to women like them — we either know them, or are their sisters or brothers, their friends, their children, their parents, their abusers, their lovers, their neighbors, or their victims. In the face of violence and grief, our first response is to ask *why*: Why me? Why now? Why did these women do this? Broadening our perspective to include theirs will bring insight, even compassion. Reading the letters may evoke sadness, pity, confusion — all responses to our increasing and uncomfortably real understanding of why women kill and why their crimes are neither the first nor the last acts of violence in their stories. Since these correspondences are one-on-one experiences with complex personalities, after reading their letters it becomes nearly impossible to cluster all female killers into a simplified category of evil.

Criminologists and psychologists who work in this field emphasize the importance of mitigation (the recognition of the background against which crimes occur, and the consideration of earlier histories that may alter later decisions) when discussing people who kill. In many cases, the violence in these women's lives can be traced, from their childhoods throughout their adulthoods. While most abused women and children do not commit violence later in their lives, most women who do commit violence have been violated themselves. The majority of violence committed against women and children goes unpunished, and even when such cases are brought to court, the sentences are ridiculously short.

Although it would not be feasible to have a window into every child's private life, proactive organizations geared toward helping to identify children in need do exist. Money spent on social programs is not only humane, but cost effective as well. Hopefully, fewer crimes, fewer prisons, and fewer prisoners would result from real investment in prevention. While we bemoan the cost of keeping a "lifer" in a state penitentiary (and execution is not cheap, either), intervention and prevention continue to be under-funded and labeled as unnecessary expenditures.

This lack of attention is shocking, considering that the Surgeon General has reported battery as the single largest cause of injury to women. By the hands of their abusers, between five and thirteen women are killed every day. While crime rates have gone down across the country, statistics for crimes against women have remained constant.

With such figures in mind, it isn't surprising that abused women can become obsessed with their survival and, as a last resort, some turn to violence. Such actions are not evil, but the only reality available to these women.

It appears that women face emotional cruelties from the legal system, on top of their personal suffering. The following women's stories show that the judicial process regularly fails to sympathize with women's needs and situations. After conviction, women are often relocated away from their families, their children, and their support systems. As recounted by the women in this book, many courts frequently ignore abuse and other mitigating factors, all signs of an extreme gender bias. The women I profiled frequently reported feeling that they had been punished by the justice system for not being "motherly" or "feminine" enough, for being single mothers, or for defying their gender roles.

While women comprise only a small percentage of the total U.S. prison population, they are in fact the fastest growing group in prison. The women's stories that you are about to read reveal what life in prison is like, but in a number of ways these women are not representative of the rest of the female prisoner population. The vast majority of women are in jail for non-violent crimes. At the same time, around 60% of women in prison are women of color — evidence of the extreme racial bias in the court system. One of the white women in this book, Pamela Smart, reports about death row inmates (based on her own experiences as an inmate), "I feel [that many] are underrepresented legally, and that racial discrimination often taints their convictions and sentences." While most of the cases detailed in this book received excessive and harmful media attention, it is also important to note that the stories that receive the most publicity are those of white women. The potential reasons for this are numerous and the most likely explanations can be found at the intersections of race, class, and gender.

Regardless of how much media attention their cases receive, the stories of women in prison are miserable. The crimes committed by the women in this book are often overshadowed by the excessive nature of their punishments. The following pages show that these killers were *taught* their rage. Without support or encouragement, many of these women lived their lives and fought for their survival within the narrow confines of terrifying and relentless abuse and violence.

There are a couple of exceptions, however: stories that follow patterns of team killings and serial violence. On the surface, the two women in this book whose crimes and motivations deviate from those cycles of abuse that are characteristic of most of these women's lives, but their letters are potent reminders that the notion of prisons serving as a place for rehabilitation is far from reality. Prison is a place of punishment, and while most of the women in this book have struggled to come to terms with the reality of their violent pasts and the harm that they have done, they are doing so without the support of the system and in spite of the realities of incarceration. One of the themes that emerges throughout the letters is the need for prison reform in order to protect the rights and sanity of all prisoners.

Predictably, the letters do not promise a resolution, though they do allow readers to approach a subject that is typically viewed as frightening with less apprehension. This information proves that evil is not innate, that these women's violent actions are the partial result of their physical, emotional, spiritual, psychological, and sexual abuse — all circumstances that are avoidable.

The cynical mind may argue that it is shameful to offer the killer a voice. Not so. Though some may feel guilty reading the words of a murderer, this is not a betrayal of the dead or some evil part of ourselves emerging, driven by a voyeuristic curiosity. Instead, we have a responsibility to try to understand the rage behind these women and their crimes. A willingness to hear them is a demonstration of tolerance. As we listen, we discover an ability to understand and even to accept women who have been rejected, ignored, exploited and violated.

Each of the women with whom I corresponded said that, at some point, she wished she had told someone about her terrors. As children or wives, they had learned to keep abuse a secret. As adults exhibiting their own violent tendencies, they bore another secret. Women who kill believe that they are alone in their deviance. This is a fallacy. Thousands of women live daily with depression and confusion, which can make them a danger to themselves and others.

But these fractured souls can be repaired with meaningful and honest intervention. Whether read from the standpoint of education, curiosity, or an effort to identify with the women, this dialogue informs us as individuals and as a society that patterns of violence must be understood and acknowledged before they can be stopped.

For sharing with us this wealth of information, the women are commended. They were brave enough to write to you, when they made their decision to write to me. These women allowed strangers to look inside their souls.

Before you judge the inmates' earnest attempts to express themselves, stop for a moment. Allow the opportunity for empathy. Do not worry: these people will not cease to be judged. The media will continue to present society with images of murderous women — "monsters" so disgraceful and frightening that they satisfy the public's need for blood, violence, and hate. And beyond the cameras women in prison will continue to suffer — violence, rape, separation from children and family, even death.

Whatever the final conclusion, these letters force an intimacy with the female killer. Seen through their own words rather than through the typically sensationalized "demonic" light, these individuals can be seen as human beings, women who lost a part of themselves along the way.

"Laney"

Or, The Making of a Murderer

This narrative was related to me by one of my anonymous correspondents. She is now sitting on death row. While the depiction of "Laney's" childhood is terrifying, her adult life is equally unsettling. Angrily using her body as an asset, she continued a life of prostitution. She claims it was next to impossible to learn another trade. She was unable to break out of this subculture, for lack of funds, education, and support.

Her rage toward men was so great, her post-trauma so severe, that she began to kill any "John" who ignited a recollection of childhood rape. The humiliation of sodomy, hitting, even verbal mockery became a license to kill.

Unfortunately, her story is not unique.

*

Laney didn't care what happened next. She'd half-assed packed the few T-shirts she could find in her cluttered room. She was already wearing her only pair of pants — torn jeans, her right ass-cheek startin' to show (her daddy'd teased her about that, he'd tickled her through the tiny hole with his big finger, making it a bigger hole, a more embarrassing problem). She grabbed her daddy's duffle bag. She started to giggle, a kind of crazy laugh. She was thinkin' about him lookin' for it — he never missed something until it was gone (including mamma), but he'd beat the fuck outta her if he knew she'd actually gone to his closet and snagged it for herself. She stopped giggling, and started thinkin' about the closet. Now she was all choked up again. Shit. She tried to not cry, but her mamma leavin' her had been the worst part of everything. And bein' in the closet, lookin' through all the crap on the floor, tryin' to find that stupid ass bag, she'd smelled her mamma.

It was goin' on weeks now since she'd just gotten up off that couch, and started walkin' — Laney thought she must be wantin' some air or some thing, but her body got smaller and smaller, and she was just walkin' away from the house, her mamma just walkin' nowhere! She must have had someplace to go, since she never came back, but her closet, she'd left those clothes of hers layin' in the closet. And time passed, but when Laney had pressed her nose against her mamma's pile of laundry, there she was again. Her "daddy," that's what he told her she had to say, but he wasn't really; and his stuff smelled like shit. Like him. He never smelled like nothin' but shit. That was what he was, anyways. Laney started shakin' her thoughts off. They weren't goin' nowhere helpful. Nothin' mattered now. Nope, nothin' mattered since she'd be leavin', just like her mamma. Too bad they couldn't have gone off on that walk the both of them, but she'd get out just the same.

It wasn't that she couldn't take her life, livin' there. She was pretty tough about it all. Who fucked her, daddy's friends. . . she could take it. But she couldn't take it from him. Smelly old sweaty scum comin' at her night after night after night. Laughin' and coughin' and climbin' on her like a dog. Laney felt her stomach get sick.

Her daddy's friends had been buyin' her time for as long as she remembered. She never got none of the money, but they give her the drinkin' — vodka. Laney loved the booze. It felt hot on her throat, and it was real quick, takin' the pain away, and her thinkin' about what was around her. Who was around her. On her. This had been goin' on since she'd turned five. She wondered how she remembered her time gettin' started, but she knew that five was pretty young, even for whores.

Now Laney was fourteen. She'd had her period for two years. Daddy's crowd had backed off some. They didn't like her growin' up. Laney didn't get that. They fucked her like a woman, but her daddy shaved her so she might look five-years-old again! None of this made much sense. And still, the men didn't want her like before. Except her daddy. He told her he deserved her, since she couldn't make no money lately. It was the least she owed him.

But tonight, before her thoughts about mamma, before the closet, and before the duffle bag and the packin', he'd come callin' on her while she was asleep, and something had hit her (besides him) so clear and hard that she knew she'd never sleep in his stinkin' house again. She didn't know how, but she'd figure some way to leave sometime tonight.

He'd come tellin' her he wants her to come inside to her mamma's bed. Something like that. She'd been asleep. But she heard him good enough. He'd said somethin' about mamma. Laney couldn't take him talkin' about her, after all the years of watchin' him make her scream like a baby, the beatin' and the rapin' and all that shit. And nothin' had helped. He'd promised her if she'd do for him he'd lay off her mamma, but he just got himself two fuckin' slaves instead of one.

Laney knew her mamma's leavin' had something to do with that last time he'd beat her. Left her mamma's mouth cut so wide open, found her teeth layin' on the floor. Laney found bloody toilet paper on the bathroom floor the morning after her mamma left. And Laney guessed she knew, her mamma didn't have no choice to leave or be killed. And now, Laney was feelin' just like that. Fuckin' gonna' get raped in her own mamma's bed.

Laney knew if he gave her the vodka it would take her thoughts away but she just kept hearin' herself whispering 'no. . .' Daddy knew what she'd sacrifice for booze, but not this. Not in those sheets.

"Lick me in your mamma's bed," daddy'd ordered. First Laney thought it was another bad dream.

"Joey's there, waitin' on you," he whispered. "Joey wants to watch me do you, Laney, and he'll give us fifty for it so move your ass out there and lick my cock." Laney rubbed her eyes. No dream. Nope. It's him again and that pervert guy, Joey. Standin' in her doorway, laughin' like a schoolgirl. The sex wasn't new, but how come he had to push her? Why in there? She shook her head.

"I'm gonna' smell your mamma all over them sheets when you do me, Laney." His breath was all boozy, and she couldn't breathe too good.

"Up, horsey head, giddy it on up. . ." That was daddy's pet name for Laney. He told her she had a head faced like a horse. Long and ugly but a big mouth good for something. Her face was already kinda' bad complexioned. Not zits, but him hittin' on her had made her face bumpy and there were lines on it. Still, she wasn't no horse — no pet for him. She pushed his head back off her face. She knew she'd either leave or die after that. Before she knew anything, he hit her to the floor, the impact of his fist on her cheek made her see dark. She could feel her nightie up, her boobs were jigglin' around and her ass was gettin' burned on the rug. Daddy had her feet and was draggin' her to mamma's room. She was wakin' up enough to see the big redhead smile down on her with his yellowed teeth. Joey was hollerin' in back of her, "make her let you stick her good! Get it good! Let's do it good!"

Laney was surprised in the middle of all this. Joey's voice behind her. She considered Joey just a watcher. He never did her. He paid to watch Daddy, but it was gettin' more violent and he was real excited. Shuffled onto the bed, she was startin' to feel her eyes were burnin'. She squeezed her lids tight. She wasn't gonna let 'em see her cry.

Her mouth ached from the men, but her mind wandered. She wished she could have a mouth full of vodka instead of Daddy. Laney thought of her mouth separate from her body, or herself. It was like this tool. Like you use a hammer, or a shovel. Her daddy made her use her mouth. The child in Laney didn't know how to argue this; in its own way, it made sense. It paid the bills. . . but it hurt, still.

Laney knew her daddy was ready to explode. She saw two cocks starin' her in the face, she heard the laughs. She thought it was weird, because she was excited, too. She figured, this was when she always got excited, 'cause this meant they'd be happy for awhile, and mostly, it would be over quick, now. Laney started screaming, "Fuck me! Fuck me!" The men loved it. She was begging for it. Laney knew in all their thrill they'd hurry things up that much more. Thank God, especially since, not gettin' boozed first, this one had been pretty hard. She was feelin' pain in her ass, and for the first time since they'd been over her, she knew they'd fucked her both places. She touched herself, and smelled her finger, bloodied from feeling her anal hole. He'd been in there. She was sick. But she was alone now in the bed. They'd gone in a split second. She took advantage of the moment to smell the sheets, her mamma. In spite of herself, she wanted to hold on to them sheets. It was twisted up. She had to let go, like her mamma, but she didn't want to, neither.

Laney got up off the bed, straightened up her nightie. Like the sheets, her clothes had got bloodied. She really needed a drink. And that's when it came to her. Daddy would do this for her — all things considered. "Daddy, go down t'market and get my vodka, we ain't got none here." She held her breath. If ever there were her moments when she deserved a favor — and just as she was turning blue, daddy and Joey walked outside, down the street!

And that's when she went for the closet.

And here she was, Laney, all packed up and ready to go. Where? At least she knew — ugly, horse-faced or not, that she was payable, fuckable. That would be a start.

Laney figured she'd make it on the streets, and so she followed in her mamma's footsteps and just started walkin' down the dark way. Gettin' smaller, and smaller and smaller. She figured she'd fuck a dog for food if need be. She'd fuck just about anything before she'd let that redheaded fuck touch her body again. Not daddy, and not on those sheets.

TERRI RACHALS

A prosecuting attorney dubbed Terri Rachals the "murderess of the century" for her ostensible role in the deaths of at least twenty patients in a Georgia hospital's ICU unit where she worked as a nurse. Charged with injecting lethal doses of potassium chloride into patients ranging in age from 3 to 89, the 23-year-old faced a possible death sentence. Despite the media's and the prosecutors' firm assertions of guilt, Terri Rachals's culpability is surprisingly open to question; the story is extremely complex.

Terri was a mother and a nurse. The initial allegations shocked her friends and co-workers, who knew her to be responsible and nurturing, at home and at work. Terri was a dependable caregiver and a regular churchgoer. She spent most of her free time with her family or with members of her congregation. Friends described Terri and her family as "friendly and sociable." Terri loved her son, her husband, and their lives together. When the news broke, everyone suddenly began to wonder what darkness might have been hiding beneath such a blissful exterior.

In truth, Terri did have a secret past, a hidden story of childhood trauma that haunted her. Terri's friends now realize that she never seemed to mention a relationship with a mother or father, though they had thought nothing of it at the time. Only at the trial, in 1986, did the truth surface and the reasons for her silence become clear. Throughout her childhood, Terri had been physically and sexually tortured by her adoptive father and abandoned by the women in her life, who were the only ones who might have had the power to protect her.

Terri's successful adult life is a testament to her strength and resilience. Hired by the Phoebe Putney Hospital in Albany, Georgia in the early 1980s, her work record was flawless. However, in the wake of the murders, hospital administrators directed their suspicions toward Terri, citing evidence that most of the overdoses were administered during her shifts in the intensive care unit. It is not uncommon to use potassium chloride on patients with heart ailments and, when used properly, the drug opens valves and aids the recovery process. If used in higher amounts, however, the medication may cause seizures, coma, even death. The murders, which happened between the fall of 1985 and February 1986, were the result of such overdoses.

When Terri was arrested, the media pounced on the story of this outwardly innocent yet possibly murderous wife and mother. The incongruity became a national fascination, with criminologists classifying her as an "Angel of Death" — before the trial. The term refers to a woman who kills for the glory that comes from desperately (and publicly) attempting to save a person's life, a woman who therefore risks people's lives just to be in a position to receive a few pats on the back. By labeling Terri as a needy killer, and officializing her guilt with a psychological term, criminologists and the media further diminished the potential for uncovering the truth of Terri's case. When such labels are applied without adequate investigation, the effects can be devastating.

The media's portrayal, coupled with comments from investigators and psychologists, drew a sinister picture of a woman who killed to get attention. "Experts" then found that her personal life fell in line with her new "profile": Terri's husband had cerebral palsy and was incorrectly described as feeble and easily controlled. While Terri's husband did, in fact, have the disease, he also ran a business and helped take care of their son. After several months in the limelight, everything about Terri's life was becoming more and more distorted, and reality seemed to be slipping out of Terri's grasp.

In a state of confusion, Terri confessed — in essence driving the nails into her own coffin. She told the Georgia Bureau of Investigation that she may have been responsible for five murders, explaining that she suffered from "fugue states," or blackouts. Terri herself reasoned that perhaps she had committed these horrific acts during one of her "spells". These fugue states were inexorably linked to the past that she had kept hidden. As was later revealed, regular rape by her adoptive father over a nine-year period had resulted in her disorder and, while separation from her abuser had put an end to the sex, the fugue states had persisted.

Later found to be the only evidence that actually held up in court, Terri's confession is a convergence of realities. When the investigations began, Terri knew that she had consciously tried to help Sam Bentley, an 89 year-old man who suffered from dissimulated intervascular clots (if you touched his skin, his pores would bleed), to die. Sam Bentley had been begging for his life to be terminated, but his family was unwilling to let him die. After his legs were amputated, Bentley was given two weeks to live. When he asked Terri to help him end his life sooner, she agreed, and injected him with a lethal dose of potassium chloride. Bentley recovered from the ensuing heart attack, but died within two weeks anyway. Knowing that she had already attempted to assist in one man's death, and recognizing that because of her blackouts large portions of her life remained unaccounted for, Terri believed in the possibility that she was the murderer — unbeknownst even to herself. Feeling trapped and under intense stress, Terri confessed to two investigators who claimed to want to "help" her. She trusted the two men, who approached her with intimidating authority, and fell into a pattern of dutiful submission by telling them what they wanted to hear.

Terri's life disintegrated further, after her confession; but the community at large now felt at ease. Her guilt was surprisingly convenient and comfortable. With the madwoman apprehended, it was now safe to go back to the clinic; Phoebe Putney Hospital would no longer suffer the damaging reputation of having a killer walking the corridors in a nurse's uniform. In addition, her confession helped the investigators to wrap up their case and quickly go to trial.

The crimes with which Terri was charged are as confusing as the rest of her case. Initially, she was suspected in the deaths of 26 patients, though seven were immediately thrown out. Prosecutors then tried her for the remaining 19 deaths, which were quickly reduced to five — only the patients who had actually died during Terri's shift. After consultations with her lawyer, Pete Donaldson, Terri entered a plea of not guilty.

Unlike the media and the public at large, who had convicted her before the trial even began, the jury had a difficult time reaching a verdict. With psychological tests backing up her claims of abuse, as well as the fugue states and emotionally wrenching testimonials from friends and family, the jury found Terri an extremely complicated woman. In spite of her childhood, Terri had persevered academically and socially. She did not come across as a potential deranged killer or an "Angel of Death," but as a woman suffering the traumas brought on by years of sexual abuse.

Finally, on September 25, 1986, Terri was found guilty of one count of aggravated assault. Discounting any mental instability and deeming her fugue states to have been feigned, the prosecution pushed for a harsh sentence despite her seemingly minor conviction. In the eyes of the prosecutors, the argument was plain and simple: Terri was a cold-blooded killer who deserved to be severely punished. In a surprisingly harsh move, Terri was sentenced to serve 17 years at the Georgia State Correctional Facility for Women, followed by three years probation. Privately, in chambers, the judge assured Pete that Terri would never serve out the entire sentence, but would most likely be paroled before long.

Three years later, and with no sign of Terri's release in sight, Pete Donaldson took Terri's case to the Georgia Supreme Court. Terri's appeal was denied on the basis of Georgia's "grid system" — a system used by the court to evaluate the potential impacts of their decisions. Looking at Terri's case, the court weighed the power of the media versus politics, public opinion versus justice. The justices argued that the public viewed Terri as a serial killer whose light sentence of aggravated assault was based on a wrongful technicality. In such a climate, the judges knew that were they to give Terri a lesser sentence, they would be attacked by the press and would risk their jobs and their political status. The justices explained Terri's extreme sentence with the generic claim that "it is for the good and safety of our communities."

Like many other women in the remote southern prison, Terri believes that it didn't matter much what the jury decided. Once she was inside the walls, she felt an ominous sense that she might never be allowed out. Still, Terri has tried to make the most of her incarceration, spending years in therapy trying to understand how she might unwittingly have been guilty of murder and how her coping mechanisms might have endangered the lives of others.

Terri has many supporters, including Pete Donaldson who still handles her case *pro bono*, and family members ranging from her ex-mother-in-law to her sisters and brothers. Describing her profound impact on his life, Donaldson writes that: "I am not the same man I was when I met Ms. Rachals. I have compassion in a way I never knew, a desire to understand why women commit their crimes; whereas, before, I only knew how to help the justice system punish them." Terri's gentle manner, her thoughtful words, and her earnest struggles toward healing provide ongoing evidence of the truth and honesty of her character. She is a woman who has overcome enormous obstacles, and whose fight continues.

After years of working to deal with her abusive and violent past, Terri now has little power over her future. Separated from her son, now sixteen, Terri has spent her time in prison attempting to heal from her long and painful history of abuse, and it is that history that actually led to her incarceration. Though she finds it difficult to address her past directly, through poetry Terri has found a window into the dark places in her own soul that had been hidden even from herself.

Such a discovery has come at a high price. She laments missing watching her son grow up and, as in one of her poems included here, expresses utter joy when he visits. She is no longer married, but she and her ex-husband remain friends. He admits that "no marriage could survive the duress we faced."

Terri's torment is multi-layered, as she deals with loss, grief, and violation in her past, in the present, and in her future. Terri's letters reveal the depth of her compassion and the criminality of the sentence imposed on her. Unable to prove that she did not commit the crimes, Terri honors the memory and the lost lives of her ostensible victims.

Their suffering, and the suffering of their families, are often in the fore-front of her mind. Terri is also committed to sharing her story with others so that other women in her own situation might know that they are not alone, and might find the tools to seek help.

Terri receives a parole hearing every three years; the latest was in December 2000. Her perspective on her life, her crime, and the lives lost, is clear and eloquent: she explains that "the victims are gone, and I can't change that; but I can work on myself and my issues with sexual abuse. More importantly, I can share the damage with others, the dangers of trying to keep it all a secret. I will grieve always, for the loss of the patients, and for my own family. I hope people will hear my story and feel motivated to get honest with themselves. I feel like, at one time, I was just like any other kid. But for all of those years of rape and humiliation, I was no longer like everyone else. I thought I was the only person on earth [to suffer sexual abuse]. Now I realize that's what we all think."

As she has struggled to use her time in prison as an opportunity for healing, Terri has felt the need to reach out — not only to other inmates and victims of sexual abuse, but also to the family of her victim, Samuel Bentley. The following is a letter Terri wrote, expressing her remorse, her commitment to rehabilitation, and her acknowledgment of the suffering created as a result of her actions. Like many of the women in this book, she thinks constantly of her victims and their families, and longs to assure them that she will never forget the damage she has done or the pain she has caused.

February 22, 1999

To the Family of Mr. Samuel Bentley,

In 1995 I wrote a letter to you through the Dougherty County District Attorney's Office expressing my remorse for the crime I committed against your family member. Since I never received any indication that you received that letter, it has been heavy on my heart to write once again to express my deep sorrow for my actions.

It has been 13 years since my arrest and conviction. Never has a day gone by in all of these years that I haven't thought of Mr. Bentley and you, his family. Never has a holiday passed that I haven't realized that I played a part in you not being able to share that day with Mr. Bentley. I have paid over these years, asking God for His forgiveness. I have spent these years seeking therapy and [participating in] various groups including Victims' Impact on Crime. For years now I have realized that my decision 13 years ago to try to help end M. Bentley's pain and suffering was *not* my choice to make. The only thing I can beg of you to realize is that this was the right and caring thing to do. I broke God's and man's law in the process and I am so sorry.

During my trial, a great deal of time was spent focusing on the sexual, emotional and physical abuse that I encountered from my adoptive father. This abuse occurred over many years and affected my life greatly. It also affected the way I dealt with pain and suffering. This is not meant in any way to try to justify or blame my actions on my childhood abuse. I am fully accountable and responsible for my actions. The abuse did affect my life and thinking processes greatly. I have received several years of Sexual Abuse Survivors therapy and can honestly say that this therapy has changed my life and helped me heal.

Because of my actions, I have hurt and affected the lives of your family and my family. My only son has grown up without his mother at home. I have never been there for him when he was sick or been to one of his baseball games. Please do not misunderstand me. I am not asking for your sympathy. I just want the chance to explain how sorry I am and that I realize how much I have hurt so many lives.

It is my fervent hope that one day you will find forgiveness in your heart for me. The act of forgiveness, I realize, is a gift and cannot be expected or demanded. I yearn for it, however.

Ten million times I have wished that I could turn back time and reverse my actions. If that were possible I surely would have done it. All

I can do, however, is to live out the remainder of my life with the knowledge of how much I hurt your family. I will serve the remainder of my prison sentence looking for ways to better myself. I offer to you the opportunity to express any feelings that you have — whether they be positive or negative. Please write to me at the enclosed address or through the District Attorney's office if you wish. I really appreciate your time and meant this letter as no intrusion to your privacy or to cause you any further pain. I only wanted and needed to relay the depth of my remorse and sorrow for my actions.

Very Sincerely,
Terri Rachals

Dear Ms. Furio,

Thank you for your letter of support. I was shocked and quite upset when I read it, however — as I knew nothing about the book. A little over a year ago, a graduate student wrote to me, asking questions about my childhood. Then she wanted to come see me. My counselor at the prison in Atlanta had her fax information and I then refused to see her because she had misrepresented herself to me throughout the entire time of our correspondence — her dissertation was on female serial killers. Can someone just do these things?

Ms. Furio, it's been over 13 years and it just seems as if it will never end. My family is tired — I am tired. I am not a monster. Yes, I had a horrible childhood and "the system" was nowhere around then. I have done everything that is humanly possible within this past 13 years to make amends and better myself. All I can say in my defense is that I never did anything with a malicious heart.

Please respond with information about this book. I guess if it is all accurate, there is nothing I can do — I have been wanting to write a book about my life but don't really know where to start — at least then I could tell my side of things, you know? My attorney said he would help, but he really doesn't have the time. What kind of writing do you do?

I know this letter sounds disjointed and rambles and I apologize — this has really thrown me for a loop — I do trust you to correspond with me, mainly because you were honest in your account of the book. I value honesty above all else.

Please write me back soon. I look forward to your letter.

> Sincerely,
>
> Terri Rachals

Dear Ms. Furio,

Thank you for your letter. I am interested in telling my story but trust, for me, comes very slowly — life has made me this way. If I may ask you some questions, maybe this will help:

How did you become interested in writing about incarcerated women?

What is your background. Are you a journalist or an *author*, or do you have a law degree?

Could you send me some excerpts from your writings — we can only have books sent from the publisher and only with a lot of red tape — but if you sent photo-copied pages in a manila envelope, I could have that.

I guess I'm trying to get a "feeling" for the kind of person you are, professionally. I couldn't bear to be exploited further. Mostly, the thought of any undue pain to my son or to my ex-husband. I have written a lot over the years — a lot of poetry. It has been very cathartic, getting the pain out on paper. I look forward to hearing from you. And hope that maybe we will be able to work together to tell my story.

I'm enclosing a copy of one of my poems dealing with my childhood sexual abuse. And how for years I'd never look into my eyes in a mirror. Through years of therapy this has changed, but it's all there and still very real. I felt so ashamed. Victims of sex crimes always do. And also, I was very angry. I still am, but I'm aware. It's not shoved deep inside of me, where even I don't fully recognize it. The fugue states were a "self-permission" to be insane — Terri the good nurse, and the deeper person who partly wanted to protect others from similar abuse, who partly wanted to kill anyone who looked like an abuser. It was so dangerous. And when I think how so many people are equally fragile. Equally abused. I hope people will know they're not alone when they read this. That's the life-changing part: taking the secrecy out of all of this.

Thanks for listening and caring enough to ask.

Terri

HAUNTED EYES

in the mirror
i'd glance at varied parts of me;
never into my eyes...
a glance revealed the memories,
betrayed the silence.
the memories.
screaming to be remembered
to be regurgitated like my food;
get it out!
get it out of me!
i'd cover the grooves encircling my ankles
etched like a brand on a cow...

now,
i glance a little and see
the unerasable terror in my haunted eyes.
they remember.
they calculated the tears,
the drops of blood fused with red clay;
they recorded the screams
replayed like an antiquated, broken phonograph
reverberating off the walls of the tractor shed...
the moon recoiled its glow
the owls were mute.

no more!
clenching my jaws the screams erupt
like drops of sweat,

> *uncontrollable;*
> *atrocities flail like newly caught catfish*
> *gasping for air*
> *as they die:*
>
> *no longer silent*
> *the truth spews forth like your semen...*
> *my haunted eyes castrate you!*
>
> *Terri Rachals*
> *10-92*

Dear Jenny,

I was thinking just this weekend that I hadn't heard from you in some time. It was a misunderstanding on my part I guess — in your last letter you said you were going to read my poems some more and then write me back and I guess I was waiting on that. I've been writing quite a bit lately and I will continue to correspond with you — I guess I don't really know where to begin. There's so much inside me, so much I'd like to say.

I saw my son today, so I am very emotionally "full" tonight. He was two-and-1/2 when I was incarcerated and he will be 16 this coming October (and 7" taller than me, and starting to *shave*!!). It amazes me how close we are in spite of all the years apart. I write to him all the time, though, and have done so since before he could read. He saves all of my letters and cards. I love him so much more than I could ever put into words if I wrote for the rest of my life! There's such a gentle loving spirit within him.

I'm enclosing a copy of a poem I've written recently, "Childhood 101." I've also written more poems of healing lately. I was diagnosed as having "fugue state" (fugue means "flight") which would occur under tremendous stress, such as that which I endured as a child. I literally ran to a "safe place" within my mind as a child. I no longer need "flight", which is a tremendous blessing. As an adult, sanity vs. insanity became a conscious choice and I believe it was because of the emotional healing I was offered, the love and support given and the prayers of Christians when I was unable to pray for myself, that I chose sanity. Had I been surrounded by apathy, like so many around me, I am not certain that the choice would have been the same.

Thank you for your encouragement and supportive belief in me. I do look forward to hearing from you soon.

God Bless You,
Terri

CHILDHOOD 101

In the early years I learned the rules:
Take the phone off the hook
Don't turn on the TV
Don't flush the toilet
Don't talk
Don't laugh
Don't walk where the floor creaks
Scarcely breathe
or cough
or sneeze lest it shatter the
safety of his drunken snores.
Life is fragile —
Hold shoulders rigid with arms lightly at sides.
Make whole existence a whisper,
Tiptoe through this life of glass
always, always scared

Terri Rachals

Dear Terri,

I just read your letter. I was happy to hear from you. The poems mean a lot to me. They allow me insight into both your despair and your hope. I appreciate that you are willing to share.

You don't have to thank me for wanting to know you better! I want to know you. I believe your allegations of sexual abuse. I believe that *that* was the "instigating factor" underlying whatever tragedies occurred over the next years of your life. But as I understand it you did so much good, too. That is so often the case. When a person comes from abuse, if you could take that damage away, that person would probably never deal with such heinous demons. I don't think in your case you knew exactly what was happening to you. I do believe you would not have acted out as you did, without your own horrors driving you to a point of insanity.

I have written about serial crime, which is your "label" — serial killer. I know that you aren't a serial killer. It's just headline news. It's not who you are. A series of crimes can be committed, without dubbing someone a serial killer. You barely knew you were acting, if at all. Your testimony demonstrates that the fugue states took away recollection. Even if you committed multiple acts, the definition of serial killer must be deleted if you blacked out (my opinion). It sounds as if I'm a quack justifying your murders. That's not it. But if psychologists were standing as judge and jury, a lot fewer women would be facing such stigmas.

I feel that whatever you did, it didn't "belong" to the real Terri Rachals. I think when you committed crimes against other persons, it was a tragic way of acting out against circumstances that created rage within you. Unresolved rage toward a stepfather who violated you; worse, he never suffered a consequence — much less offered an admission of guilt. That would create mental dismantling. In spite of all this, you tried very hard to carry on a loving life with a husband, child, friends and church.

I am very much centered and focused on my own family, our church and our life there. Spirituality is the core of our existence. As a Lutheran, I believe in grace alone. I am not a "holy-roller," but I know what my priorities are. I think He would want others to look at you with grace. You are not evil, and you deserve to be loved. In fact, the biggest difference between you and me is that I was never tortured as a child. And not all who have been abused will kill, but many will suffer related disorders. You did. It's Russian Roulette. Anyone is a possible candidate for impaired thinking, dangerous thinking, if they live a life of such unspeakable violation.

Is such a theory acceptable? Not acceptable? I only can say that I see the rationale.

I hope I don't come off too strong. I think I tend to be too straightforward. Let me know.

Jen

Hi Jenny,

How are you? It was great to receive your letter today. I love to hear my name at mail call. No, I don't even hear from any of my old friends. I'm long forgotten to them. I love to write letters but it seems it has become a lost art in this fast-paced society where e-mail sites are given instead of addresses now! The only real penpals I have are in prison, and you. It's lonely to be so cut off from the outside world.

Abuse as a child — a young child — did damage my inner ability to trust and yes, as you indicated, there is a real battle at times within myself — it is as you described, however, it's been like that all of my life. I wouldn't know how it felt not to have to weigh out every minute situation. God is working greatly in my life and I have come so far in learning to trust Him as my Heavenly "Father." I have been doing a lot of Bible study and have been in touch with Joyce Meyer of Joyce Meyer Ministries. She was abused as a child and is so anointed of God. I can relate to her — she is down to earth and most importantly she has "been there!"

In answer to my divorce. . . I believe it was the constant stress that broke up my husband and me. He wanted to have a life again. He stood with me through *everything* that happened, never wavering; then, after it was over, after the appeals, he just couldn't take it anymore. I will always love him. He has raised my son — never saying a negative word about me — into a sweet-spirited, strong, Christian young man. Yes, I love him and I hold no ill feelings toward him for divorcing me, for I know my actions brought to him a suffering and constant torment for years.

Thank you so much for being a "constant" friend. God is helping me untie all the knots I've been tied into for so long. The fact that you care about me astounds me at times — I wonder why I've been blessed by your continuous care and your belief in me. My son's birthday is a difficult time for me, switching around here. . . please pray with me that this year will be easier. I'm enclosing a poem about my son, "Silent Truce."

Again: *any* organizations that you think might help me, I will write. I want desperately to reach out, Jenny — sometimes I struggle in knowing how. I want to help others and get help also. I am very thankful for your support and efforts on my part.

I guess I'll close for now, I've got several letters to write. We are going to be allowed to order from the Steakhouse for a Christmas dinner on Dec. 10 as a part of the Honor dorm. Although I don't eat much meat, I'm looking forward to a baked potato! Anyway, I hope to hear from you next week — I hope you and your family are well,

Love,
Terri

SILENT TRUCE

Bugle boy pants
high-top Reeboks
psychedelic cap of purple and green
seven years old
flesh of my flesh
grown under my heart and it is...
Visitation is over
time to say good-bye
silence...
so much to say... You talked of Braves' Games
your best buddy Bret
diving into the swimming pool
Daddy
your brand new red bat
tell me of when I was little, you said,
of when you were at home...
I talked of lullabies and rocking chairs
cups of water thrown from your bathtub ship
Giggles over things you've now outgrown...
Home...
you never ask anymore
afraid of the repeated reply;

silence screams with unspoken pain.

Two sets of green eyes meet

to reiterate the truce;

as the unrelenting war

rages on in our kindred souls.

by Terri Rachals

Dear Jenny,

Hi. Thanks for your letter and the bio. I'm enclosing your letter back so that I can make corrections in some areas that are marked. You're right in that I really do not know what I actually did. Most of my memory of my time at the hospital and of my childhood (*stress times*) is in images rather than actual chronological, step-by-step remembrances. I think that's why my poetry is so vivid. I remember feelings and "snapshots" if you will. I do know that whatever I did, it was not with malice. I know that, with everything that is in me. I know now it was not my choice to make — my attorney, and several of the psychologists believe that I sought a way to end my patient's suffering in a way that I had wanted someone to end mine (as a child). I remember begging God to make my Daddy stop — and I could never understand why God didn't answer my prayers. Finally I decided God *didn't love* me. It has taken *years* to work through this area and be comfortable with the idea of God as my father.

I hate the way the media exploited my husband. Yes, he had cerebral palsy. But he was capable without me, though the media used his disease to further exaggerate my "need" to care-take, and then kill. Label for this: "Angel of Death." On that term alone, I stood as evil, convicted. My husband needed *no* help from me on a daily basis. He raised our son — *alone* — and he owns his own business, which he operates himself. He walks with a slight limp and very slightly he slurs. To hear the media portrayal, he is/was an invalid that I was taking advantage of to satiate my own sick desire to be the superior nurturer. If anything, it was him who has nurtured me.

I am not evil. I love God, I am living normally. I am the victim of abuse. It was extreme and so was my response. I can grieve but I no longer ignore the roots of my disorders. Today I work in the law library. I would like for people to see me as I am Jenny. Not an emotional crip-ple because that is no longer me. That WAS me before therapy, before God fixed the broken places. Thank you for helping me.

Terri

Dear Jenny,

You asked me for a commentary, something over-all about my life. I looked over the letters of mine that you sent back. I don't know if I told enough in my letters to make people really sit down and think about what damage can come from sexual abuse. That was what I had wanted to do. Then I thought about it, and beyond that, there is all that has happened since that first day, the day I was initially interviewed as a suspect. The spiral into Hell. I use my poems to get my feelings out. My counselor thinks — knowing that blackouts are still a part of how I *can't* remember certain things — that the poetry is good for me. Writing has triggered things, too. It has made me realize that I am scared of this place, this system that had the power to hold me. There is more I want people to know about my life here. Please include some of these last three pieces if you can. Thank you for everything and hope these help.

Love, Terri

WORK #1

The day was Thursday. I went to work as usual at 2:30pm, after baking chocolate chip cookies for Roger and Chad, and taking Chad to the baby-sitter's house. After being escorted to talk with the GBI (GA BUR INV) by Mrs. Diane Hall, the head nurse in SICU, I sat in the 9th floor conference room waiting to cooperate with the agents. It never entered my mind to request that an attorney be present while I was being questioned. I wanted to help in any way that I could.

I remember very little about the actual conversation in the confer-ence room, on that day that turned into evening before I was finished. It was then that I decided that I just wanted to die. I had been convinced by those agents (Sweat and Musick) that I had committed murder repeatedly. I was so confused and in a state of shock. I remember Agent Musick telling me that his wife was a nurse; he wanted to help me. Agent Sweat talked quickly, telling me the evidence against me in rapid-fire sequence. I remember asking for Mrs. Hall to be allowed to come into the room with me while I gave my statement on tape. I was so devastated by this time that I just wanted someone with me that I knew. After that was finished, I asked to see Dr. Douglas Calhoun, a surgeon whom I respected and who was my personal physician. He came up to see me and after talking to me, called Dr. Turner, a psychiatrist, because he felt I was suicidal. Dr. Turner admitted me to the Psychiatric Intensive Care Unit at the hospital. I was given medication (a sedative) and later re-medicated because I would not stop crying. I could not sleep. I think Roger was called and came to the hospital that night. I don't remember what I said to him. I only remember him asking me, "Terri, what did you tell them?"

The next morning Dr. Turner gave me a physical and talked to me about how I was feeling, asking if I wanted to die, if I had thought about ways to do it. Later, he stated that he felt that I was only trying to avoid spending a night in jail.

Shortly thereafter, I met Pete Donaldson. I was sitting cross-legged in the psychiatric unit in a blue and white hospital gown. He walked in, introduced himself and asked me what I had done and whether I was guilty. He preceded this by telling me that it was very important to tell him the truth, and patiently explained the attorney-client privilege. I looked at him and said, "I don't know." At about 10:00 I was taken downstairs to the hospital boardroom, where the Board of Directors were meeting. One of them was Ms. Mamie Reese, an active, voting member of the Pardons and Paroles Board. It was there that the arrest warrant for one count of murder was read to me and handcuffs were placed on my wrists for the first time.

I was then taken to the Dougherty County Jail and booked. I was placed in a solitary confinement cell on the guard walk. I stayed there until the following Monday, until I was allowed to take a shower, and then only at Pete's insistence. I remember very little of those days, except the harsh feel of the wool blanket, having to use the restroom with anyone walking by being able to see me, and the spectacle that was made by keeping me in my nurse's uniform for the 5 days that I remained in jail.

WORK #2

We had a shakedown today. This is where the officers come in and pat search everyone, have you stand outside your door with your shoes off and they go in and go through every item of your property. The shakedowns are done at random and they try to keep the inmates from knowing when they will occur. Usually they don't succeed in keeping the "secret", as the officers involved usually tell one favored inmate and it goes from there. The shakedowns serve a very valid purpose in controlling "hard contraband," such as drugs and homemade knives and weapons. When nothing is found, often they nit-pick, hunting for something to have a problem with. We are allowed to have so little personal property these days and yet an extra lipstick or too many letters can be grounds for a major embarrassing scene in front of the entire hall of inmates. Some inmates laugh it off and go on. Others get mad and argue, which is pointless since we are not in a winning position. Still another group gets very upset and often cries. I used to cry and still do at times, but now it is more out of frustration and the weariness of it all; the pleasure that is derived by some of the staff at rifling through our things and taking what they can, the screaming. I do try really hard, however, never to let them see me cry. This seems to fuel the power and control syndrome that plagues many of the staff once they begin working here. I feel the same anxiety and fear, stomach rolling, and heart beating in my ears, reminding me of the feeling of getting off the school bus years ago and walking up the dirt lane to the house. I feel relatively certain that the officers are not going to hurt me physically but the tension is so intense. I have always been fairly fanatical about following the rules of the institution and trying to make sure my locker is perfect, according to the diagrams they give us to go by. I never keep contraband but it really still gets to me. They had no problem with my locker today and that was a blessing. My roommate and I prayed together before they got here, asking God for a hedge of protection for our room against any harmful intrusion.

It's the not knowing when or if you're going to be singled out or wondering what they are going to find a problem with. I keep a saying taped to one of my manila envelopes that says, "What may seem like nothing to you, may be all that I have to live for. . . " Several officers have remarked over the years that this sentence has really made them stop and think.

The shakedowns are the worst, yet the daily open-locker inspections are fear-inducing also. Usually I am at work in the Law Library, but I know that they still go through my things. At least my detail lets me avoid the anxiety of standing at attention, wondering if everything is OK. I have the very real desire at times for invisibility (again, as I did as a child). It is not as bad as the terror of my childhood, but the similarities are there. There are more objects of scrutiny, but it is also difficult for me to watch someone else be screamed at or degraded because I know how it feels.

The dining hall is another area of anxiety for me. We have 10 minutes to get a tray, sit down, eat and leave. It becomes a matter of deciding what you want the most and eating in that order. Rarely do we receive the allotted 10 minutes and even when we do the officer (usually a Sgt.) is hollering the entire time, "Row 1, Row 2, your time is up!" This is all in a very loud, authoritative male voice. My food tends to have a really hard time going down. If I am upset about something, I do not even bother to go eat because I know my food will not stay down and I will leave more upset than when I came in. The women with poor dental conditions have an even harder time, and are often left hungry.

One night, recently, I was especially excited to receive a large piece of strawberry cake. I rarely eat meat of any kind, so I was eating my carrots and salad when Sgt. Busbee (change name) started screaming for us to get up and leave. I was very upset. Normally I never say anything because it doesn't do any good, anyway, but this night I went up to him on my way to take my tray to the window with my cake uneaten and said, "Sir, permission to speak?" He nodded affirmatively. I said, "Do we no longer have 10 minutes to eat?" He bellowed, "You had

10 minutes! Go stand over there and finish eating." He was pointing to the area where the trays are turned in which is surrounded by garbage cans. Much to my dismay, tears sprang to my eyes. I put my tray in the window (cake and all) and left. Many women will stand next to the garbage cans to finish eating. I cannot do it. Maybe it is pride, I don't know. . . it is just too degrading. They have taken so much from me; I would rather go hungry than to allow them to snicker because I am eating my food over the garbage.

There is a lady in my dorm that quit eating, period, because it made her so upset being screamed at. She lost 30 pounds before Mental Health stepped in, and now she eats all her meals in the infirmary.

It's the screaming that gets to me the most. When you come from an abusive background (as most female offenders do) it is difficult to endure the tension of this place. It seems, oftentimes, that prison just picks up where the abusive husband/partner/father, etc. left off — emotionally, anyway.

The officers have no idea what you are going through or dealing with and yet they scream and scream and scream. Walking down the sidewalk they scream. Eating, they scream. It is impossible to describe how it feels to endure year after year after year, day after day, being screamed at.

A friend, Carol (changed name), received a 5-year parole denial the other day, after serving 15 years. She'd been really upset for most of the day and as we were walking back to the dorm from our detail, an officer screamed at us for not walking single file, in a straight line. We were behind one another, but we were not perfectly straight. The officer threatened her with a D.R. (Disciplinary Report). She said, "You know, I just don't care. This is so petty. It is impossible to walk perfectly straight. I'm so tired, I just don't care." The officer then realized that she was really upset and backed off, asking if she was OK. Maybe they are supposed to be "in our face"; it's just difficult for the longtimers to endure this, year after year.

Receiving a Disciplinary Report, to a lot of inmates, doesn't mean anything to them. Usually, unless it is a major assaultive type of D.R. it won't affect your release date. But to those of us who live in the Honor Dorm it is a very big deal, as we will be moved out if we receive a D.R.

and are found guilty in Dis. Court. I have only received one in all these years. I received it in April 1998 at Metro State Prison in Atlanta, GA. It was for "Unauthorized Contraband" for having a homemade address book.

WORK #3

Nights are scary. That's when nothing else can vie for my attention and it's just me and the what-ifs and what-might-have-beens. The memories of the pain I saw in the SICU plagued me for years. The patient's eyes held the fear, anger and agony. They often had endotracheal tubes or tracheostomies, and were connected to ventilators. These tubes prevented the patients from talking and their hands were secured to the bed rails with soft ties to keep them from pulling out tubes and other lines. They often had tubes in every orifice. The tubes and lines had their purposes, however, and that was to monitor or assist in the recovery process. The sickest of the sick were in the SICU. We housed those who had had major surgery on vital organs such as the heart, lungs, or vasculature. We also cared for all the neurological patients whether they had had surgery or not (i.e., closed head injuries, etc.) Many times the surgical patients were just in the unit overnight for observation post op — to make sure their vital signs were stable and to be weaned off the ventilator.

I was working in ICU when the first coronary artery bypass surgery was done at Phoebe Putney. We all underwent extensive training and were all both excited and proud to have this program succeed. I trained additionally to be one of the patient liaisons. The day before the patient surgery, after they were admitted to the hospital on a regular surgery floor, I would come in and meet them and their family and explain to them what they could expect the next day and during the days following surgery. It seemed to allay their fears and the fear of the family members when they knew what to expect. I told them about the ventilator, and that they would not be able to talk while it was in, but said that a nurse would be with them at all times. I explained about the pain they would experience and how it would mostly be in the leg where they took the vein graft from, and very little in the chest. I told them they'd most likely be up and sitting in a chair, the day after surgery. I documented their anxiety level and how receptive they were to the teaching and about the support of the family. If they were extremely anxious I would spend extra time with them. Many times I'd come to work early the next day in order to check on the family before reporting to work. Many times, whoever did the pre-op teaching would be the primary caregiver for that patient, post-op. The patients usually recovered so rapidly and felt so much better post operatively that it was a joy to work with them.

Hi,

The poems were beautiful — as usual. Very impacting. The three pieces you sent were also very powerful. It all helps me to understand you better. You are much more than what has happened to you. I almost feel shame that people won't step up to the plate and give you the opportunity to live outside; perhaps with some recognition of your soul, this will happen. Make sense?

I feel you are innately good (we are capable of evil — but it must be provoked). I understand you went through so much but I can't fathom what it must have been like. You worked so hard to rise above your pain.

I'm so sorry for those who fell victim to your own victimization. I'm sorry that you had to watch your son grow from afar (a mother's greatest fear). You are the epitome of "Victim Equals Victim."

Enough sadness. I hope you had a nice holiday. I didn't send out cards. Sorry. I was busy and something had to be eliminated. But my prayers are with you, and my relentless support of discovering who you are, all the good within.

Jen

Journal Entry
3-16-2000

This is the first day of my 15th year of incarceration. It is unreal

43

that it has been this long. In one sense it seems like it hasn't been that long, but in another, bigger, bigger sense it seems like I've never been anywhere else. The flowers on the front of this journal resemble honeysuckle in their coloring and were the reason this particular book was chosen for me, a gift from the heart. Honeysuckle, my favorite flower — a weed actually, it is unique but strong, sturdy and will grown between the rocks along the rough places. I like that. The smell is magnificent and floats on the wind, reminding me of years past when I was fascinated by the honey-filled flowers and the way they twisted into a vine, a crown I could wear; barefoot, as I skipped across the red, clay-carpeted fields in Hopeful, Georgia. It is awesome to realize that the horror of my childhood was enveloped with this beauty and carefree play.

I looked out on the guard line last summer and was enchanted to see a honeysuckle vine growing up through the razor wire fence. It stood strong, unintimidated, almost glamorous in its stance, even surrounded by the deadly metal. It's been uprooted now, but grows nearby. I know, because I smelled the fragrance yesterday, prancing on the breeze, almost a message. I will survive. I will thrive. A fitting present for the closing ceremony of 14 prison years.

I was trying to explain this love of honeysuckle to another inmate. She said, "Oh no, honeysuckle doesn't bloom this early. Way too early for it." I smiled and knew then that it was a symbol to me from God, a sign, like the rainbow was for Noah.

Strength is sent in the small things, I have found. A smile, a touch, a letter from a stranger, or simply, the fragrance of a favorite flower.

Terri Rachals

KRISTINE BUNCH

Other stories in this book involve confessions, denials, obvious instances of insanity, and that gray area where imprisonment comes as the result of another's actions. We can make some sense out of these cases. Yet, if ever there existed a story that could force the greatest skeptic to reconsider cynical views regarding a convicted person's plea of innocence, it would be the case of Kristine Bunch — a young mother imprisoned for the death of her son in the fire that consumed their small trailer home.

On June 30, 1995, 21 year old Kristine Bunch fell asleep, after an exhausting day of parenting her three-year-old, Anthony Maxwell, and working at a nearby factory. Before collapsing on the couch herself, she had been lying on the cushions, watching her son fall asleep beside her. Once Tony had drifted into a peaceful sleep, Kristine picked him up, put him to bed in his crib, and settled back down on the couch.

Though she was always tired and often lonely, her future was hopeful: Kristine had plans for herself and her young son. She was weeks away from certification as a machinist, a good position considering she had worked only as a temp in the factories outlying her hometown of Greensburg, Indiana. From working in "personnel", Kristine had forged relationships with people who would help her get a more secure job position. Increased financial stability would also help her to finish the "Impact Program," a state-assisted educational format that would provide her with access to better-paying positions in the future.

Although she tried to keep in touch with her son's father, Ronnie, he did not pay any of their bills or contribute to other expenses related to his son. In fact, he had practically cut off contact with Kristine and Tony since she had applied for state assistance; the government had begun to try and track him down. Though Kristine was ambivalent about her relationship with her son's father, the state wanted Ronnie to pay his share of child support. Kristine had recognized early on that Tony's biological father was incapable of parenting or settling down with her, so rather than lament the situation she counted her blessing, Tony, and focused on creating a life for the two of them.

Though not very glamorous, Kristine had shaped her life to best provide for the needs of her son. She moved into her mother's 22-year-old trailer in the Crestwood Mobile Home Resort so she would have extra help with bills and childcare. The trailer was built on stilts, with a kitchen crammed between two tiny bedrooms, a toilet and bath, and one extra "room" created with dividers. Along with Kristine's 17-year-old brother who "came and went", the two women and the child managed an existence not much above poverty-level. Her mother had lived a difficult life, divorcing three times and leaving Kristine's father when Kristine was just ten. As a young mother herself, Kristine didn't judge her mother's relationships, but still she knew that she wanted a more stable life for herself and her son.

Throughout Kristine's struggles, her mother was a source of support, and living together was exactly what Kristine needed. With her mother, she found a place to relax and to truly put her work into creating a viable and successful future for herself and her son. Such efforts — working full time, completing certification programs, and single parenting — were exhausting, and on this particular night she fell asleep within minutes.

Neighbors and a fire expert currently working on Kristine's case believe that Tony, alone in his crib, got hold of a cigarette lighter (a frightening habit of Tony's) and set his room on fire. Kristine slept through her son's death. When she awoke to flames and smoke, Kristine immediately ran down the hall towards her son's room. Already, however, the smoke had grown thick and choking, and flames consumed the thin trailer walls. In a panic, Kristine fled the trailer. Her mother was gone. Kristine immediately ran to Tony's door and saw the flames inside. Panicked, she started throwing things at the door, then ran for safety. There was no way to run through the blaze — Tony, her baby, died, while Kristine survived.

Within six days, Kristine was arrested on charges of both arson and murder. Still traumatized by the loss of her son, it did not even occur to Kristine that she might be the prime suspect in his death. The transition from mourning mother to suspected felon was sudden: after only a 30-minute "survey" by the fire marshal, resulting in an arson charge, Kristine was arrested and jailed. Later, the judge released Kristine on a $5,000 bond, citing "lack of evidence and no tendency to run, no motive, no insurance money."

In a matter of days, not only was Kristine's life shattered, but her past and her future were irrevocably distorted. It was not long before the media got a hold of the tragic story, and the debate over Kristine's guilt or innocence became a relentless headline.

It is hard to overestimate the impact of media coverage on Kristine's trial. For example, on the night before jury selection, newspapers falsely stated that Kristine had "confessed." This was not only a fallacy — Kristine had actually been ordered by the court not to speak of Tony at all — such a claim was an outright lie. Kristine was too frightened to express her intense grief over the loss of her son, much less make a full confession to a newspaper. Kristine was so distraught by media misrepresentations of herself as cold, stupid, and guilty, that she elected not testify at her trial. Kristine's public defender had never tried any case more serious than petty crimes, and didn't realize the magnitude of this lacuna; Kristine's testimony could have been crucial. To his credit, he recognized the potential impact of the intense media hype and attempted to secure a change of venue. His request was denied. Months of conjecture had already spread and before Kristine's trial even began, she was in many ways a convicted murderess. The jury knew the woman as a cold-blooded killer, "tired," as one paper stated, "of being a mother."

In February, 1996, Kristine went to trial. Her attorney, Frank

Hamilton, Jr., explains that Kristine "found herself in fairly hopeless poverty, living as a single mother with her child, with, as I recall, little to no assistance from the child's father. Kristine Bunch was very quiet and some viewed her reaction to the death of her child as 'not what they thought it should be.' She never cried, not even at the scene. Perhaps shock, personality, I am not sure. But I doubt it was callousness. Yet this is how it was viewed: cold."

Evidence supporting Kristine's plea of innocence was plentiful. The single gas can found alongside a lawn mower and other outdoor equipment on the property came back clean of fingerprints, suggesting that Kristine's hand hadn't touched it. Attendants questioned at gas stations throughout the area had no memory of seeing the young woman at all — much less of her purchasing gas or kerosene. As explained in a letter by Kristine's father (included) recounting the trial, the type of chemical suspected to be the cause of the fire, heavy petroleum distillate, could also be found within the components of the trailer itself. For example, the trailer had been heated with fuel oil, and the kerosene that investigators cited matched the kerosene lighters that were found. Still, fire experts argued over the origins of the fire.

Except for her grief, Kristine was found to be psychologically of sound mind. She had no hidden issues originating from childhood or from her relationship with her son's father. She was not motivated by an insurance policy. Her mother had no money and no policies.

In all areas, Kristine's life had been looking up. Prior to the fire she had become involved in a new relationship, which later proved to be a great source of support for her during the aftermath. While out on bail, she relied on her boyfriend for support and, though using birth control, became pregnant. Kristine needed someone to lean on and she found a sense of safety in their relationship. Unfortunately, when Kristine informed her lover of her pregnancy, he confessed that he was married and had no plans to leave his wife. Shocked and hurt, Kristine let go of the relationship, and allowed herself to feel blessed with the pregnancy. Knowing that the father did not want the baby, and that Kristine might not be free to care for it, her mother agreed to take custodianship should Kristine be sent to prison.

The jury felt little empathy for Kristine, and the court failed to properly present the case: while the evidence was judged circumstantial, the jury members were not instructed to follow a circumstantial format. Kristine received sentences of 60 years for murder and 50 for arson. In Appellate Court, however, the arson charge was vacated under the confines of Double Jeopardy, and Kristine received 60 years for a single charge of murder. Her earliest possible release date is November 26, 2025.

Kristine gave birth to her second son while serving her sentence. Now three years old, Trent visits his mother in the Indiana prison where she is incarcerated as often as the prison will allow. Although it has been several years, Kristine has yet to become accustomed to prison life. She feels she is wrongfully imprisoned, and has difficulty concentrating on anything outside of her conviction and years of Trent's life that she is missing.

On the advice of a cellmate, Kristine began writing to me, unsolicited, and as our correspondence continued her willingness to do anything to be with her son, Trent, became clear. She is willing to write to anyone who might help her find justice. She recounts the details of her story, no matter how painful, because she believes that the truth lies in such details. Her letters are a balance between pain and hope. Now 26, Kristine is not the only person who fears she will wrongfully deteriorate in a cell. Fortunately, a fire investigator has taken on her case, *pro bono*, and prison reform advocates are working to secure her a re-trial. In the interim, Kristine works on her education. She has earned an AA from Ball University, as well as a cosmetology license. She explains that she is determined to have work skills when she is proven innocent.

No matter how distant her freedom may seem, Kristine's focus remains on providing for her child. She has lost one child to death, and in many ways she feels that she is dead to Trent. Her absence as Trent's primary caretaker, as well as her unresolved grief for Tony, weigh heavily on her. "The grief [over Tony] is still so evident and it has been almost five years now. The grief won't ease because I can't really mourn in here. . . I wasn't allowed to, before. . . I can't really say 'Good-Bye.' Plus, there is the added emotion because of Trent. I feel as if I have lost both of my boys. It seems that my immediate family hasn't healed either, because we aren't together."

Dear Ms. Jennifer Furio,

My name is Kristine Bunch. I am incarcerated at the Indiana Women's Prison. Hope Rippey (your correspondent) is a friend of mine and she gave me your name and address.

To be honest, I really don't know what to say. I'm not exactly sure who you are, who you know or even what (if anything) you can do.

The reason Hope offered your name is because I confided in her that I am going to write to a television producer to see if I can get my story publicly aired and hopefully (I pray) get some help to get out of here. That's when Hope mentioned you and said, "that you know some people." I don't know what that means, exactly, but locked away, I'm desperate for help. I need someone to help me, even if it means becoming another television tabloid freak. I'll do anything. Let me start with what's happened.

On June 30, 1995, my mother's trailer burnt down. My 3-year old son, Tony, and I were the only ones there. I awoke early that morning to smoke and flames. I couldn't get to Tony. I freaked. I ran out to get help but, it was too late. I lost my son.

On July 5, 1995, I was arrested — charged with murder and arson. The Fire Marshall concluded after 30 minutes that the fire was an arson and only an arson. This trailer was 22 years old and still had all of its original wiring, floors and ceilings. Ten samples were taken. Only four tested positive. The positives tested as heavy petroleum distillates which include Kerosene, fuel oil, and jet A aviation fuel. The trailer was heated with fuel oil and at several times it had had kerosene heaters in it.

I was released to my family on a $5,000.00 cash bond. The Judge said I was "no risk to flee and there was a lack of evidence." There was no motive. There was no insurance of any kind. My mom and I lost everything. . . including my most precious gift, my baby.

In February 1996, I went to trial. I didn't testify. To be honest, I wasn't in any shape to. A lot of conjecture and hearsay was allowed into my trial. The day before we selected a jury, the newspaper ran an article that said I had admitted it. The Judge denied a change of venue. My public defender hadn't ever had a case (murder) like this.

The fire experts couldn't agree on where the origin of the fire was, they had no container that carried an accelerant except for a one-gallon gas can that had a fingerprint on it that wasn't mine, they could find no gas station that said I purchased anything, and their chief witness — a fireman who recovered my son's body — changed his story at the trial. I was convicted of murder and arson. The Judge sentenced me to 60 years for the murder and 50 for the arson, but then he merged them, giving me just 60 years. I'll never forget him saying I "didn't deserve to raise a baby." He was so disgusted by me. I felt naked and ashamed, I had no time to feel the loss properly.

My bail money, which should have been returned to my family (they are very poor), was given to the State by my Judge. I have two letters from my prosecutor to one of my witnesses that speaks of jury tampering, but nothing was done. In appellate court my arson conviction was vacated under Double Jeopardy. What I don't understand is: if there is no arson, then how was there a murder? My case was strictly circumstantial, yet my jury never received circumstantial instruction. I feel the judge was sure of my guilt before the case began. The newspapers had sort of "hanged me."

I apologize for my writing. I have a lot of pain inside of me. I am very confused about many things. While on bail, I became pregnant. It was an accident, I was on the pill. My mom has my three-year-old, Trent. I'm frightened you'll judge me as promiscuous. But please know, the relationship didn't mean I was not thinking of my boy; I think I was running from pain and the pregnancy was never meant to happen, yet it's the only blessing to come from this black hole.

Ms. Furio, I am trying to fight to be able to mourn and grieve for my baby, Tony, to be able to visit his grave; and I am fighting to be with my other son, who needs his mom. I don't know how to fight or even where to turn.

I have a fire investigator who is right now looking things over *pro bono*; but the investigator can't do anything without an attorney. I don't have the money for an attorney. That's why I am trying to get some awareness. Thus, maybe, I'll get some help. I don't mean to sound ungrateful, but I know that my case was biased because of money. My whole life I have been poor. That has been okay; I was working on making that better for Tony and me. But my family had always been lower-class. There is a stigma with that. I just couldn't believe it went into the courtroom with me. As if poor equals dumb. And I love my children as much as anyone, and I know I deserve a fair trial as much as someone with the means. But the two seem to go hand-in-hand. I don't think I'll have the money anytime soon, so what else are my options?

I thank you for your time. If there is anything you can do or even some advice you can give me, I would be forever grateful.

Sincerely,

Kristine Bunch

Dear Kristine,

I just received your letter, as I am still in California — a trip I never anticipated lasting so long. You can continue to write to me at my permanent address. I was moved to respond to you when I read your circumstances. I have enclosed an example application for the organization, the Prison Activist Resource Center. Perhaps we can get your story on the Web? There are many branches and persons available to help those like yourself. It is satisfying to know that there are places to go where people can offer solutions.

If what you say is true, I pray your situation is salvageable. There are no miracles, but I am a firm believer in the power of advocacy. I know that women can be wrongfully convicted, as well as rehabilitated.

You are right — poor women from poor families with little education have less chance to get a fair trial. There is a lot of bias out there. But you sound sincere, and I hope to be of some help, if only by helping you get your story out there.

My only doubt would have been that you might have killed your baby because you had been impaired in some way. For example, isolation (which can occur with entrapment or abandonment by a family member — usually a spouse/partner, resulting in a state of fear or panic, leaving one to feel that a child would literally be better off dead) can often be a trigger or contributing factor to crimes women commit against their children.

This doesn't sound like you, at all. And now you have a child at home who does need you, a mother who will grow to depend on you and a gravesite that needs your spiritual tending. You don't sound like a woman who needs any further punishment (especially considering your "testimony" lends itself to the possibility of wrongful conviction).

Circumstance took your child away, something I can only pray I never experience as a mother of two myself. But to *convict* rather than to *heal* seems unproductive. Even had the courts found holes in the case, as an activist I question the extreme nature of your punishment, and then by proxy, your son's. So many options: house arrest, parole, temporary custody with a family member; but separation from your son will only damage him further, in the long run. The courts are so bent on punishment, they lose sight of the children who do not benefit from such absence and loss of bonding.

I would like to read your court transcripts — I will send them right back.

The most important "strengths" are your lack of motive, lack of isolation and seeming lack of any psychological abuse. More "concrete," the feeble structure of the trailer as you described it. And, of course, the lack of quality defense (a big one — just a few things).

I hope to hear back soon.
Jennifer Furio

Dear Jennifer,

Thank you so very much for getting back to me. Any chance, any possibility, any hope and I am going to grasp for it. I am *very* willing to work with you.

I want to show people that I put my time to good use. I used to work hard, paid for systems like this. I don't want to be a burden. I am the wrong person to be in here. I know you hear that, but I will repeat it until I die. It also keeps me "well," you know: thinking about my son Trent, who is out there with my mother. Thank God for that, but he needs me. More on that. . . I have acquired my cosmetology license and will graduate this May with my Associate's Degree from Ball State University.

I do have another person who can give you some great insight into my case. He is the fire investigator who is helping me, for free. The problem is money for legalities. I am including his name, address and phone number. He knows and has agreed to help in any way he can, with whatever I decide to do. His name is Frederick S. Goethel.

I thank you for your time. It means a lot to me that someone just listens to me, let alone offers to try to help. I am *very* grateful for that. I can't even find all of the words to tell you just how much I appreciate it!

Before I end this, I wanted to tell you one last thing. There are no psychological issues surrounding my case besides the ones they tried to fabricate. I was in no abusive relationships. They tried to substantiate a motive by saying I was tired of being a mother, yet they had no evidence to back that up.

If there is anything else you would like to know. . . please, feel free to ask.

I look forward to hearing from you again. Take care.

Sincerely,
Kristine Bunch

Dear Jenny

First of all, I apologize for taking so long to get this letter out to you. I want you to know that I'm not dragging my heels at all. It is very important to me to do whatever I can to get some sort of possibility of getting out of here.

Now to answer your questions. . .

The fire took place in Greensburg, Indiana. The trailer was in a park called Crestwood Mobile Home Resort, or it's also known as Lake McCory. The fire happened on June 30, 1995.

The trailer was built in 1972. It had two tip-outs on it, so it was several feet short of being a "double wide". At one time there was a divider in one of the bedrooms which made it a four-bedroom. When my mom and stepdad purchased it, the divider had been removed and it was just 3 bedrooms. The back bedroom was my mom's room; it had the water heater and breaker box in its closet. It opened to a hallway. On the right of the hallway was the bathroom. The bathroom contained a sink, tub, toilet, washer and dryer. Directly across from the bathroom, on the left side of the hall was the backdoor. There was a set of steps behind the backdoor and the fuel oil tank. Before you reached the end of the hallway, to the right there was a door that opened up to a small closet that encased the furnace. At the end of the hall to the left was a small bedroom. To the right and straight ahead was the kitchen. The kitchen table set up against the wall of the small bedroom. From the end of the hallway to the right was the telephone, the oven, the sinks, the refrigerator, and then a closet. Directly across from the closet was a built-in china cabinet. Between the cabinet and the closet was the walkway into the living room. On the right, right next to the closet was the front door. Outside of it were cement steps, a deep freezer (chest type), lawn mower, gas can, and various other stuff that belonged to my mom and stepdad.

The living room was the largest room in there. Off of the living room was the bedroom that at one time had been divided into two bedrooms. This is the room where Tony died. The trailer didn't sit low to the ground. It was about 3 ft. off of the ground. I would have to stand on something to even look into the window. I am 5'4". My age when this happened was 21. I am now 26. My son, Anthony Maxwell (or Tony) was 3 when he died. The son I gave birth to in here, Trenton Michael (or Trent), is now 3 years old.

Tony's father, Ronnie Snider, took off when I was 5 months pregnant. His family (his mom) came around from time to time to check on me. She also brought things for Tony. Ronnie left me and got with two other girls. Within three months after I gave birth to Tony, these two girls each gave birth to Ronnie's children! Before Ronnie left me, we had already decided that we both knew we couldn't get married or stay together just for a baby. I told him he could always come around and we'd always be friends. Ronnie was trying to keep a low profile because he had gotten aid from the welfare for Tony and they were after him for child support. Ronnie is the first to admit I never "begged" for him. I watched my mother's relationships as a child. My focus was my child, not some guy.

My mom and dad divorced when I was 9 or 10. My mom remarried and divorced two more times after dad. My dad remarried and he's still with her. With my mom, things weren't always easy growing up. Financially, things were difficult, and there were times mom was on public assistance. Yes, I have contact with all of my family members. None of my family members, including my mom and dad, ever doubted me.

Tom Claxton is a close family friend and lived close by my mom's trailer and still does. He baby-sat for Tony. At one time, Tom was dating my mom. Tom. . . well, I consider him my family. He has stood by me through all of this. He even helped my family with the bond money.

There was one journalist from Columbus, Indiana. His name was Scott Olsen. He didn't ever meet me or talk to me, but he was the only one who printed a factual story. Otherwise, no, there wasn't hardly anyone on my side. I didn't really have a lot of friends because all of my time was spent on bettering myself and being a mom.

Yes, I had worked before. I worked through Personnel Management in temporary factory jobs. At the time the fire happened, I was just about to receive my certification as a machinist from Versailles. I was in an Education Program to get a better paying job through the Impact Program.

I am enclosing Tom Claxton's E-mail in case you want to get in touch with him. He wants to help in whatever way he can.

I thank you for all you are trying to do. I really appreciate any glimmer of hope that can be offered. Take care of yourself. I hope to hear from you soon. If you need anything else, please let me know.

> Sincerely,
> Kristine

Hi,

It was good to talk by phone. We are almost finished with a final manuscript. I feel very good about getting you "out there," loud and clear!

Since we have known each other, you have struggled through birthdays and Christmas holidays, always in mourning. I'm sorry for that. I know it's been such a struggle for you to try and be a mother from your cell.

Frederick Goethel wrote to me and, like everyone else involved in your case, wrote to me that: "Kristine was, in my opinion, shafted the first time." He suggested that he had new information on your case, which could be really positive for you.

I have also spoken with Tom Claxton, and he seems to be a very kind man. He really is concerned about you and your son, and would like to see you released as soon as possible.

You have always felt that you were different, trying to concentrate on studies but obsessed with Trent. Let's just pray that the court will recognize your circumstance as one that is deserving of a review. There are so many holes, so many biases, and let's not even go into the lifer thing. You were a little girl. You can't be a grandma when you get out of there!

God Bless,

Jen

Following are a letter from Kristine to Mr. Hass, her attorney, detailing the night of the fire and the months leading up to her trial, and a letter from Kristine's father to the Governor of Indiana, describing the circumstances of her case. Both letters were submitted to me by Tom Claxton.

Dear Mr. Hass,

. . . I thought I would tell you a few things before you read the list of events.

First off, Tony, just as Trent is now, was my whole world. A lot of events are blurred and fused in my mind. I will try to write things out as accurately as possible. But this is still the most horrifying memory I have and probably always will be.

I should probably tell you that I do not feel responsible for Tony's death. But as a mother I feel guilt because I wasn't able to get him out. I also feel like a total coward because I have never been so afraid in my life as I was at that moment. For awhile I was desperately hurt that I didn't die with him. I would have gladly given up my life for Tony.

Keep these things in mind as you read through these events. Contrary to what's been said I am not and never have been a cold-blooded, calculating, psycho killer. . .

Sincerely,

Kristine Bunch

June 29, 1995, 6:00am: Got out of bed. Dressed for school. 6:20am Woke Tony up. Fixed Tony breakfast. Cleaned up mess and got Tony dressed. 7:00am Took Tony to Tom Claxton's. I stayed until 7:20am (just talking to Tom and watching cartoons with Tony). 7:20am Left for school. 7:55am Arrived at Versailles Vocational School.

4:00pm Left school.

4:35pm Arrived home. Went directly to Tom's. Tom and Tony were playing ball and watching Angles in the Outfield. I got a glass of pop. Went back over to my mom's trailer and got the lawn mower. I tipped the gas can up to the mower because when I shook the can I thought I heard a little in there. None came out of the can. I set the can on the table next to the steps so I'd remember to either get gas in it or have Tom get some gas.

5:20pm Tom went to town for something for his antenna. Tony and I mowed Tom's lawn. Tony had a plastic lawnmower that he followed me around with.

About 6:00pm Tom got back. Tony and I were playing ball. I told Tom I was leaving the lawn mower there so he could lower the blade. Tony and I stayed over at Tom's till about 7:30pm Tony asked to stay all night and I told him I wanted him to stay with me.

7:30pm Tony and I ate chicken, rice and mushrooms in front of the TV. After eating, we took our bath. Done a load of laundry and washed dishes. Talked to my mom on the phone and Tony talked to Nanna, too. We made plans for July 4th. I hadn't turned on the air conditioner when I left that morning — so the house was hot. Tony and I laid down on the couch and I tried to get him to go to sleep. He said he didn't feel too well. I just thought he didn't want to go to bed. I read him a story and we sang songs. I think he finally went to sleep somewhere around midnight, with the two kittens. I covered him up and laid down at the opposite end. Tony woke me up about 3:00am. The dog was barking. I took Tony to the restroom and on the way back opened the door. I told the dog to shut up. Tony and I got back on the couch. He went back to sleep as soon as I handed him his kittens. I was very tired. I had taken two allergy pills. I decided to go to school late so I shut off my alarm clock and went to sleep.

June 30. I don't know why I woke up. I thought I heard something but I'm not sure. Everything happened so fast. Even now just writing about it my chest tightens, my throat closes and I can't seem to think. I know that I saw fire and smoke. I know I saw Tony standing on the bed. I know that I threw a blanket on the fire in the doorway of the front bedroom. It melted in my hands. I know I picked up a pillow and tried to hit the fire — the pillow burned. I kept trying to think. I ran to get the fire extinguisher. I couldn't find it. I started back to the bedroom. The fire was on the ceiling. I ran out the door screaming for Tom. I knew I couldn't get in the side window even though I tried. I went to the front window and busted it out with Tony's tricycle. I started to go in. Someone — I thought it was Tom — pulled me back. At this time the flames were through the roof and the tree was on fire. Someone told me it was too late and he's gone. I remember looking around and there were a lot of people around. Linda walked me to the ambulance. All I knew and all I was thinking about was I couldn't find Tony. I talked to the medic — just answered her questions. Candy got in the ambulance with me. They wouldn't tell me anything. All I wanted to know was if they had found him. I already knew he was gone, but I didn't want him to be lost, too.

I asked for Tom. Tom got in the ambulance. I asked him if they had found him. He told me that they found him. That's all I needed to know, as long as he wasn't lost. Went to the hospital. In the emergency room the nurse let in JuDena. She told me she was sorry. Then she left because my Dad came in. I told Dad my baby was gone. Then a sheriff came in to question me. I had only been at the hospital a short time. The sheriff left. I don't really know what all he said, I was crying too hard.

I was admitted and taken to a room. I was given some Xanex and my step-mom helped me take a shower. Even after the shower I could still smell smoke and fire. My hair was black. Everyone kept telling me to sleep. I just couldn't. Every time I closed my eyes I saw it again. More officers came in to question me again. I'm not sure what-all was said, I was just so upset and confused. I got much worse when they told me that Tony was murdered in cold blood and they thought the same was supposed to happen to me. They finally left. They wouldn't let my family stay in with me. So when they left, my family came back in. I asked to leave the hospital. My mom took me to Tom's after getting my prescription of nerve pills. At Tom's I still couldn't sleep. I took another nerve pill and went to bed. I just got to sleep when the sheriff called and told my mom to bring me in.

10:00 pm I had to go barefoot because my shoes were all gone. My mom was told to wait. I was taken into a little room with the cops. They yelled at me and called me all kinds of names. I came out of the room and made mom promise she wouldn't leave me alone again.

July 4. Back in the sheriff's office again. He's questioning all of us again. Mom and Tom didn't leave me alone with them again. I tell them I'll take a polygraph test. I don't know what it is, but if I take it they said they'll leave me alone. I go back to Tom's. People keep driving and walking up to look at the burned out trailer. I can't believe it. I get real upset. They shouldn't look at it like a freak show. Don't they realize my son died there? I go to my Dad's and stay there overnight.

July 5. Dad and Deb go with me for polygraph test. I was very scared and nervous. Tired too — the nerve pills make me sleepy. The test was weird. The operator kept changing his voice. I felt like he was sneaking up on me because I was strapped in the chair facing the wall. Finally it's over. He turns me around and tells me he knows I killed my son and I'm just a cold-blooded killer. I looked at him and told him I wanted a lawyer.

I was taken back to Decatur County and arrested. Charged with murder and arson. I thought I would talk to the media. Before I could, Frank Hamilton was appointed as my lawyer. He told me not to speak to anyone. I didn't speak to anyone the whole time I was in jail, except my family. I had to write to the judge after I had been in jail for two months, because I had only seen or spoken to Frank Hamilton Jr. for twenty minutes. I was afraid of everything. I had never been to jail before. I thought my lawyer would explain things to me. He didn't.

Oct. Released on bail. The sheriff and everyone are mad because they don't know anything about it. As I walk out of the jail, a reporter snaps my picture.

Oct. 31. My mom takes me to Columbus. She tries to cheer me up. This is the night I got pregnant with Trent. It wasn't planned. I didn't even think I could get pregnant.

Nov. 26. Between then and now, we were staying at my aunt's. I don't feel comfortable going anywhere. Every time we do the police harass the people we are around. They are still following us everywhere. I decide to stay with my Dad. I feel safer going to see my lawyer with a family member. Every time I step out of the car in Greensburg, someone yells "Baby Killer" and points to me.

We did depositions one week before trial. Sheriff Jon Oldham admitted if the fire experts weren't saying this was an arson there wouldn't be a case. Jim Skaggs and Brian Frank differed on how things actually took place. My investigator, Tom Hulse, gave a deposition as to what they'd found. After that the prosecutor offered me a deal to drop the murder charge if I pleaded guilty to arson. I couldn't do it. I didn't do anything but freeze up like a coward because I had never faced a fire before.

Feb. 16. Jury Selection, but first Frank asks for a change of venue because an article came out the day before my trial which stated that I was guilty. Change of venue denied. Jury selection begins. Prospective jurors sit up there talking about how I'm just another Susan Smith. My lawyer took care of picking jurors without my advice. He took care of my testimony and he said none of my family could be in the courtroom.

I was convicted. On April 1, I was sentenced. I have been in Indiana Women's Prison ever since. Yet people who testified for me, such as Kim and Tim Hubbard, are still being harassed and threatened...

... I apologize for this being so sloppy. It's very upsetting to remember. I try to remember only the good things. In a way, and I have admitted this, I feel guilty. God gave me such a special son and I feel I failed them both. If I wasn't so frightened maybe I would have gotten him out.

I tried to remember as much as I could. I hope this helps.

Kristi

March 13, 1996

Governor Evan Baye
Indianapolis State House
Indianapolis, IN 46222

Dear Mr. Baye:

I am writing to you because I feel my daughter, Kristine Bunch, was given an unfair trial. Her lawyer has done nothing. I have provided you with just a little information on the things that went wrong. I have enclosed copies of a few items to help prove to you that her trial was unfair. There are many, many more. This is why I am asking you to please, do an investigation. Please help us get my daughter a new and fair trial as quickly as possible. She has suffered enough.

Kristine's trailer was found on fire on the morning of June 30, 1995. Kristine lost all her material possessions; but more importantly, she lost her son. On the morning of the fire, Kristine was transported to Decatur County Hospital. There she was treated for smoke inhalation and all the burns that were found. She was also give Zanax to calm her. Being at the hospital with not even enough time to be properly admitted, she was questioned in the emergency room. She was questioned three or four times during her short stay at the hospital. She was even woken up after only having an hour of sleep to be questioned. How much can a mother be expected to remember after losing her son? How much of that will be perfectly clear?

Kristine was arrested July 5, 1995, very shortly after the burial of her son, on the suspicion of arson and murder. She was told she would receive a criminal lawyer out of Indianapolis. Instead she was appointed a local lawyer, Frank Hamilton, Jr.. Hamilton had no prior experience of a case such as this. The prosecutor asked that no bail be set. The judge agreed and Kristine was placed in Decatur county jail. There Kristine was forced to wait.

After receiving very little information from her lawyer, Kristine wrote Judge Westhafer a letter to request a new lawyer. She felt that her attorney was withholding information from her, was not doing everything he could, and was working, literally, against her. She went before the judge on September 26, 1995. The judge denied her request. He stated that he felt that her attorney was doing his job. Shortly after requesting a new lawyer, Hamilton made a request for bail. Kristine was granted bail because there was little evidence and she was not considered a flee risk.

On January 18, 1996, Kristine filled out a complaint form to Indiana Civil Liberties Union. In this complaint, she stressed how unconfident she was in her lawyer and that her request for a new lawyer had been denied. She also stated her ignorance of the law and how she felt like she was being taken advantage of. She mentioned the fact that she had asked her lawyer and the judge to explain her rights to her and asked several questions; neither could answer her questions. Civil Liberties responded to her complaint and told her she had the right to a new attorney.

Greensburg's local newspaper, the *Greensburg Daily News*, has printed several one-sided articles. These articles have all insinuated that Kristine was guilty. The first was right after she was arrested and another was printed after her release on bail. An article was printed the Saturday before Kristine's trial was scheduled to begin. Kristine's fear of an unfair trial due to all the publicity resulted in her request for a change of venue. Judge Wasthafer denied her request. He said that he felt that the jury was fair and unbiased. However, is it not Kristine's right to feel the same?

The prosecution's list of witnesses started out long. However, many of these witnesses were scratched off that list. One fireman's testimony revealed that he had forgotten the fact that he had to climb over a chair to reach the bedroom. However, in two prior statements, he only mentioned having to crawl over a ceiling tress and ceiling debris. I find it odd that he needed eight months to remember that a chair was blocking his path. I overheard the fireman's father, who happens to be an undercover cop for Greensburg, ask, "Did you do any good?"

A medical doctor gave testimony that Kristine could not have been burned if she had not been in physical contact with the fire. He also said that x-rays might not show that she had indeed inhaled smoke, due to the fact Kristine is a cigarette smoker. However, Krisitne was coughing out soot, bringing the prosecution's theory that Kristine was not in the trailer during the fire into disbelief.

William D. Kinard, Forensic Chemist with the Bureau of Alcohol, Tobacco, and Firearms (BTF) also took the stand. Kinard had examined the ten samples that were taken from the trailer. He stated that *properties* of a heavy petroleum distillate (HPD) were found in *some* samples. Kinard gave six examples of HPD including: kerosene, No 1 fuel oil, Jet-A (aviation) fuel, solvents for some insecticides, diesel fuel, and No 2 fuel oil (home heating oil). However, he neglected to inform the jury that household items such as: grease, soap, detergents, wetting agents, and many more can also show these same properties. If you study the results of the tests on the samples (Enclosed), you will notice that no properties of HPD were found in the fabric, carpet, carpet padding, or fiber material. However, they were found in five of the wood samples. It is impossible for something to be able to be in the wood and not on the carpet or carpet padding if directly poured on.

I conducted a few studies on my own and found that the items listed above are not a complete list of items containing properties of HPD. I also discovered that it is possible for properties of HPD to stay in the wood forever. Bringing me to the theory that whatever was found in the wood samples could have been there before the trailer had been purchased. Also, a Nathyic Distillate will show properties of HPD if it is added. A test will show if a distillate was just put there or if it had been in the wood for a long period of time. However, a test was not done on the wood to show how long the properties had been there.

. . . As you can see, there is plenty of reasonable doubt. We beg you to please conduct a formal investigation. You will be surprised by your findings. Besides the examples given earlier, there are several more. For example, three state fire marshals that testified for the prosecution's side, all had different opinions on where the fire started and what was supposedly used. Not to mention the fact that the jury requested to listen to nine of the testimonies. They were permitted to listen to only three of the nine tapes.

We also feel that Kristine was not given proper representation. The town had been given a one-sided story by the media that pointed a guilty finger at Kristine. However, I feel I am part to blame. We were told by Frank not to speak to the media and now I wish I had. No one was told the truth and our side. We again ask you to please help us get a new, fair trial as quick as possible. Not only for Kristine and her family, but for everyone who is affected by this case. Justice must be served for all.

Sincerely,

Arthur M. Bunch

Note: A representative of Governor Baye's office responded by informing Mr. Bunch that the governor had no jurisdiction over such complaints, and that the matter must be addressed through the judicial system under the guidance of an attorney.

PAMELA SMART

Pamela Smart became a media star — presented in the papers, in magazines, and on television as a "vixen" who used her sexual prowess to manipulate men into committing murder — when she was charged with conspiring to kill her husband, Gregg Smart.

On May 1, 1990 Pamela came home from a work meeting to find her condominium ransacked and her husband shot to death. Pamela's tragedy, however, did not end with her husband's death, but continued throughout her trial, through the ongoing media hype that has distorted and exploited her life, and her life in prison where she has been beaten so severely that she needed reconstructive surgery. Pamela herself is an articulate, educated woman pursuing a graduate degree in Criminal Justice.

At first glance, Pamela's story seems straightforward. She married young; when her husband had a one-night extramarital fling, she responded by having her own affair with a teenager, five years her junior. When she tried to end the affair, he blackmailed her into a continued sexual relationship. When she confessed to her husband and they agreed to work out their differences, Pamela's young lover shot and killed her husband. Pamela's involvement in the murder itself is ambiguous, and will probably remain unresolved forever. While the gunman claimed that Pamela personally enlisted him to murder her husband, Pamela herself claims she is innocent. No one but Pamela and Bill Flynn, however, will ever know the truth.

Pamela's story became more a media circus than a quest for the truth. As Pamela notes, during the investigation and trial, "The media picked me apart, head to toe. . . my waist size, my favorite shoes, my hairstyles. . . . I had watched stories on television of men standing trial for murder, but no one had ever remarked about the outfit he wore to court that day. . . nothing made sense."

For months, the press was glued to the attractive women who had worked for eleven schools as the Director of Media Services. Contrary to popular belief, Pamela was never a teacher, though many arguments against her have been based on this fallacy and her perceived misuse of authority. A college graduate aspiring to a career in the media, Pamela's ambitions exceeded her age but not her talent. At age 21, Pamela had already earned a bachelor's degree in media and communications from the University of Florida, had married, held a challenging full-time job, and had worked through marital difficulties with her husband. The press made Pamela's accomplishments into evidence of the cold, heartless nature of a woman driven to succeed at any cost.

Beyond the camera's glare, however, Pamela was grieving over the loss of the man she loved and the life they had been struggling to build together. Pamela Wojas and Gregg Smart's relationship began when they were still in their teens. Even before marriage, the couple faced conflicts as they strove to define their identities, both together and apart. They enjoyed rock music, partying, going out with friends, and, above all, being together. Nevertheless, after graduation Pamela left Gregg suddenly and moved to a different city in Florida to start a new life. Gregg followed her, confessed his love and pledged his support, and asked her to marry him. Pamela accepted, and the couple began their married life buoyed by hope, and with only a bit of trepidation.

Marital conflicts soon arose, however, as Gregg expressed his desire to have Pamela home when she needed to be at work. While Pamela began to realize that her own needs weren't being met within the marriage, nothing prepared her for Gregg's December 1989 confession to a one-night affair. Pamela felt unable to deal with Gregg's infidelity, and her self-esteem plummeted. Pamela turned on herself, picking apart her character and appearance.

Unfortunately, the solution Pamela eventually sought out was more destructive than she could ever have imagined. Through her job in the local schools, Pamela had been working with a 16-year-old student named Bill Flynn, who had developed a crush on the attractive, successful young woman. Feeling rejected and betrayed by her husband — the man whom she felt she should have been able to trust unconditionally — Pamela reciprocated Bill's attentions. They began a short-lived affair, which Pamela thought would boost her self-esteem. Any confidence she gained, however, was quickly countered by intense guilt. When she tried to break off her relationship, Bill threatened to tell Gregg, and he blackmailed her into a continued sexual relationship. Pamela felt violated by Bill's manipulation and his continued sexual attentions.

By April 1990, however, she had finally had enough, and moved to end the relationship and reclaim her marriage. She confessed to Gregg, and the couple decided to work out their differences.

On May 1, 1990, Bill Flynn and three of his friends, Pete Randall, Vance Lattime, and Raymond Fowler, shot and killed Gregg Smart in the condominium that he and Pamela shared. Pamela claims she had only met Bill's three accomplices in passing, and that she had no long-term relationships with any of them. Still, the courts and the media targeted Pamela as the manipulative mastermind behind the crime, and viewed the young men as "innocent boys" simply carrying out her wishes. The courts also took the standpoint that Pamela had convinced the boys to carry out the murder by promising to share the proceeds from Gregg's life insurance policy.

Many of the arguments used to convict Pamela Smart would be unconvincing now, just ten years later. In 1990, young adults were still viewed as incapable of committing heinous acts. Today, a series of school shootings has alerted the general public to the reality that white, suburban youth can be vengeful and deadly. The public, and the court system, are slowly coming to realize the violent capabilities of younger generations.

Had such information been available during Pamela's trial, and had the jury fully understood the power of Bill Flynn (as specialists understand the power of violent youth today), Pamela's case might have been approached very differently from the start. At the time, however, Bill was perceived as meek, cowering and complying with Pamela's whims. In fact, Bill was willful enough to stalk Pamela, smart enough to use blackmail to force her into a continued sexual relationship, and cunning enough to devise a plan between four boys that resulted in murder. Bill knew power. His own court testimony summed it up best when he confessed the "power and thrill of killing." Bill had little difficulty in pulling together a killing team. But the fantasy notion of a handful of lads at the beck and call of a cold-hearted beauty fed the media's representation of Pamela as "the Bombshell Killer," and distorted the administration of justice in her trial.

The relentless media attention surrounding Smart's case continues to this day. She has been portrayed in at least one feature film and one television production, along with countless television news or investigative reports and numerous newspaper articles and "exposés". During Pamela's trial, even the judge was taken in by the hype, and was later reported by witnesses as fantasizing about "when this is made into a movie."

The exploitation affects not only Pamela, but her friends and family as well. In May, 2000, Pam's mother Linda Wojas sent me an e-mail message that illustrates just how obscene the media's attention has become: "Dear Jennifer, I burst into tears after the show on Court TV, out of sheer frustration. . . I called John (my husband) and he assured me it wasn't 'that bad' but I felt it was. . . [the news anchor who claimed to want to interview Pamela and me] only wanted to address the eBay b.s. — (jerks selling Pam's autograph. . . awful) — so unimportant I told her I would not give five seconds of precious air time to some individual who is so small as to profit from our pain. . ." The interest surrounding Pam's case seems in no way to be waning. The anomaly of a beautiful, educated, articulate, and thoughtful woman imprisoned for a scandalous crime of passion continues to fascinate the public.

A third-year law student at Barry University School of Law, Todd Bober, has written his senior thesis on the hype surrounding "megamedia trials"; he identifies Pamela Smart's trial as the first true example of the kind. The brief summary of his thesis, included here, touches on many of the same points addressed by Pamela in her personal accounts. He argues that Pam's trial occurred in an environment which, because of widespread negative media attention, was "deeply hostile" to her. He redirects the issue from her guilt or innocence to the manner and viability of her trial, and asks the hard question of whether, "with such widespread community outrage being communicated directly to each juror [who were not sequestered] every evening on the news, and every morning in the paper, her jury [can] still be considered impartial." Todd Bober, Pamela, and her family believe that the answer is no, and are seeking a new trial.

As recounted by Linda Wojas, the questions surrounding Pamela's case are numerous, including not only the media coverage but the integrity of the New Hampshire judge assigned to Pam's trial and the New Hampshire court system itself. In a copy of her 1998 testimony before the New Hampshire Legislative Committee on Judicial Conduct, Linda describes the numerous ways in which Pamela's judge repeatedly jeopardized the outcome of her case. Pamela's case is not unique in that, but it is a clear and highly-publicized example of how easily the integrity of the criminal justice system can be tainted.

Despite everything, Pamela's perseverance and focus on her education are impressive. She admits that her prison experiences have changed her profoundly, and that, should she be released, she is dedicated to working as an advocate for those who have been abandoned by the system. She writes that "I have seen too much to ignore. . . I know that even if I ever leave prison, the prison will never leave me. The pain and suffering of confinement will forever be etched as a permanent part of my soul."

Jennifer,

Hi, I got your letter. I have received mail from all over the world. The letters help me realize that I am not forgotten, and that the injustice I am suffering angers many.

I'm trying my best to stay strong, but this has been a long nine years. I work as a teacher and tutor here. I enjoy helping others so I do a lot of work in the school building.

I am also in a correspondence law program. When I finish I will have a Master of Science in Law with a specialization in Criminal Justice. The work is very difficult, but so far I am maintaining an "A" average in both of my classes. I have two 40-page papers due in the next two weeks, so I am pretty busy with all of the work.

My appeal is currently in front of a federal judge in New Hampshire. I have been waiting for his ruling as to whether or not I will get a new trial. I pray that he grants it because I am truly getting weary of this fight.

To answer your questions, I am not guilty of having anything to do with my husband's death. I miss him deeply, and I often wonder what our lives would be like if he was still here with me. I have no feelings for the people who killed my husband other than anger. I try not to focus on it because there is nothing to be gained that would be positive. Letting myself get angry would only serve to hurt me. Instead, I try to focus on the positive. Well, I must end for now because I have to work on my paper.

Take care,
Pam

Jennifer,

Hi. I tried to write up a synopsis of events. There is so much to say I could write an entire book. I don't know, but it's a start. Let me know what you think.

As far as the education goes, anyone who wants to help can send the money to me or my mother. I need money for two more semesters. Books, postage to mail my papers out, etc. . . .They should just write that the money is for educational purposes. Any help, anyway, is greatly appreciated. I've been busy reading and writing papers. I got an "A" on my first paper on Aristotle. I just wrote another one on Natural Law. I have to turn those in later this month. I'm also working on a big project on the death penalty. So if you see any info out there maybe you could send it. It's hard to get a lot of outside info because I don't have Internet access.

I'm going to close because I want to get this out to you. Thanks a bunch.

Pam

Pamela Smart

I am a 32-year-old woman and I am serving a life sentence in prison for a crime I never committed. My story is both tragic and complicated, but nonetheless inspiring in its own way.

I am in prison because I was wrongfully convicted of being an accomplice to the murder of my husband. I was tried and convicted in the most publicized trial in New Hampshire history. One made-for-TV movie, one motion picture, four books, and thousands of news stories have purported to tell my story, yet they all fall terribly short of that aim. Millions of dollars have been made at my expense. I have been labeled an ice princess, cold-hearted, unfeeling and unemotional, calculated, selfish. . . yet I am none of these things. I have been left to die in prison. I am Pamela Smart.

My tragedy began on May 1, 1990, and it has yet to end. It was on that day, nine years ago, that my husband Gregg was murdered. He was killed by Bill Flynn, a young man with whom I had an extramarital affair. Bill Flynn and three of his friends planned and executed Gregg's murder and set this nightmare in motion. It is now close to ten years later and the truth remains unseen.

I married Gregg because I loved him more than anything or anyone in my life. He was everything to me, and I made every effort to make him happy. Our life was pretty much routine, until December of 1989 when Gregg told me that he had engaged in a one-night affair with another woman. Needless to say, I was devastated. My whole world seemed to crumble beneath me and I began to find fault in myself in an effort to place the blame somewhere. My self-esteem plunged and I considered myself fat, ugly, stupid and inadequate. It was during that time that I first met Bill Flynn.

I was 21 years old, and working as the Director of Media Services for eleven schools. Bill Flynn was a 16-year-old student in the district's high school. At first, our relationship was innocent enough. Bill began to develop a crush on me, but I did not really consider it to be anything but flattering. However, as the months passed, I found myself feeling something beyond that. When I really thought about it, I considered the idea crazy.

However, something in my heart was telling me different. I now believe that I was very vulnerable because of how Gregg had betrayed me. In my confusion I made a horrible decision and became sexually involved with Bill in February 1990. Our relationship only lasted a few weeks, because my conscience would not permit me to continue the affair. I tried to break it off with Bill, but he told me that if I broke up with him, he would call Gregg and tell him about the affair. Because I feared losing Gregg, I continued to see Bill. In April 1990, the pressure became too much to bear. I told Gregg that I had had an affair, but it was over. At first he was obviously very hurt and angry, but in the end we decided to work things out. I told Bill that things were truly over, and that I had told Gregg about the affair. I had no idea that would be the impetus of his plan to murder my husband.

On May 1, 1990, I returned home and found my husband lying on the ground and my condo ransacked. It appeared that my husband was unconscious — he didn't respond to me — so I frantically searched for help. When the police arrived and investigated the scene, I was informed that my husband was dead. At 24 years old, his life had been ended by an unknown assailant. The notion that the murderer might have been Bill Flynn never even entered my mind.

When Bill Flynn and his friends were arrested about a month later, I still had a hard time believing that he had committed the crime. It was too awful for me to face. I was also contending with my own guilt and grief that I had had a relationship with the person who murdered my husband. At 22 years old, my life seemed shattered. Sadly enough, things would get worse.

On August 1, 1990, I was arrested and charged with being an accomplice to my husband's murder. I have not seen freedom since. An onslaught of negative publicity pursued me from every angle. My life was no longer my own. Every nuance of my life was fodder for the feeding frenzy. The media commented on everything from my hair to my nails, to my breasts, my waist, my taste in clothing, my shoes, etc. I have yet to understand the purported relevance of any of this. Nor have I seen any male defendant who ever encountered such scrutiny. My judge, himself caught in the media frenzy, commented to the jury that he hoped Clint Eastwood played his part in the eventual movie. His comment showed his obvious lack of concern that my life was literally in the balance. Throughout all of this, my jury remained unsequestered, and was free to roam through the community saturated with negative publicity.

Against this poisoned backdrop, on Good Friday 1991, I was judged guilty and sentenced to life in prison without the possibility for parole. I was only 22 years old.

If it wasn't for the love of my family, friend and supporters all over the world, my spirit would have died that day. Today, it is nine years later, and I still feel the same pain.

In 1993, I was transferred to the Bedford Hills Correctional Facility in New York State, where I remain today. I have never been told why I was taken from my family and moved so far away. I expect that the move was retaliatory in nature so that I would be unable to effectively work with my attorneys or maintain close ties with my family and friends. In 1996, while here in New York, I was assaulted and brutally beaten by two other inmates. I suffered a broken nose, a blowout fracture to my facial orbital bone and trauma to my knee. The injury to my face required plastic surgery where a plate was placed in the facial bone. Because I have a nerve trapped in the fracture, I will never feel anything in the left side of my face again. A cyst developed in the back of my knee, and that was surgically removed as well. A nerve, damaged in that injury as well, causes me constant pain in my right leg. Five ugly scars remain where the surgeon entered my body, but none of them compares to the scar across my heart.

When I reflect upon these things, it is hard for me to believe that I have survived all of this. The parts on paper don't even tell half of the story. There is so much more. Yet, I continue to survive. Sometimes year by year, other times minute by minute.

Since my incarceration, I have worked in the prison as a teacher and tutor. I have worked with students in the ESL, Pre-GED, Pre-College and College Classes here. I graduated, with a 4.0

average, from a Criminal Justice Program through the University of Alabama. I acquired a Teaching Apprenticeship from the New York Department of Labor. I am now in my second semester of a correspondence Master of Science Program in Law. The work is extremely difficult, especially under these circumstances, but I am hopeful that I will somehow complete the program.

My federal appeal is currently in the District Court of New Hampshire. Judge Steve McAuliffe has my life in his hands. I am asking for a new trial. The appeal is complex but includes issues regarding the publicity's effect on my right to a fair trial, the length of my sentence, the judge's illegal conferences with the jury, evidence that was not given to the jury, and the immunity deals that tainted prosecution witnesses. I pray that this man has not only the wisdom to see the injustices, but the courage to do something about it. My life literally depends on his decision.

Pamela Smart

Jennifer,

Here's the extra info you asked for. Thanks, I really appreciate your help. Pam.

More Info About the Teen:

Bill Flynn was 16 years old at the time he murdered my husband. He enlisted the help of three of his friends, Patrick (Pete) Randall 17, Vance Lattime and Raymond Fowler, both 16. All of the boys traveled to my house together on that night, but according to their testimony, only Bill and Pete entered the house. I did not really know Raymond at all. I only met him briefly, once or twice. I did know Vance and Pete. But barely at all. Of course I knew Bill Flynn because of the relationship we had.

When the crime occurred in 1990 public opinion about juveniles and crime was very different than it is today. Back then, I was portrayed as a scheming manipulator who coerced these innocent "boys" to commit these acts. Nowadays, with the juvenile murder a daily occurrence, and situations like the Columbine Massacre, the public is becoming increasingly aware of the fact that juveniles are quite capable of premeditating and committing first degree murders of their own volition. In fact, even at the time of my trial, Pete testified that he had hoped to be a "hired assassin" when he grew up. There was also testimony that immediately after the murder, on the way back in the car, Bill bragged to his friends about the "power and thrill of killing." These are hardly the words of an innocent kid who was manipulated to murder.

Looking back on the situation, I now believe that I was the victim of Bill Flynn's out-of-control obsession with me. When he realized that he could no longer keep me with him by threatening to tell Gregg about our relationship, he concluded that he could never have me as long as Gregg was here. It was then that he devised a plan to eliminate Gregg, making me available to him alone. When that still didn't work after Gregg was gone, we all were arrested and Bill was facing life in prison. The prosecutors gave him a new opportunity to "keep" me forever, and that was by sending me to prison for the rest of my life. He testified against me to avoid his own life sentence, and his testimony secured the fact that I would no longer be available to anyone. In the end, Bill Flynn took both Gregg's life and mine. In his sick mind, he concluded that if he couldn't have me, no one would.

On Dealing with Circumstances Here:

I do the best that I can to remain positive in this environment, although it is extremely difficult considering the oppressive nature of confinement. That is worsened by the fact that, because I am a high-profile inmate, I am always being watched and singled out. Some officers take great pleasure in being the ones to write Pamela Smart a misbehavior report, as if that alone makes them famous in some way. I also often feel like a monkey in a zoo when I am pointed out to new corrections employees when they first arrive here. Some officers and Sergeants are mad that I am continuing my education and working on a Master's Degree. They don't like intelligent inmates, for obvious reasons. We are more likely to challenge and expose their corrupt practices. So whenever they can, they do what they can, to try to prevent me from going to school. This often causes me undue stress and makes me wonder if it is all worth it. I am glad to say that for some reason, fighting against the odds makes me want to fight even harder.

If I wasn't behind bars I would be working in some capacity to help people in prison. I would someday like to be an attorney for death row inmates because I feel they are underrepresented legally, and that racial discrimination often taints their conviction and sentences. If that is not possible, I know I would somehow work in the capacity of an advocate for prisoner's right. I have seen too much to ignore. I would be a voice for those who are silenced by their conditions. I know that even if I ever leave prison, the prison will never leave me. The pain and suffering of confinement will forever be etched as a permanent part of my soul.

Pam

Jennifer,

Hi. I have been totally swamped with my papers. I am in the process of writing a forty-page paper. My room looks like a bomb hit it. There are books everywhere. I don't know how I'll ever get through all of this, but I'm trying. I'm in the middle of a lot of stress right now because a few of these officers and Sergeants are really harassing me. It is so hard to understand unless you are here, but they are all power struck. Being a high-profile inmate is not easy because they get joy out of messing with me. This is probably the only time where they have power over women. There is so much injustice. Nothing makes any sense in here, and it all becomes so frustrating because we have no power to change things. Boy, when I get out of here there won't be a microphone big enough for all I have to say.

To answer your question, all I know about Bill and his crew are that they are in a Maine prison. They asked to be moved there, right after the trial. They are closer to their families because it's right on the border. He blamed everything on me because that's what the state wanted. They used the affair to say that I manipulated him through sex. We are supposed to believe that he was weak — yet life circumstance proves his strength. He was persuasive enough to convince three of his friends to commit murder with him. And I am the one accused of manipulation: nothing makes any sense.

I really have to get back to my schoolwork so that I can complete these papers.

Take care, and Happy Holidays,

Pam

The following is a piece written by Todd Bober, who contacted me at the advice of Pamela Smart's mother, Linda Wojas. Approached from a legal perspective, Todd's work complements and further develops Pamela's own analysis of her trial and sentence.

To: Jennifer Furio
From: Todd Bober

I am writing today at the request of Jennifer Furio to assist in her current project of studying women's issues relating to criminal cases. At this time, I am a third-year law student at the Barry University School of Law, where I am in the process of writing my senior thesis. I have chosen to focus my attention on the issue of pretrial and trial publicity. I chose this topic because I believe that the modern mass media through recent technological advancements has developed to a point in which it has the ability to influence the outcome of a criminal trial. Given this ability, the media — while practicing its first amendment right to a free press — jeopardizes a criminal defendant's sixth amendment right to a fair trial by an impartial jury. These two very basic and most coveted constitutional rights are in a more direct conflict than ever before; the US Supreme Court should be acting to protect the criminal defendant's rights.

To illustrate the current constitutional conflict, I decided to focus my thesis on a study of the case of Pamela Smart. The trial of Mrs. Smart is the first in a series of trials that I have dubbed the "mega-media trials." What makes a mega-media trial different from previous notorious trials is the amount of publicity and the degree of hostility that it generates. Before the Smart trial, criminal trials were mostly covered by newspaper reporters, and perhaps received 30 seconds of air time on local news. While talk radio shows may have devoted more time to discussing an individual trial, their limited audience prevented them from having much impact. However, the rules changed for the trial of Mrs. Smart.

The only local television station broadcasting in the area took a direct interest in the case. One of its reporters, Bill Spencer, launched his own personal investigation, which resulted in a television special based on the case, entitled "Anatomy of a Murder." Although this program appears not to have revealed anything new about the case, its timing — just a few days before jury selection — was clearly not in the best interest of the defendant. The same station, WMUR 9, preempted normal broadcast programming, including the high-rating soaps, to run gavel-to-gavel coverage of the actual trial. While the electronic media was running with the story during the day, the print media was preparing its own stories. The result of all this coverage was a media blitz on a scale that had never been seen one before. Reporters later described the coverage as having taken on a life of its own.

Even the most basic analysis raises the question of why this trial received such extensive coverage, while others before it did not. Of course, one aspect is that the facts of the case contained "sex, drugs, and rock and roll", everything modern America craves for in drama. But such cases have occurred in the past and have not received nearly so much press attention. I propose, in my thesis, that in 1990 the press for the first time had the ability and the motivation to extensively cover this perfect story.

I believe that the media industry as a whole changed in 1980, when Ted Turner launched the Cable News Networks. CNN was like nothing that had been tried before. For the first time, Americans could get their news 24 hours a day, often with live coverage. Because CNN mainly focused on international and national news, the local broadcast network affiliates had to shore up their falling ratings by covering more local issues. It is common knowledge that in television, ratings are everything. WMUR had ample motive to cover, or exploit, the story for all that it was worth.

In order to cover live breaking news, CNN style, the local affiliates including WMUR had to purchase expensive equipment to allow the live coverage. The primary investments were often satellite trucks and mini-cams. This equipment, once reserved, by cost, to only the larger markets, now enabled even the smallest stations to put men in the field to cover local breaking news live with clear video.

The above conditions led to an environment in the media industry in which each news department was vying for as large a market share as possible to justify its very existence. While competition in the free industrial market leads to increased quality at a lower price, in the field of journalism it often leads to sensationalism. This was the very environment in which Mrs. Smart found herself on trial for her life.

My thesis shows that while Mrs. Smart's trial was, for the most part, conducted in a proper mechanical manner, the environment in which it was held was deeply hostile to Mrs. Smart. Her jury was not sequestered and the media coverage was so extensive that it would have been impossible for even the most civic-minded juror to ignore. It is all but certain that the media conveyed the community's hostility to the jurors. With such widespread outrage communicated directly to each juror every evening on the news, and every morning in the paper, can the jury still be considered impartial? Unfortunately, the Supreme Court in its recent series of decisions on this issue appears to indicate that such a jury may still be held to be legally impartial. However, Mrs. Smart still has hope; her case still stands as unique in American jurisprudence and ironically such fame may prove to help her win an appeal in federal appeals court, where her case is currently pending.

The following commentary was sent to me by Linda Wojas, Pamela Smart's mother, in response to my request for further commentary on Pamela's case and judicial experience.

Jennifer,

It was nice to speak with you today. This is the text of my testimony given under oath before the New Hampshire (NH) Legislative Committee on Judicial Conduct on August 20, 1998:

Seven and one-half years ago Judge Douglas Gray violated my daughter's constitutional rights in his courtroom. 1200 press articles created an atmosphere so hostile that no person, however diligently they might try to avoid it, could fail to be affected. The trial court's failure to sequester the jury, and the New Hampshire Supreme Court's failure to remedy this error, cost all of us a part of our freedom. Judge Gray flatly refused to sequester her jury, change the venue or continue her trial until the publicity abated. Instead, he had a room built in his already tiny courthouse to house the media and invited television cameras from around the world to film the entire trial, this never having been done before in New Hampshire history.

He has been called an arrogant bully for his courtroom conduct and I saw this arrogant side when we appeared before him requesting a new trial recently. Yes, in this state you must go before the same judge and ask him to admit his mistake. I believe it takes a bigger man than Judge Gray to admit a mistake. He will admit he was wrong in the press but not in a court of law, where it counts. It may be that he knew his outrageous actions would be rubber stamped by his brethren in the New Hampshire Supreme Court. Now, suddenly, without explanation, we begin to see changes regarding cameras in New Hampshire court-rooms. Even Judge Gray himself has issued media coverage bans. Seven and one-half years later and much too late, he banned cameras from my daughter's hearing for a new trial. What message is he giving us? Ban cameras for a hearing, but when you are on trial for your life they are acceptable in the courtroom? I think not. I think he got the message that his erratic behavior was unacceptable, but no one in our court system has the integrity to admit this mistake. For admitting it would mean a new trial and maybe an innocent person who has already spent eight years in prison will be set free. And how would New Hampshire look, then? As you may know, cameras are banned in federal courts. Supreme Court Justice David Souter said, "The day you see a camera come into our courtroom, it's going to be over my dead body." Television cameras in courtrooms serve to sensationalize, not to educate. The New Hampshire Constitution states, "Every citizen is entitled to a fair trial, free of outside influence." When Judge Gray invited the eyes of the world into his courtroom, it was at his discretion. When he refused to put in the safeguards to go with it, it was an abuse of his discretion.

When the frenzy of the press finally rolled into a tidal wave, all decorum in Judge Gray's courtroom was lost. He finally announced, "The press is out of control." But it was much too late. This case was never about finding the truth. It was about winning at all costs. The person who murdered my daughter's husband took a plea bargain in exchange for implicating her. She has a death sentence; and the murderer will be your neighbor some day. The final insult occurred at the end of the trial when Judge Gray turned to the jury and said, "I hope

Clint Eastwood plays me in the movie" which told me he was more interested in the filming of the upcoming movie than obtaining the truth. Any man who cloaks himself in the robes of justice and utters such a callous remark should be defrocked.

We'll never know what Judge Gray said or how he said it, as no record was made during three ex-parte communications he had with her deliberating jury. When asked, he fumed, leaning forward and pulling his glasses from his nose, "I took an oath concerning my office, that's how you know." Judge Gray did indeed take an oath and that oath stated he would protect all defendants who come before him, but nowhere does it allow him to waive anyone's rights. While the jury was deliberating and the vote was 3 guilty, 3 not guilty, and 6 undecided, Judge Gray told the jurors if they did not reach a verdict they would be sequestered. Shortly after, on Good Friday, they reached a unanimous verdict. Why was my daughter's life not worth the safeguards our Constitution entitles us to?

We should all feel free to speak out against injustice in any form. However, the price one pays to do so can be steep. In order to punish me for speaking out, the state has moved our daughter three states and a nine-hour ride away from us, claiming she is a "security risk". The only "risk" to our security is the states' lies. We do have a maximum security prison for women right here in New Hampshire.

Respectfully submitted,
Linda A. Wojas

Note:

The day after I gave the above testimony, Judge Gray announced his plans to retire five years early, with full pension, on August 21, 1998.

There are 631 Judicial Conduct Complaints filed against judges here. . . only 8 have been adjudicated. . . All the others are hiding in the NH Supreme Court. Despite the fact that we have a right-to-know law and a sunshine law, these files are closed to the public. The NH Attorney General brought a 35-page damning report which prompted the resignation of Justice W. Stephen Thayer. During the recent impeachment proceedings, all these files were subpoenaed, but to no avail. Of the 5 sitting NH Supreme Court Justices: one has "resigned rather than face indictment (Thayer); one has been impeached (Chief Justice David Brock); three others have suspended themselves pending investigation (Justices Horton, Broderick and Johnson).

DIANE BOWERMAN

Diane Bowerman's story is one of violence, confusion, and regret. Incarcerated since 1987 at the Washington Correctional Center for Women in Gig Harbor, she is serving a life sentence without possibility of parole for her part in the murder of her lover, Matt Nickell.

In legal and activist circles, Diane's case is considered unique; it is currently being reviewed under the terms of a new statute regarding the sentencing of individuals who commit crimes in response to their own victimization. As several of the cases within this book demonstrate, these circumstances are not in fact unique, but are more common than many would like to believe.

Abused sexually, emotionally, and physically, Diane has only known non-violence since she was placed in state custody. This can only be described as an ironic tragedy.

Abuse was formative to Diane's personality and beliefs about the world. She first received the message from her father, a police officer (who repeatedly beat and raped her) that it is common to hurt people, regularly and without consequences. His continuous threats kept Diane quiet and his crimes went unpunished. As an adult, Diane's intimate relationships followed a similar pattern of violence. When her boyfriend, Matt Nickell, beat her — just as her father and her past boyfriend had done — Diane was already accustomed to hiding and denying her victimization.

The depth of Diane's feeling of isolation and acceptance of her victimization is representative of the experiences of women across the country. In one notable instance, just six months into her relationship with Matt, Diane was hosting a party at her house for some of her co-workers. Matt returned home and began beating her. He hit her and yelled at her, while her friends watched. Once the guests realized what was actually going on, some of the men pried Matt off her and kicked him out of the house. Concerned for her safety and well-being, some of Diane's friends stayed overnight at the house. The next day at work, however, no one talked about the incident, and Diane herself was too ashamed to bring it up. Unfortunately, Diane interpreted her co-workers' and friends' silence as approving or at least as condoning of her life choices.

Diane's isolation was more emotional than physical. Outside of her intimate relationship with Matt, Diane worked full-time as a manager at a hardware retail store and maintained a more distant "layer" of friends, but tried to keep the abuse a secret. When Diane's friends found out about her increasingly frequent beatings, they responded with shock and anger. Daryl Seaver, a motorcycle gang member, even offered to hurt Matt for Diane. At first, Diane dismissed Daryl's offers, but as Matt became more violent, Daryl's suggestion began to seem more appealing.

Diane's co-workers were shocked by the "thoughtful young woman's" horrible boyfriend, but none of them suspected the degree to which Matt's violence was affecting Diane's reasoning and emotional stability. Matt, who drank and dabbled in drugs, was beating her severely. He was also abusive during sex, often sodomizing her. Yet, Diane continued to play caretaker. She helped him try to kick his drugging and drinking habits. When rehabilitation programs failed and no amount of "love" stopped the violence, Diane was at a loss — where could she turn for help?

Still, Diane tried to maintain the relationship. Though Matt battered her severely, she depended solely upon him for her sense of self-worth — a common dichotomy. In such cases, the batterer dehumanizes his victim so thoroughly that she needs him, to regain a sense of self-esteem. Without her batterer's approval, a woman learns to feel worthless and her life feels meaningless without his attentions.

The possible results of this devolution into a dependent battered woman are numerous: the woman may remain in the relationship until her batterer either kills her, or injures her so severely that she is compelled to leave, rather than die. She may stay in the relationship for the rest of her life, praying that the violence will stop. She may manage to leave, and seek outside support such as counseling, crisis services, and battered women's shelters. Or she may eventually strike back — though it is not always her batterer who is the victim of her violence.

Unique to Diane's case were the "friends" who surrounded her. Several persuasive people, including Daryl, were continually pushing her to teach Matt a lesson. When Diane gave in and finally agreed to let Daryl develop his plan, she felt a sense of relief. She did not believe that she would be "safe" from Matt's physical violence, but rather hoped to be "safe" from his abandonment. Diane only wanted Matt to love her and need her, and she knew no other way to secure his affections.

When she told her friend, Diane Peterson, about the tentative plan, the woman encouraged her to let her own boyfriend help. Peterson's boyfriend, James Hutcheson, was looking for extra cash and thought that Diane and Daryl's plan would offer some easy money. Diane trusted James, because she trusted his girlfriend. Like her conceptualization of "love," Diane's understanding of trust was distorted by the years of violence and victimization she had endured. Diane Peterson's approval and James's involvement made her feel more comfortable. She looked upon James as having a sort of authority. Diane was certain that when Matt was hurt, he would run back to her for love and healing.

Despite such assurances, Diane wavered about actually giving James the go-ahead. It was Matt who finally pushed the vulnerable woman over the edge. He informed her that he had been having an affair with an ex-nurse (fired from several hospitals for stealing drugs), and told Diane that he wanted out of their relationship. The news disoriented and enraged Diane. Rather than focusing her anger on Matt, however, she displaced her rage onto his new lover. She felt caught in a bind between love and hate: she needed Matt to feel valuable, yet his treatment of her threatened her life and safety. Terrified and depressed, Diane began to fail at work. She was frequently too embarrassed to even show up at her job because, as Matt became more reckless with his violence, his beatings left visible bruises on her face. In addition, Matt had begun to show up at her work place drunk, and her boss had told her to either stop the stalking or she might need to find a new job. With her life going to pieces around her, Diane was prepared to do anything to regain her self-worth, and that meant regaining Matt's affections. In desperation, she told James to go ahead with his plan.

Diane was more shocked than anyone when the beating resulted in murder. She had survived her beatings; it seemed only logical that Matt would survive his and would then come back to love her. Of course, Diane was in such distress that none of her thoughts made sense.

Psychologists involved in Diane's defense later testified that Diane was actually suffering from conditions known to result from severe violence and battery. One forensic psychologist who testified at Diane's trial stated that when Diane committed her crime, "She was suffering from at least two diagnosable disorders: PTSD (Post Traumatic Stress Disorder), caused by exposure to events that are physically or emotionally frightening, [and] secondly, a dependency disorder." The roots of dependency disorders are more vague than for PTSD. It has been confirmed that dependency disorders render their victims highly vulnerable to suggestion and prone to poor judgment in interpersonal relations.

Unfortunately, the same poor judgment that allowed her to believe that beating up her boyfriend would bring him back to her also affected her initial responses to police questioning. At first, she denied all involvement with Matt's death. As James, Daryl, and Diane Peterson all began to reveal their roles in her life and the murder, however, Diane changed her story. Police and the prosecution at her trial later used her indecisive answers to argue that Diane was actually trying to manipulate her way out of accountability. In a letter, she explained that she "didn't think the man [James] was a killer. I loved Matt and never meant to have him dead." Investigators did not believe Diane would pay money for a simple "roughing up," but that she acted as a scorned woman who arranged her boyfriend's death out of revenge.

In reality, there is overwhelming evidence to suggest that Diane's changing stories were not only typical for battered women in her situation, but are normal responses for an average person of conscience who is suddenly confronted with evidence that his or her own actions have led to someone's death. Psychologists even go so far as to suggest that women like Diane, who have killed their abusers, often cannot comprehend that they have constructed or carried out a murder. Explaining Diane's case, one psychologist offers her observations that: "after consultations with a colleague who debriefs police officers after shootings, [there is a clear] indication that police officers who have shot someone engage in similar confused, distorted recounting of events, even though they are usually engaged in a non-criminal and socially sanctioned act." Like the police officers described, Diane's horror and fear at her own actions made it highly unlikely that she would initially tell the truth about her participation in such a violent crime. Brown's statement also suggests that, under similar circumstances, most people would first respond to accusations with panic-induced denial. In application, whether they are police officers or battered women, the effort of integrating into their self-concept the fact that they have killed someone is, for each individual, a slow and painful process.

Despite such testimony, prosecutors insisted during her trial that Diane was "clumsy" but manipulative. Lawyers argued that Diane knew exactly what she was doing when she paid to have Matt beaten to death. Psychologists called by the defense, however, countered that such interpretations contradicted Diane's personality as well as her history. Evidence suggests that Diane was too impaired to accept the notion that she was responsible for Matt's death. During the time leading up to her trial, she remained unable to integrate into her soul the fact that she was a killer.

Diane never expected that the law would come into her life in such a way, since none of her past encounters with violence had drawn any attention from the criminal justice system. After a personally grueling trial, Diane was sentenced to serve life without parole at the Washington Correctional Center for Women in Gig Harbor, Washington State. From being arrested, to being charged, to being incarcerated, it has all been beyond belief. Diane remains in shock. Like other women in this book, Diane's prison experience has been one of contradictions: while incarcerated, she has finally had the space to examine her own life and take responsibility for her actions. At the same time, the chaos and violence of prison life have impeded her healing.

In her letters and in our personal conversations, Diane has demonstrated success in realizing that her delusional nature and her actions leading to Matt's death must be faced continuously. Though she knows she cannot allow herself to fall back into a weak state of disbelief, she still feels that she loves Matt. She misses him, and feels painfully guilty. At the same time, she is learning to differentiate the state's conviction from her own true motive and actions.

Diane's psychologist, continuing to be involved in the case, insists that although Diane killed once, she is not a risk to society at large. Diane had no prior history of violent acts and no desire to engage in violence. Since childhood, people had been exploiting, wounding, and violating Diane. The violence in her life was primarily committed against her.

Diane's inability to decipher her criminality influenced the sentence she received. Diane has rehabilitated that part of herself that was traumatized into believing that violence was not only acceptable but rewarding. Since her incarceration, Diane has overcome the disoriented thinking that rendered her a prisoner both emotionally and physically.

Diane's story should not end with her imprisonment. Doctors and reform activists alike feel that Diane's life has been plagued with enough environmental stressors. In prison, Diane is often frightened by the violent behavior that surrounds her. She is ready to move on to the next step in her healing, yet without a safe place in which to do so, she will be unable to develop her full emotional and personal potential. For those who believe that, somehow, prison will continue to do justice for Diane, an analysis of the mitigating circumstances must persuade them that if real justice had been offered to Diane early on, she would not be forced to live in a world of violence and chaos today.

As Diane writes, the confinement and petty rules and protocols of prison life are real obstacles to her attempts to deal with her past. In one of the first letters she wrote to me, she described her life story in the following terms: ". . . if I discuss my love for him, the prison sees a delusioned response or something. I do love Matt, but I realize he is dead, and I realize it's because I told someone to kill him."

Dear Jennifer,

How nice to hear from someone who cares about women in prison. I know Veronica Compton "very well." She has told me about your work with her. I am proud to call her a friend of mine. Looking at her, and knowing how long she has been here, only makes me feel "more hopeless" about my case. I wish we could meet because I'd like for you to have a better impression about me. I am no criminal and have never hurt anyone or done anything (as far as the law) wrong. I *did* ask for Matt to be scared, not murdered though. Now I take the responsibility for his death. I am not a "murderer."

The bottom line is, you have to get people to listen to the "truth" and that's an impossibility, right there. The next thing is, they made me look like such a heinous, dangerous person you'll never be able to change people's minds. I see more *sick, evil* people running our justice system; the truth and justice will never prevail. I don't mean to sound negative, I'm just a realist. And that's the way our country is. Prison is a big, big industry. Taxpayers are being taxed to death while "big" politicians are getting paid more and more. This is what I see and believe. This place is amazing, I have a harder time than most because I just don't fit in. Maybe this is too much to be saying in my first letter.

No, I have no children, I think that is one of the things that hurts the most. However, because I'm here forever, maybe it's best. I've worked hard all my life to establish a good career, and make something of myself. Before I came here, I was a supervisor at Kenworth Truck Co., in the paint department. I made very good money and considered myself to be well-off. I was ready to attempt having children. I was scared because of all the violence in my life, but it only seemed normal because I knew nothing else. I was very confused and sick before this happened to me. I never drank, did drugs, or smoked anything. My only focus was to be successful and healthy: Matt, my boyfriend of 7 years, was an alcoholic, drug addict, and a gambler, but more important than that he was "violent." Please don't get me wrong: he had his good side too, which always blinded me to his bad side. I took care of Matt and loved him very much, more than anyone in my life and even to this day I can remember or think about how much I still do love him. I love him and he loved me very much, that will never change in my mind.

I consider myself a "practicing Christian"; it is hard for me to love these women in here, but I do try. I have so many friends that have still stuck by me in my almost 13 years of hell. My family (some of them) have been very supportive to me. I have an identical twin sister whom I have *nothing* to do with *at all*. She is very sick-minded. I have been on several talk shows such as: *Current Affair*, *Geraldo*, *Northwest Afternoon*, *Sally Jessy Raphael*, and others. My story (according to my twin) has been in *Women's World Mag.*, *World Weekly*, and others. I was portrayed as the "evil twin" while she is the loving "good twin." This is so far from the truth. She's only interested in being famous and rich at my expense. Most of my family have nothing to do with her.

If you were ever able to see me, I could show you some of the material and stories that made me look so "bad". You'll be very shocked. I don't know how much you want to know about me, I think I've skimmed the surface on some things. It's always nice to know someone who cares.

I've sent my story and a copy of the report by one of my psychologists, I hope you get them. Maybe this will shed a little light, please let me know what you think. Thank you again for having compassion for those women and myself. It's nice to know some of us are not forgotten.

Respectfully,

Diane Bowerman

Dear Jenny, (From the start:)

My name is Diane Bowerman. I am currently serving life without possibility of parole at the Washington Correction Center for Women. I have been incarcerated since August 4, 1987.

My story is about a man named Matthew Nickell. I met Matt in April of 1980. And we were attracted to each other immediately. I am awkward sharing this, because if I discuss my love for him, the prison sees a delusioned response or something. I do love Matt, but I realize he is dead, and I realize it's because I told someone to kill him. That is my point. I do take responsibility now, but at the time, I had no idea that Matt would really die. I'll try to explain as we go along. It's enough to say I thought I could hurt him enough to need me.

I saw Matt as a helpless young man with a serious drinking and drug problem. He saw me as a person he could always depend on — which I mistook for love.

It didn't take long for Matt to show me his drinking and drug side. I was never into alcohol or drugs, but I knew that I could help Matt (or so I thought, at the time). Since we both worked at the same place, it was easy to get to know each other's friends. Matt was usually the center of attention and was always fun to be around. I was the responsible one, who always drove the car and took care of him.

I had no idea he was so cruel. I might have seen the signs, looking back. I'd always been hurt by men. My father included.

More later,
Diane

Diane,

I think that your story in particular is going to affect many women who are sitting at home with men banging at their doors. Women afraid of beatings. Afraid for their children. How do they appease these men? How do they protect themselves? As I write to you, women are wiping their cuts, or calming their frightened kids. All the while, terrified of literally being killed.

The police come, and then they leave. The man always can "maintain" his composure at least enough to get away. But the woman knows her fears are real.

Do you relate to this? I think your message is so powerful. Your words. There must have been a moment in your relationship with Matt, a beating, when you could have walked, but you didn't. Was it charm, fear? I don't want to put the words in your mouth. You are explaining everything so well.

Jen

Jenny

Yeah, I remember our first big one: it was in the car and I was driving. Matthew put his hands around my throat and started choking me. I had to pull over immediately so we wouldn't crash. I did feel scared to death, but it was like old news at the same time. Try to understand, this was the way men always ended up treating me — the ones I loved. I don't know what I did to deserve that. No one deserves that.

He talked crazy as if everything was my fault. He scared me so bad that I started crying and was begging him to stop choking me. I could never fight back because his words always stuck in my mind — "women never fight." That wasn't different than my dad — because he always said to keep it a secret. So either "don't fight" or "shut up", it's the same thing, let it happen. I thought "real" women could overcome this kind of anger. It was like I thought I must be doing it to the guys around me!

Matt was violent every time he drank. You are right. He didn't show his problem until into the relationship, either. Drinking had a big role in his beating me. I would be in bed, he would jump on me and start choking me. It was all I could do to get him off me and get to the bathroom. He would pound on the door trying to get to me. I would wonder what I'd done. He would leave and call me in the morning to pick him up. He usually went back to the tavern and there some women would feel sorry for him and take him home. In the morning, he would call, as if he was helpless, to come get himself home. He said he didn't remember. Matt was quite attractive and getting a woman's attention was not difficult.

I always believed he was sorry. I wanted to be his partner. I would get jealous. It made him seem a catch. He just didn't show his violent side to the others. Still, there were good times.

Diane

Hi Diane,

Thanks for being so candid. I hope this is "good" for you, as painful as it might be. I think the more you probably hear yourself talk about the damage, the more you will heal. What a nightmare, but one so many women will read, and nod their heads with an understanding.

More than you realize, you are helping people right now with your words. Battery is universal. Women in prison for murder are, by 90%, there for trying to defend themselves and their own from a beater. That means only 10% of women who kill do so for another reason! This is incredible to me. There is no rhyme or reason. And no one does much: There is very little help. And some women never try to get help, anyhow. Not with the belief that they are bringing it on themselves.

Well, thank you for sharing so much of yourself. I know that your story can make a real difference.

Jen

HOPE RIPPEY AND TONI LAWRENCE

When four teenage girls from Madison, Indiana, went out for a ride one January night in 1992 and finished their evening with a brutal murder, their actions shocked the nation. Hope Rippey, Toni Lawrence, Melinda Loveless, and Mary Laurine Tackett were all arrested for the murder of twelve-year-old Shanda Sharer. Suburban parents across the state and the nation wondered how such an abominable crime could be committed by such young women. To friends, family, and neighbors, they had always been the girls-next-door.

The following letters from Hope Rippey and Toni Lawrence reveal the different ways that the young women have confronted the grave darkness of their actions. Underlying the "normalcy" of their early lives is a story of peer pressure and of the way that individuals can too easily lose themselves to the momentary thrill of power.

As violent as the murder of Shanda Sharer was, the motive and context of her death are equally disturbing. Mary Tackett was jealous; she originally set out to kill her former lover Amanda, who had recently become involved with Shanda. Planning to kill Amanda for her betrayal, the girls went to her house, but Amanda's mother told them that her daughter was asleep. Having already devised an intricate death plan and eager to act out their fantasy, the girls decided to kill Shanda instead.

The two instigators, Melinda and Mary, were young women full of pain and anger. Melinda's home life was incredibly violent. She had been molested by her father since she was a little girl, and she witnessed domestic abuse so severe that her mother was hospitalized. Mary Tackett claims that she was battered by her mother and forced to follow her strict religion. Mary was an angry young woman, dealing with issues of sexuality and identity without emotional stability from the adults in her life.

Together, the girls had created a place where they made their own rules: the Witches' Castle, an isolated spot otherwise known as Mistletoe Falls. Sitting near the bank of the Ohio River by the town of Utica, the Witches' Castle had once been a building, though by the time the girls claimed it as their own only a few serpentine walls were left. Legend had it that, at one time, the nine witches who had controlled the town of Utica had lived there. The townsfolk had burnt down the building, and — as Melinda and Mary believed — buried the witches under the ashes. When they practiced their own versions of magic and the occult, the girls believed that they were tapping into the power of the witches who had once lived, and were now buried, there. No matter how out of control their lives felt, the girls could find safety, security, and trust at the Witches' Castle. Their secret retreat would soon become something much, much darker.

When they knocked on Shanda's door and asked her to go with them to a concert, and told her that they would meet up with Amanda later (a lie), she immediately agreed. Being younger, she envied the older girls and felt honored to be invited out by the same teens who usually had little to do with her. Recently, the girls had even written her a threatening note. Wary and excited, Shanda told the girls that she had to wait a while before leaving, but that she would be able to sneak out soon enough.

When Mary, Melinda, Hope, and Toni returned to pick Shanda up, two of the girls hid in the back seat of the car and later positioned themselves to prevent Shanda's escape. With Shanda safely in the car, the girls informed her that she would be going to the Witches' Castle with them. Hearing this, Shanda became frightened and began to cry. In the first act of physical violence, a blow to the head, quieted her. At the Witches' Castle, the girls tortured, beat, and humiliated Shanda.

The violence continued for hours, as the girls next put Shanda in the trunk of the car. Despite their grisly efforts, she was still conscious, and pounding. Driving around, the girls delighted in stopping to take turns knocking her out. At one point they even sodomized her with a beer bottle. Toni Lawrence recounted how she will never forget the look on Shanda's face when the other girls opened the trunk during a stop at a gas station and Shanda sprang up, her hair matted with blood, bone, even brain, and whispered, "Mommy. . ." In the end, no matter how hard Shanda fought for her life — and her efforts to survive were awesome — the anger and violence of her four young killers were too powerful. To ensure her death, the girls lit her on fire and watched her burn. Later investigation would show that, based on the way her fists clutched the remains of the blanket that had covered her, Shanda had still been alive as the fire consumed her.

Leaving the young girl's body, the teens went to McDonald's to eat and "celebrate." Hope and Toni weren't so celebratory. Back at Hope's house, Toni told Hope's mother that they had "hurt" Shanda. When Hope's parents went to Toni's house to share the girls' story, they found that investigators were already aware of the kidnapping. Toni was "high" on valium throughout the night and forgot that she had "confessed" from a gas station pay phone while Shanda was still pounding on the lid of the trunk.

Throughout the events surrounding the murder, Toni Lawrence was the least enthusiastic about the plan; in fact, the plan itself was a surprise to her until she was already in the car. Once the tragedy began to unfold, she begged the other girls to stop; yet even her best friend, Hope, was swept up by the savage mood.

Hope Rippey, shy and a follower, was responsible for pouring gas over Shanda's little body, the act that finally and irrevocably ended her life. Mary and Melinda were sentenced to 60 years in prison; Hope was sentenced to 60 years but had ten suspended for mitigating circumstances; and Toni received only ten years for a charge of "criminal confinement."

Three of the women were held at Indiana Women's prison (referred to by Hope and Toni in their letters as IWP), a maximum security facility. While still in county jail, Toni attempted to commit suicide and was sent to Kosair Children's Hospital, where she almost died. Upon recovery she was transferred to Rockville Correctional Center. Hope, Melinda, and Mary are all still housed at IWP together, and Hope has expressed her fear of Melinda and Mary and their proximity, both in her letters and during our phone conversations.

Toni feels the need to rebuild her life and to come to terms with her past. On the other hand, although Hope detailed her feelings in her letters, Melinda and Mary were across the way while she wrote, staring at her. Still involved with their darker sides, Mary dabbles in the occult and Melinda shows no sign of remorse to anyone. Hope seems to want to change herself, but as long as she shares prison walls with these girls, she will be tied to them — and horrified of them.

The letters written by Hope and Toni reveal the different ways in which this crime and their punishment has affected their lives. While Hope still worries most about her future trials, and "hurting her case with misconstrued words," Toni is plagued by her sense of remorse. She is willing to do or say anything to "keep Shanda's memory alive, to stop others from giving into peer pressures. . ."

Toni has become an articulate and sensitive young woman. When discussing her upcoming 2001 release date, Toni mainly expresses fear and concern. She is unsure of how others will treat her and how she will adjust to a completely new environment. Having spent the last eight years in prison, Toni feels separated from the outside world. She knows that, even after she leaves the prison walls, the memory of Shanda will continue to haunt her. At the same time that she knows that her life will be a struggle, she also knows that she can use her own experience to help teach others.

Looking back over her life and her crime, Toni recounts that: "In many ways, we were like lots of other teenagers — we relied on each other more than our families. We were loyal to each other, and frightened of each other at once. We aren't alone. Look at Columbine. There are hundreds of teenagers hanging out with kids capable of killing. You don't know when you're going to be in the car, when the jokes will become real. People need to first feel sorrow for victims, but they need to know this is not an enigma anymore. . ."

Note: The following letter was sent to both Hope Rippey and Toni Lawrence.

Hi,

I know you don't know me but I am going to write to you any-how! I know it's bizarre when you receive a letter from a complete stranger. Regardless, here goes. . . I have read quite a bit about your situation. It isn't that I am naive to the crime committed, but I would like you to know that, as one who studies crimes, there are people out here who are dedicated to shedding light on "the other side." People, of course, want to hate you. On the other hand, some people, with prob-lems of their own, may write and tell you what you did was "cool. . . " It takes all types.

What do I think? I think that it is a tragedy — the victim, her lost life. But in all honesty, there is another sort of victim in any circum-stance where such damage occurs in the first place. This is hard for people to understand. The pressure to go along with what is happen-ing, the way an idea can get entirely out of hand. The way we can feel rage, and the way it feels good to release it for awhile; but the side no one gets, living with how we deal with our rage for the rest of our life, haunted by our actions.

Everyone acts extremely shocked when there is a murder among young people. This is strange to me. It's a time in life when we feel so much rage, jealousy, sexual confusion. Sadly, hate often seems to ac-company such emotions.

As a teenager, I was lucky enough to learn that rage didn't really get me anywhere — I know that sounds cliché, but I looked around, and realized how quickly we allow ourselves to get caught up in these emotions. But it's a vicious cycle, landing one back at the beginning. Hate, punishment, and back again. No clearer for any of it.

I am writing to you as one who advocates for the rights of those in prison for murder — or at least one who tries to show their human side. If you would let me help you, I would certainly like to try. I think your position is quite sad but hopeful. I never mean to disrespect the dead, but by defining you as some perpetual murderer is erroneous. I think the act was singular, and you are going to have to live with that.

You deserve to. Still, you have many years ahead of you. How do you want to use them? I hope you would want to see things change, not just for yourself, but for anyone who has ever made a really horrible mistake, and wants a chance to show they can start over.

Please write back if this interests you. I know there is much we can learn from each other.

Jennifer Furio

*

HOPE RIPPEY

Dear Jennifer,

Hello, I'm sorry I took so long to respond to your last letter. I was glad to hear from you again. I'm still not exactly sure what it is I'm supposed to do but I guess I'll figure it out as we go. Before I go on, let me say that I don't mind you using anything that I say or anything that you learn about me in order to *help* me or someone else. I'm a suspicious person by nature, so it's hard for me to trust people. I've never talked to anyone about my case because for one I'm ashamed of it and also because I don't want people to hound my family or anyone else involved.

Us and Shanda's family and friends. I guess I don't know how to go about this, in part because I don't know who I became that night. I was the one in the group to usually go along. Maybe that's why I got "so" involved. I was, I'm sure you know, the one who poured the gas over her body. I can barely say that in a letter. I get scared. It's not easy, years later, it's like yesterday, whatever people may think. I know she can't come up and "get me," but in a way, that's what I deserve.

Her family will never know how much I really feel that. I wasn't really "having fun," but Mary, the rest — not Toni, the other two, they liked it or enjoyed it. They wanted her dead, and they got more excited torturing her. It was like it wasn't even happening. Everyone that knew me was shocked, including Toni. I still love her, but I think it's hard for her because I didn't have much courage at the time. I let her down.

Another reason I feel leery to do this, although I will, is because people betray me for money. I've seen many words come back to haunt me but I also feel like it's time for me to get over this hump. I've been dealing with this basically on my own for over 7 years now and I feel like it's time if I'm going to do anything, I may as well do it now. I pray a lot that God will turn this whole sordid ordeal around and maybe this is the beginning, who knows. I don't expect people to understand what happened or what's happening now — there's so much that I don't understand myself. I don't know what's going to come out of all this but it can't be anything worse than what's already happened.

You said many people would want to hear my story. What would that do? I don't mean to sound stupid, if I ask a lot of questions, but honestly I don't know a lot about anything that goes on outside my surroundings. I know everyone's not against me although sometimes it seems that way. But I don't know what my name would do. How will people receive me? I'm not real *keen* on the idea of another book — even one from my perspective. Actually, Jennifer, in all honesty, I'm afraid to take part in a book. I've seen so many things get twisted and I don't want that to happen, okay? So much is played up, dramatized and ran with; I don't want my words or my actions to cause any more hardship to anyone, including myself. I plan on going back to court one day, probably not for awhile, but when I do, I don't want two or three words that I used misconstrued and used against me when I don't have malicious intents. That has happened before and once it's done, nothing I can do or say further can straighten it out. I don't know what else to say right now. If you'd like I'll call you so we can talk. I would prefer that to writing because then maybe you could explain things better to me. I would want you to be careful in a book and if you are using my letters, I don't want to be made out as some evil creature. I'm not.

Let me know —

Hope

Jenny,

I feel like it's easier to talk to you by phone. I am always being stared at by Mary and Melinda when I'm in my cell. They haven't changed much. They are here, doing time, but they still have the ability to think how they want, which has to do with witchcraft, their girl-friends and things like that. They kind of are in control. I wonder if I will ever get out from underneath that, because we live together, you know? We have to get along. So when we get some privacy, sort of, on the phone (not always then, either) I am safer to tell you about myself. When they see me writing, they ask to who, stuff like that. I envy that Toni got moved to a different facility. That's because of what she did, or didn't do, to Shanda. I think, anyway. She was the worst one, or I mean, the best of us. I went along. I looked like I was enjoying it. I think I am just the worst at knowing how to be myself, who I am. But that would hurt Shanda's parents. I helped kill a girl because of my own need to be liked, and that's about all it comes down to. So what good am I?

I guess there are other girls out there who feel a need to be part of a crowd. This is the truth about what can happen. Girls are always talking about how much they hate another girl. One day you are "in" and the next day you are "out." I am not good at that. So I got into Melinda and Mary. Thinking that I was really in. I don't want to con-tinue this, though. I know it sounds shallow, and I am so afraid it will hurt me in court or hurt others. I'm here forever because I wanted to be "in." People could read about the case, and I did the fire, so I look pretty evil, and I don't have an excuse. I feel helpless to be of any good. And the truth is, I still have to be here, and these people are not so much into "prison reform" as you are. Writing and making friends with you just hurts me in here.

Sorry,

Hope

Hope,

I'm glad that you called me. I am sorry to hear how "timid" you sound about where you are. I'm sure that it would be strange to think of facing these issues, because of the backlash involved. It's not as if you would have loving followers, but you could hope for a better life with some understanding. You probably are more courageous than you think. More powerful. In your case, your "weakness" is your cover. I don't think you are ready to take on your life, and what you truly did to

Shanda. When we speak, you skirt around her, and your part, which was huge, considering you had the capacity to burn her tiny twelve-year-old body. But that's the same reason you seem to be hiding. It was horrific, and you aren't one to like being disliked, even if it should mean living a life around people who accept you the way you are, honestly, knowing what you did.

To reach for sincerity is bold and graceful, and there would be a response, but fear is in your way. I don't condemn you for that. I would probably be much like you, had I ever experienced such trauma, or should I say, inflicted it?

I don't think your true concerns are with Shanda or her family. If you grasped their perspective, you would feel more compelled to take a step back and try and help them, even if only by providing more knowledge. They have nothing but the "why's"... no daughter. You took that.

All you can provide is a semblance of what might have gone through your head, and how to help people look closer at people experiencing whatever you were going through. What were you afraid of then, that allowed you to act so savagely? Fear brings us to rage. That's a fact. Mary and Melinda, I know they still watch you from their cells, today. That must be quite confining and frightening. I'm sorry for you, Hope, but you will find your way.

Jenny

*

TONI LAWRENCE

Hello Jennifer

How are you? I hope that you and your family are healthy and in good spirits. I'm as good as can be expected.

Sorry it's taken so long to respond to your letter — I get burnt out on letter writing, every blue moon.

Your letter was deep — real deep. When most people hear about a murderer, they usually conjure up an idea of the person. It's always the dope dealers, or crack fiends or devil worshippers — this is a myth. Actually most of the women here for murder weren't on drugs or making a sacrifice. Most of them are here for killing their abusive husbands or lovers — they saw murder as their only way out. There are so many who went to the police for protection — they weren't protected — so they took the law into their own hands. You'd be surprised, most of the women in for murder are over 50 yrs. old. More [are] over 30 than under 30. The dope dealers are all murderers too — they push the drugs that the junkie or the newcomer overdose on. They aren't serving 50-year prison terms. God only knows how many people died from the dope he/she dealt. Murder is murder — the executioner who presses the buttons to put the prisoner to death is no better than the man who shot his enemy.

You're a blessing in disguise for many people — there aren't many people who would do the things you do for those who are doing time. It's sad but true.

How does it feel to be going home soon? — actually, I don't think about it — it's still too far away. To think about it now would make the time harder and [make it] go slower. I'm scared — not of people — because I've had the same set routine for almost 8 years now — it'll be a hard cycle to break — I'm lucky tho, I have my family to stand beside me and pick me up when I fall down. Yes scared is a very strong emotion.

The music that [I remember] was out then — Metallica "Unforgiven" and Guns and Roses. . . I like the Cure, also, and Enigma and Nirvana — I like all music, tho. I've never had a preference — we can have 10 tapes and mine are all rap and R & B except two, and they're country. I love to listen to a guitar — my boyfriend, before my case, would call me every night and play "Purple Haze" on his guitar, yes, it's very very calming. I missed it for a long time, but I got over it —

Anyway, I'm gonna close this so I won't put off mailing it.

Take care,

Toni

Toni,

Congratulations on your work continuing your education. . . from one who knows, college is like a meal ticket. You really need a degree to go anywhere or have much power over your life choices. I hope you do well. Have you picked a major?

. . . Tell your friend I'm really sorry about her sentence (the woman who shot her abuser). Recently, a gal I know went to work at a place where the previous owner, a woman, was murdered. She had begged the police to get her ex to stop threatening her for months, and nothing (as usual) was done. He came to her door a few months ago, and said he was going to kill her new boyfriend. She stepped in front of this man, and when her ex shot, it was her who was killed. Nice story. I don't really know what people expect, when the stats just keep proving that the majority (over 90%) of all women in prison for murder are there because they felt forced to take matters into their own hands.

You are still searching for why what happened, happened — to you and to Shanda. Like you said, "All these years, for fifteen minutes." I hope someday you can understand the part of yourself that went along with them, because I think it will be an incredible experience, a release. I just don't get this feeling that it was "you," but perhaps that part within us that allows others begin to take over our own power, to allow ourselves to be guided, good or bad. Many of us know that feeling.

What happened to you probably makes that sound very trivial, but I just feel it can happen on all levels, and sometimes in your life, you will trade in some of your own personal responsibility (you have always felt remorse, responsible), and maybe begin to question other factors, like why you chose the friends you chose, or things that were happening at home, anger or confusion you were acting out. That would be incredible for you and you deserve to have that peace sooner rather than later. And yes, you are an incredible "story," about a multitude of issues — about anger, about recklessness, about consequences, about peer pressures, about self-forgiveness, about responsibility, about adapting, evolving — you will teach people and redirect those who may be right now where you were before. Or parents who need to take a second look at their own family dynamics. Communication, love, affection. All that psychobabble. But it's true, Toni.

You say you wish Shanda were alive. The reality of murder probably was so far away from you. I don't know how close you were, the four of you, or if you were feeling more and more powerful being a part of something bigger than yourself, but I just don't think you really got that your actions would mean forever. I'm sure that the haunting has made that clear. It gave me chills, the small ways she enters into your life everyday, playing cards or whatever. I'm glad that you can look at what happened, allow yourself to think of her, and find yourself smiling. I believe that God forgives and so do the dead. It's important that you grieve. It shows you aren't that same person, that it is crucial for you now.

. . . I never knew anything about the details of your suicide. And yes, I can imagine how that brought your own family closer. The idea of losing you. I guess if ever there was a time to begin to appreciate your loved ones, it's at the brink of death. Will you tell me more about that? The other *prying* question I still don't understand, is *who were you*, when you did what you did. With the other girls. To Shanda. I want to understand what was in your head. I see it as something planned, based on something deeper that built on rage. But I'll say it again, I won't read the books, so tell only what you feel you can, and know I'm shooting in the dark, because I truly know so little about the actual case. I only read if I want to find out where someone is, what they are guilty of. Books inevitably embellish, unless they are first person. True crime is not fiction.

Well, was this long enough? Probably and then some. Thanks for the picture.

Jen

Dear Jen —
Hello —
College — yuck — yes, it's my meal ticket — it's also my way for an early release. I like to learn, just hate the lectures and homework, especially in the boring classes. No minors or majors here — classes are limited [because] not all teachers will teach here, through the college I attend. So I'll major in general studies. At IWP I was majoring in Anthropology — there are NO anthro classes here. I'm basically getting all the core classes out of the way and then when I get free I can go back to school.

Family life before prison, I was daddy's girl but when I hit 13, I didn't need them in my everyday life anymore — I talked only when I

108

needed something or wanted something, like to go out somewhere. Usually I did what I wanted, with or without their approval. The only person I was close to was Hope. I felt like you — a very lost soul.

Spiders, they are here at my workplace. Big ones. Like big like a quarter, just the body itself. I always just stand stuck in the spot, and I'll just say "a spider, a spider, a spider," til someone comes and saves me. Ha. My friend Angie killed one the other day and I was like 5 feet away and I heard it crunch. It was a big one. Then after I was sure it was dead, I picked it up in a paper towel and looked at it under a scope. It was *so* ugly!

The last week or so I've been thinking about the past a lot. Of the crime — about Hope. I haven't wrote her in about a month and that's unusual for me — but my heart won't let me. It's like something finally snapped in me and let me see for the first time that when she could've helped me during sentencing and she flat out said no — then she said to me before we got arrested — "we'll either sink or swim together" — those words haunt me. Just a lot of things are hitting me about her. I'll always love her but today I'm feeling much dislike towards her.

I'm also glad Shanda haunts me — it keeps me in check with reality — the haunting used to be horrible — but the thoughts now are peaceful. A couple weeks ago it was brought to me that this girl that just moved into my dorm had been talking about my case. Well, I walked up and sat at the table with her and asked her if she'd like to talk about it with me — and usually I get angry to the point of shaking, well, she was tongue-tied and stuttering, so I couldn't even be mad. I just laughed at her — until — she said Shanda's name wrong. I got mad then and I swore at her and I told her how to say it right and I made her say it over and over. I snapped. Not because she talked about me but because I felt it was so disrespectful to Shanda. Usually, I just correct people, but that day it went deeper.

I thought that I knew a lot — but when I get your letters, you help me find more peace with my past than I've ever been able to. Thank you.

I agree that an all-loving God judging homosexuals is unreal. No sin is greater than another... blah, blah, blah — I'm not religious, have I ever told you my thoughts and views on religion and the whole God thing in general? Let me know. . .

Yes, I have someone in my life right now. Her name is Whitney. She's not in here, she's free. A good girl (never been in trouble). She came to see me today. And we were gonna take pictures but the picture girl had just left and she had to leave before the other girl came in. I'll send a picture of us when we take some — next Wed. is when she's coming back. I met her at IWP — I did a tour and gave a "talk" to a government class and she was in the class. We've been friends since — over 3 years. We've been talking relationship-wise since Feb. . . My parents have met her and approve. She makes me happy.

The isolation here gets unbearable at times — it gets easy with time. You get used to it — or I have. Some people don't try to get used to it and they get in a lot of trouble. At IWP for the first 2 years we could hold hands and hug, and when they took that privilege away it hurt, because for the most part it wasn't sexual, it was just to feel loved — I always held Hope's hand. I never really got into the prison relationship games — I haven't had a girlfriend inside in almost 2 years. We were together for 6 months. She got angry and scratched me across my neck — I didn't talk to her until the day she went home.

I overdosed on Aug. 16th 1992. I saved my meds for 8 days (Xanax, Sinoquans, Tylenol 4 w/codeine, Lorazepam) I don't really remember much — I was told that after I talked to my lawyer I was in good spirits — I went to my cell and I remember sitting at my little desk taking the pills out of my pop can (where I was hiding them) and taking them. I was found on the floor by my "beanpole" where I *always* sat — they came to give me my medication, amazing, eh? Anyway, I was comatose — Dick (the jailer) called the ambulance and held me until they came — they took me to the C. hospital — I died there for the first time. They brought me back and then overdosed me on charcoal — I was asphyxiated — the charcoal filled my lungs and made them collapse — I died again — they flew me to Kosair's Children's Hospital in Louisville, they kept me breathing manually. The next time I woke up was 8 days later — I had been in a coma — I was hallucinating — I thought that someone was trying to kill me — I was strapped to the bed. There were flowers. Balloons and tons of stuffed animals — but there were all these scary looking machines — my body — what I could see was black and blue from over 100 IV's. I had a track down my throat and there were all these machines. The next second, my mom walked through the door. And she just started crying. That was the happiest moment of my life. She screamed in ICU for my dad. Not only did my dad come but every nurse and doctor on shift came, too — I started crying because all those people scared me. They finally left — after removing the track. My dad left to call the family, the doctor only gave a 5% chance of living and if I did live he said I'd be a vegetable. My mom untied my hands. They were so stiff. She asked me why I did it and I told her Shanda needed my help. I asked her why I was strapped to the bed? Because I fought the doctors and nurses, I pulled out a chest tube and when they first strapped me down, I got my sister to unstrap my hand and when she did it I fought her and pulled out some IV's — needless to say, I was NOT trying to live.

Three days later I was sent to my first mental health facility. I have 7 scars — 4 from chest tubes and 3 from heart tubes. I've seen pictures from when I was in the coma — I was 3X my normal size from the drugs. It was really ugly. I had 3 stays in mental facilities. Two in one and one in [another]. Suicide is no longer an option for me. Self-mutilation was another way of life for me. I get urges now but I don't do it. There's obviously a reason for me to live — that's how I see it now.

Toni, the old one, the one that night, she was nothing. The normal (whatever that means) 15 yr. old out for the night with her best friend. Yes, it was planned — but Toni was not in on the plan or a part of the plan. I had *no* idea. I went with Hope. When I wanted to leave, Hope wouldn't, and I wouldn't leave her nor would I go alone with strangers (2 guys we met before Shanda was brought into the picture). All I knew until we got her, was that they wanted to beat her up. That's usual with teens. When things got bad, I blacked out. I was there but not there. Ya know what I mean? They kept asking me to help and I kept saying no. My only words to Shanda were "I'm sorry" — but I was scared, too — I got back in the car and crawled up inside myself where I felt safe.

Here are a couple of pictures — you can keep them — I have more.
I'll close for now. Sorry it took so long.

Toni

Hello Jen,

Hope you're doing well. I'm okay — stressin' over finals — I took
2 this week in communications and psychology. I turn in my Ethics paper Monday and I have my geology final on Thurs. I did my Ethics paper on "Does one have the moral right to judge or impose a moral value
on another. . . ?" I thought I could write and thought I had a little sense
but the teacher of this class doesn't agree with me. It's a really difficult
class. It's a junior class.

I'm sorry my letters exhaust you. Ha! It's not my intention. I have
a problem with being overly honest. It's a good thing. For the most part,
I will tell you this, you are the only one I've ever talked to so openly
about Shanda. I owe you a lot of thanks. I feel better about it now that
I've talked about it. Some would look at me crazy for talking about the
victim. You know? It's weird to me still.

I'm getting ready to go to Bingo — we have it four times a year.
We get prizes that we don't have on commissary! It's a good thing, they
don't give us much here. . .

There are four girls, me, Hope, Mary and Melinda. The two guys I
spoke of — Hope and I met that night at the Skate Shop where the concert was. They weren't involved in any of it. Yes, the whole thing was
out of jealousy. Shanda was seeing Melinda's ex-girlfriend, Amanda, so
Melinda planned it. But the actual plan was called the "Amanda
Plan" — Melinda had planned on doing to Amanda what she did to
Shanda, but Amanda fell asleep before Melinda came to pick her up.
This was brought up at Melinda's sentencing hearing. It was before I
knew anything about Melinda — actually it was concocted with a
whole different set of people. Jealousy was the only motive. Hope, yes, I
backed her. . . I didn't get the same in return. You said that Hope told
you Mary and Melinda were still "tough". . . She just stopped communicating with them. She used to follow Melinda around like a little lost
puppy. The whole time I was at IWP I spent more time with Mary than

I did with Hope. Mary was a toughie until her dad died. He was her world. He was the only one that ever believed in and supported her. She changed after that. I think his death was a reality check for her. She shared her feelings with me and she is very remorseful, under her "bad girl" mask. She recently hooked up with a girl who is into black magic and devil worshipping and she's gone downhill from there. Back to Hope. Yes, her heart carries more guilt — Hope poured the gas on Shanda, took Shanda's watch and when Melinda made Shanda take off her clothes, Hope put her bra on then and there. She's remorseful, she's still a follower — whereas I have changed — I no longer follow, I now lead. That night does own us — we're known as "the four girls from Madison." I hate it but it will forever be. . . Hope did betray me — she broke my heart with it. She's not swimming — she's floating — a letter from her not too long ago said that I am her lifesaver. She stays above water because she hangs on to me. Me — who she told to sink or swim with her. She is using me to stay afloat. I found it humorous. Such is life. I feel like this — she'll need me before I need her.

Religion — I'm agnostic. I believe there is a God, a higher power, I'm just undecided about *who* it is. I have a problem with God, for there to only be one he must have multiple personalities or something. He's viewed in so many different ways, colors, styles, plus I have a hard time believing the Bible. I think it's man's work — all of it. And if he is so forgiving, then there really is no sin — you can do no wrong in his eyes — cause no matter how bad it is — he's gonna forgive. Religion is something to put your faith in, to believe in, but you can do that to anything. . . do you understand?

Your daughter — at six — is very smart. Kids grow up so fast these days, be thankful that while she's older than her years it's in a positive way. Most kids who grow up fast go on the wrong trail. Yes, she could end up in my shoes. . . peer pressure is a very strong leader. There's no way to see it coming, but being your daughter, and you doing what you do, I believe that she'll go the right direction. You have an open relationship with her — that's something I was lacking — but it was my own choice. Keep the lines of communication open at all times with her. I think life is predestined — what happens happens for a reason. I think about these things too. I want a child, and I often wonder if it's really worth it to bring an innocent child to this hard cold world, a world that, like you said, allows rage. Even more, the world provides rage. [The world] teaches us rage and how to act out in a violent way. Then when it happens no one tries to understand. They just judge you and throw you in a cell to form even more rage in your stir crazy mind. "It could never happen in my family or my circle of friends. . . ."

It can happen to anyone. . . but no one understands or believes it until it does happen. It's sad.

BORN, 2-16-76 Cape Cirardeau, Missouri, two older sisters. Made decent grades in all grades up to 10th. Met Hope in grade school — bonded quickly with her. She moved away for awhile, when she came back to Madison we picked up where we left off and stayed best friends until the case.

Molested by my grandfather one time, July 4, 1985.

Molested by "family friend" over some time — can't remember how long. . .

Ran track, cross country, soccer, softball, bowling, gymnastics, pool.

Always had friends — always had a boyfriend, lost my virginity from the guy who raped me at 15.

At 13, drank whenever alcohol was available, smoked cig's and weed when available.

Bulema-rexic for 9 years (haven't for over 5 years).

Self-mutilator from age 13 — ? Fascination with suicide from 13 — 16, when I OD'd in jail.

Snuck out my bedroom window at least twice a week from age 13 til arrest. Usually with Hope.

Talked to parents and sisters usually only when I wanted something.

Met Mary in 7th grade but never associated with her until 9th — we would cut ourselves in class together.

Hope asked me to go to a concert in Louisville with her and Mary. I asked parents — they said no, so I told them I was spending the night with another friend and went to school Jan 10, '92 like every day — after school Mary picked me and Hope up. On the way to New Albany I was told about Melinda — picked her up, where I learned about the plan to beat Shanda up. Went to Shanda's — she couldn't leave; she told us to come back at midnite and she'd sneak out with us. Went to Louisville — on the way learned real plan was to kill Shanda. Went to Skate Shop, the music was too loud, too hard, and shop was too packed. Hope and I went to the car — met 2 guys — tried to leave with them. Hope wouldn't leave with me so I stayed with her. Midnite — parked down the road from Shanda's and Hope and Mary went to get her while Melinda hid in the floorboard of backseat under blankets — Mary got in back. Hope drove and Shanda got in middle of front seat. I sat by the door (my charge of criminal confinement came from this). Mary started talking about Amanda who was at the "Witches Castle" waiting for Shanda. Melinda jumped up and put knife to Shanda's throat — knife went thru my hair. Took Shanda up to the "dungeon" of the "castle" — Mary and Melinda tied her hands and ankles — I stood in the background. Cars started going by. Mary decided that wasn't a good place. Untied Shanda and she walked by herself to the car. Now she got in back with Mary and Melinda and me and Hope in front. Hope driving. Stopped to get gas — I made a call to a friend — told him what was going on — and that I was scared. Got back in car and went to an old logging road by Mary's house — everyone got out of the car — this is where I told Shanda I was sorry. . . Hope and I got back in the car. This is when Melinda made Shanda take all her clothes off except socks and Melinda gave her a t-shirt to put on. I can't remember if she made her take off her underwear or not. Mary and Melinda tried to slice her throat — the knife wouldn't cut. Hope got out and helped get her on the ground — she got back in the car; when I asked her why she was helping, she said she wasn't. Mary and Melinda choked her til she passed out and they put her in the trunk. Drove to Mary's house. We went inside until Shanda started pounding on trunk and made the dog bark. Mary and Melinda left, Hope and I wouldn't go. We got in bed and hid under the covers. . . we were scared. They came back — I don't know how much time had lapsed. They were laughing and joking and there was blood on their hands, faces, clothes and in their hair. They had gone country cruising and every time Shanda made a noise they'd stop and open the trunk and beat her with the tire iron. Mary's mom got up, so we were leaving — drove to a burnpile behind Mary's house — they were gonna burn her there. Mary's mom came out on the back porch, so we left. Hope drove to an old abandoned road in the country. Oh, before that we stopped at a gas station. I had to take my med — they told me to buy a 2 liter — I took my meds and gave the 2 liter to Mary; she poured the pop out and filled it with gas. Then we went to the road. Mary, Melinda and Hope got out, opened the trunk — someone sodomized her then — no one will admit to it and I was in the back seat, out of it — they tried to get me to help get her out of the trunk [but] I wouldn't. They finally [got her out and] she was wrapped in a blanket — Hope poured the gas — no one set her on fire. Mary thinks that an ash fell off her cigarette when she was bent down beside Shanda. They jumped in the car — we drove and turned around. Melinda jumped out and poured the rest of the gas on her — I looked at her. . . I can still close my eyes and see it. We stopped at McDonald's — everyone ate but me. They took me home where I got ready for work. I went to work but I couldn't function so they let me off early — Hope's mom came and got me cause my parents weren't home. Hope went to my house with me — neither of us wanted to be alone. We went to the bowling alley where we saw two friends Chris and Shawn and we told them what happened — we went back to my house and then to Hope's — I was gonna stay the night, we were watching movies with her mom — I fell asleep on the floor and kept screaming out with nightmares until Hope woke me up. We called a friend and there was a lawyer at her house playing cards with her parents. Hope told him. He said to go to the cops. We told Hope's mom — and then me, her and her parents went to my house [where] her parents told mine. We didn't tell them she was dead, tho. We said that she was alive when they left. . . I don't know why or whose idea it was. My parents took me to the police — I told them what happened — they had already found her body — 2 hunters did, I knew the hunters. Shawn and his father had already told the police. Shawn was there when I got there but I didn't know it. I got questioned for a long time. Then they sent me home. They didn't know who the victim was. They picked up Melinda and Mary that next morning (middle of the night). They were in Melinda's bed together. Melinda acted like she didn't know what was going on and the only thing Mary said was "are we on Candid Camera?"

I try not to think about the happenings so I gave only a run-down. . . stream of consciousness. . . but it's basically how it went. When I bring it up I have nightmares.

I'm closing,

Take Care,
Toni

Dear Jen —

Wow — this was the shortest letter I've rec'd from you. I didn't think possible!

Hi — well today is the anniversary of Shanda's death. I cried myself to sleep last night — when I could finally close my eyes. I was scared to go to sleep. I hate nightmares. I think that I cried so much that when I finally did sleep I slept too hard for any dreams, good or bad. I've been in a world of my own for a few days. I get this way every January. I have a few friends that tried to keep me from the depression. My mind wandered all day — what Shanda would be like if she were alive.

No, Shanda wasn't seeing Melinda's boyfriend, Amanda was the reason for Melinda's jealousy. Were Hope and I involved? I'm not really sure. Drugs and weird stuff. . . she says yes, but I've either blocked it or she's exaggerating.

I understand your need to want your kids to know right from wrong, how to deal with peer pressures. It's everything, as a parent. Like with my nieces and nephews. My nephews know that I was bad and that I'm in jail. I talk to them about it. And Tina (my sister) talks to them about it too. They live in Madison so I'd rather them know from me than to hear it elsewhere. My nieces — they are a different story — Teresa (other sister) doesn't feel they're old enough to know or understand. They're the same ages as my nephews. I don't know what Teresa tells them. I don't talk about it — I tried and she got mad. We aren't as close as Tina and I.

What did I lack most: Self love. Not to be confused with self esteem — cause I thought I was cute back then. I just didn't love myself. So I didn't care what happened to me for the most part. I had everything that I wanted for the most part.

Do you think the book/articles will help? I'd just like a copy when you are through. I'm gonna close till I hear.

Toni

Toni,

Got your letter. How sad for Shanda. She would be in college by now. I'm sure you have thought all of these "would have" issues through. I don't need to do that to you, for you. Nothing will bring Shanda back, but I will always feel convinced that you are paying for being there. Nothing shows me that you were even capable of feeling stimulated. Some may never initiate, but will get turned on and participate (maybe Hope?), but you were, from the minute you found out what was happening, scared to death. You aren't masochistic. Sadly, this means you will suffer more than the girls that initiated her death, that got off on it — for whatever reasons.

Please know that I see it, and many others will, too. Most importantly, somewhere Shanda knows that. I have learned a lot from you. You are candid and honest, and you prove that no matter how good you are, the most awful things can happen. Compared to Hope, it is entirely different communicating with you. You have really evolved. I understand that Hope is frightened, but it is everything I believe in, I mean, what you represent. That people aren't evil and that they act in malignant ways, but then can move forward. I'm proud of you. I would choose to be your friend, in spite of the past. You have that kind of strength.

No matter what happens, I hope you feel you can always write to me. I hope to continue corresponding with you. I want to see you graduate and go on with your life and make it a valuable one — twice so — once for yourself, and once for the life lost. And I'll be around, to watch you grow.

Pretty mushy, Ugh, Gotta run.

Love, Jen

Jen,

I can't believe how soon I'll be getting out of here. All the other girls involved still have a lot of time. I hope I can do this. I'm so used to being here, it's frightening to consider being out there, with people knowing, or just aside from that, trying to get work, not being told what time the lights go out.

My mother is trying to be supportive. I have learned from you to try and be honest about what happened. I can forgive myself and move forward if I stop lying. It helps me stay closer to Shanda, too. My mother thinks my nieces and nephews are too young to understand "jail." My one sister and I are having problems. It all seems bigger when I know I'll be getting out, going to my own place, alone to deal with everyday issues. Other people have learned over time. It's a crash course, just like coming here was a wake-up call. But you get used to things. Now I'm used to this.

Well, I want you to know that this last year, you being here for me has helped me. I think your sincerity will be something I can hang on to when it gets rough. I hope to remain close to you? I guess that's about it,

Toni

BRENDA SPENCER

Brenda Spencer was born in San Diego, California in 1963. Now in her late thirties, she was only a teenager when she committed her spree killing. Her case speaks both to those who are shocked when violent behavioral histories are ignored by social service programs, schools, health providers, and law enforcement, and to the widespread confusion created by the increasing numbers of suburban youth who kill.

Until Columbine was hit by its own teenage spree killers, no one had paid serious attention to the fear and anger expressed by outwardly "normal," suburban white youth. Now, we look closer at the Columbine Massacre; it is always easier to point out murderous behaviors in retrospect — obsessions with bombs, dark or secretive clubs, websites dedicated to the message of "cleaning up our culture." In the wake of such unexpected violence, everything from the family unit to school intervention policies are scrutinized. The media bombards the public with revelations of dysfunction as a possible cause or influential circumstance. Like other suburban youth who have killed at schools recently, the Columbine boys were portrayed as victims of society, as outcasts who simply needed a little more understanding, kindness, and attention.

In contrast, when Brenda Spencer committed her act, no one cared to consider mitigating circumstances or family problems, even when Spencer herself pleaded for understanding. There is no excuse for the lack of intervention by the adults and service providers in Brenda's life. From truancy to theft to suicide attempts, though Brenda acted out for attention and survival, no one seemed interested or able to help the tortured teen.

Brenda was not keeping secrets; her stories of abuse and terror were simply ignored. Brenda was introduced to violence while living with her father after her parents' divorce. Over the years, Brenda had been physically and sexually violated by her father on a daily basis. Looking back, she recalls that the "touching, beating and emotional abuse was coming from the person [she] should have been able to trust most in the world." Brenda was angry and frightened, but not incapacitated. She openly sought a way to escape her father's brutality, yet Brenda's visit to a school counselor resulted in what she recalls were simply "a bunch of notes but no action... No help came from anyone." The message was clear: she was helpless and unimportant. After her counseling farce, Brenda's anger escalated, along with her sense of betrayal. No longer able to trust authority — How could she? — Brenda lost interest in school and in life.

Finally, she was arrested during a 1978 burglary attempt. Ironically, it was a good thing. Her probation officer demanded a psychiatric evaluation of both Brenda and her father. Brenda felt "relieved... someone would know, now, and stop the sex." Testing confirmed that Brenda was so depressed she posed a danger to herself and others. The diagnosis suggested a hospital stay and Brenda was the first to agree. She had tried suicide unsuccessfully and continued to think of ways to remove herself from her father. For her, prison or death did not seem as bad as home. In comparison, a hospital stay seemed like a great option. The possibility made her feel more secure and encouraged a renewed belief that authorities took her pain seriously. Unfortunately, because he had too many secrets she could expose, her father would not comply, and the young woman's hopes were dashed.

Instead of giving Brenda her health (and wary of the damage her revelations could cause to his own life), for Christmas her father bought her a rifle and 700 rounds of ammunition. Brenda's first thought was to stick the barrel in her mouth and pull the trigger. She thought again: suicides always failed. Brenda explained her thought process in a letter, confessing that: "I'd probably live, be a quadriplegic and be trapped even worse with dad than I already was."

Across from her home was the Cleveland Elementary School. From television, Brenda had assessed that the cops always showed up and killed armed individuals in crowded areas before any damage was done. She devised a plan to become a sort of sniper herself, sure that the police would kill her — they never missed.

Brenda wrote out a letter detailing the reasons for her actions. She wanted peace and saw no choice for herself. She also left a will. Though her father found the papers, ripping up her letter and filing away the will, he never confronted her about her plan. Brenda was determined to die and her father's disinterest was a license to go ahead. Obviously he was not going to go to the authorities with any parental concern.

On Monday, January 29, 1979, when she was only fifteen years old, Brenda got loaded on drugs and alcohol (nothing new for Brenda), then grabbed her rifle and ammunition and hid in the bushes outside the elementary school. She intended to aim her gun into the sky, and for twenty minutes she fired drunkenly, waiting for the police to shoot her. By the end of her assault, the principal, Burton Wragg, and the custodian, Michael Suchar, had been killed as they opened the school gates. Nine children between the ages of six and twelve had also been wounded. It took Brenda another six hours to surrender to the police. Still high, her mood was volatile. The media took less than a minute to shove their microphones at her. "Why?" they hounded. Because the real answer was too complex, Brenda retorted, "Nobody likes Mondays."

That singular comment erased years of tragedy at the hand of her abuser. Brenda became known as a cold-blooded, flippant killer. The pop band, The Boomtown Rats, penned their song, "I Don't Like Mondays," after her statement. The media coverage caught more than the band's attention, however. Brenda may not have liked Mondays, but the jury at her trial *hated* Brenda.

Bias during Brenda's trial became particularly blatant when the court refused to look at previous psychiatric records and recommendations. Her claims of sexual abuse were thrown out after her father made the grim statement that the allegations "were just more lies." Brenda was sentenced to life without parole.

Two decades have passed. In spite of the frenzied prison environ-ment Brenda continues to rehabilitate herself. She is no longer her fa-ther's victim. He recently visited — a surprise to Brenda. He spent their time together telling her that she was a loser, and subtly reminding her of past traumas. Even a nearby guard overhearing their conversation shook his head with disgust. But today, she can distance herself from his comments. In a world full of insanities, she has managed to find and hold onto her own sanity.

Brenda has a good job as a mechanic, close friends, and a partner, Chris. She deals with chaos and restrictions, but Brenda is the first to say that her childhood prepared her for a not-so-perfect world. She la-ments the state's refusal to allow her to confront the families of the people she wounded and killed: "They probably have questions. It's not much, but it's the only thing I could do — answer some of their ques-tions."

Some counselors suggest that Brenda has not only been rehabili-tated, but that prison life has little to offer this woman. An inmate since her teens, she has grown up in women's facilities. Brenda has come of age behind bars and, in a way, it is the only — and safest — world she has known. Reflecting on her early prison experiences after her sen-tencing, she writes that "The first month I was in custody, it hit me. I hadn't been beaten for a whole month!"

Brenda's letters provide insight into what it means to *live* in prison. She recounts not only her crime, and the abuse that drove her to seek escape through violence, but she also describes the daily abuses committed against herself and against those around her within the prison itself. Over the years Brenda has learned to accept the reality of prison life, and her letters blend her sense of humor with her deep re-gret and honest sensitivity. For example, she berates the media for trivi-alizing the lives of her victims, while at the same time recognizing that, when confronted with a microphone and harassed into a response, her words have often been callous and obscured her true intent. With her typically honest and straightforward style, she admits that: "I do go bal-listic with the media, all they want to do is sensationalize my crime and harass my victims. There is nothing good about my crime and I feel my victims should be left in peace so they can go on with their lives. . . ." In nearly every paragraph, Brenda describes realities of prison life which are as bizarre as they are heart-breaking.

Brenda has so much she would like to do for the society that she took from. She is earnest when she says she cannot stop thinking about her killing spree. She is plagued by guilt; in or out of prison walls, she will never escape her actions. For Brenda, telling her story is one of many acts of recovery and acknowledgment that she continually seeks out as she attempts to rebuild her life and come to terms with her past. In an intimate way, Brenda's letters reveal what it means to be incarcerated for life, and what it means to hope for a future without ever attempting to escape the past.

Brenda,

I am sending you this letter because I just read a sensationalized synopsis about you in a book I don't dare mention the name of, for fear of a lawsuit; suffice to say it could have been entitled "Big Murdering Mamas" or "Killer Babes." That's the kind of intellect we're talking about. Still, it did provide me with information about you, thus this letter.

I was upset when I read the excerpt about you. Upset by both the crime, and then, the tabloid way it was presented. The article almost poked fun, and the killings were horrible. From your mouth, how come it happened?

So who am I that you should open your mind and heart? My name is Jennifer Furio. I'm married, pretty happily. But the really wonderful thing is that I have these two incredible kids, Frances and Dennis. In fact today is the "last day of school." My daughter graduates from kindergarten! She thinks it's pretty big stuff. It is, actually. When I think of you, I realize we are close in age. Under different circumstances, you might have a daughter of your own, or four strapping young boys. Instead, you're locked away for firing a rifle at an elementary school. I suppose that's part of my connection. When my kids look up with those huge, brown, bear eyes, I think they assume that I'll see to it that their world will always be safe. They won't have to think about another schoolmate firing shots in their school.

Your crime speaks to these times, these issues. Not just selfishly. We have become obsessed with Columbine — I suppose with good reason. But we are a society in denial if we categorize such incidences as only committed by young white boys living in suburbia with chips on their shoulders and computers with intricate web links. Rage is rage. We believe that school violence is new — and epidemic. You are alive and well, here to discount such beliefs. You were a young female. You lived alone with your father, no computer, no cult. Just seemingly damaged. How? The connection isn't about cults or computer freaks, it's about rage.

So I write and I lecture and I hope that I can make some tiny little statement about violence and hate, and about how futile it is to live in a cycle of perpetual hate-punishment-hate-punishment — unless we also are examining the issues deeper, the core to rage and violence. Then we can stop the cycles. I know I sound like a hippie chick with a lot of fluff ideology. I'm a woman with, I believe, a lot of common sense (and okay, maybe I'm a hippie, too).

So do you have something to offer? Do I make sense to you? If so, I realize you have been hurt by talking to media. But I'm not tabloid. You can talk to me. You can fight exploitation by just being honest.

Jennifer Furio

Jenny,

You sound like someone I might want to talk with. I have tried to carve out a life here. It's hard to let people in because I have to prepare for more judgments. I don't mind talking about my crime, I wish more people would listen. I think it's the least I could do. I know what I did was wrong. I won't say anything except how sorry I am. That won't make it better either. . .

So a kindergarten graduation? Big stuff! Treat your daughter well. I would love to have some sweet kids running around. Another story. You're right: Thirties would be great, with kids and everything. Out there, free. Hard to believe sometimes that I committed my crime as a kid myself, but I'll pass my "golden years" in this place.

Please elaborate. I don't really know where I'm going with this. Is it enough to say I would like to correspond?

You were really nice to reach out in a non-hateful way. Thank you for that. I will say, I'm not who the media thinks I am. There's more to what happened.

Brenda

Dear Jennifer,

Sorry it's taken me so long to answer. I appreciate your card and I better catch up. I've been really busy at work, it seems like old home week because a bunch of my old friends are all coming now and I've been running around in here making sure they're OK and we've been having a major heat wave and I've been falling out in seizures. No excuse for not writing, I know, I just wanted you to know I haven't been just laying around on my ass, doing nothing but not writing. Calm, that's kind of cute that you said I sound calm. I guess after living in a place for twenty years, seeing people act in the most bizarre ways imaginable, you do pick up a certain degree of calmness. But then, no one ever listens to a hysterical woman. . . I do go ballistic on the media, all they want to do is sensationalize my crime and harass my victims. There is nothing good about my crime and I feel my victims should be left in peace so they can go on with their lives. But yeah, I do get kind of irritated when you shove a mike at me, a camera into my face and start rapid firing stupid questions at me.

Your "punishment" question isn't a bad one at all. Actually, I don't feel twenty or twenty-five years is too much, so I'm doing the punishment I think I deserve. The only thing I would change is being able to have a fair chance at parole and a second chance at life, so I could prove to my victims that I haven't just been wasting time here. I'd like a second chance to prove to society that they haven't wasted all that money just keeping me here, but that they've also done a lot of good and helped me turn my life around.

I have a significant other. I would like the opportunity to spend at least part of a normal life with this person. Going through life with a dad who kicked me in the head was just the luck of the draw, he should have been punished for what he did. I killed two people and wounded nine, putting people who didn't deserve it, innocent people, through years, if not a lifetime of pain and suffering. I'm doing the punishment I deserve. After all this time though, you sort of have to be OK with life and circumstances, otherwise, you never get anywhere. It doesn't mean you have to necessarily "like" it, you just adapt.

I learned a trade, mainly so I wouldn't have to rely on someone to repair things for me, should I ever get out. I don't have to really deal with men, I've been gay my whole life. Maybe I was born gay or it was because of how my father treated me, I don't know. In prison, it's considered a "genetic queer" as opposed to a "generic queer." Genetic queers have been gay their whole lives while generic queers come in, have husbands or boyfriends and are only gay while they are in prison. Some of the slang terms in here are really strange. It's almost a language in itself. Anyway, my wife has visions of her coming home from work and finding me in the kitchen, with a book, tools and the pipes all torn out trying to fix a leak. She knows how I get. Why call someone when I can do it myself and save the money? And yes, I have given my wife quite a bit of gray hair already because I am so independent and a bit headstrong and stubborn.

Men do think differently but from my side of life, women can be worse. At least men are somewhat predictable, while women can just go way out there for no apparent reason. I think it's a hormonal thing, I don't know. I've had girlfriends in the past that make Freddie Kruger appear normal. But the one I finally settled down with, we're very much in love with each other and we get along quite well. We bring out the best in each other, she just overlooks the bratty side of me. Well, let me get this in the mail to you. Before your address changes. I'm not the queen of organization either, as you can tell.   Your curiosity doesn't make you a nutcase. I've seen those, they wander around the yard here, talking and hugging the bushes, sometimes eating dirt and I don't want to know what else. Take care of yourself and your family. Hope to hear from you soon.

Sincerely,

Brenda

Dear Jennifer,

Sorry I haven't gotten back to you sooner. It's been kind of hectic. "Hectic, in prison?" you say? It happens here too. Anyway, how are you? I hope everyone is fine, you and your family. I don't know where your last letter is so please forgive me for not answering anything in it. I know I had lapsed a long time in answering in the first place, I'm sorry, I'm really unorganized. So please forgive me all around.

Don't worry, you don't bug me at all. I do enjoy your letters very much and from the way you write, your tone and sense of humor, etc., you'll probably be stuck with me as a friend for a long, long time. We do have a crappy mail system oh my! There are stories there! You'll hear them all eventually.

OK, coffee is made, want some? I'm sitting on my bunk, locked in right now, watching "Maury Povich." This will probably be a rambling letter, so bear with me. It's been a long month. First, my father showed up for a visit. And I thought, "Well, what the heck, where there's life there's change. Maybe he's changed and is an OK person now." But, nope, he wanted to argue. Tell me a bunch of crap, how good I look in prison, don't write anyone in the family, on and on. The cops stood there with their mouths hanging open. They sent him out and the cop at the desk said, "My God, that was your father?! I'd never say such stuff to my kid. . . " I said, "Well, that's the difference, you really ARE a father, not just pretending."

I won't lie, I was angry, upset about the whole thing, called my honey and bawled and cried on the phone to her. Which I try not to do, cause she just doesn't know how to handle it when I cry and she kind of freaks out cause she can't be right here and protect me from what is upsetting me. Big, macho babe. She's funny. So, we got through all that.

Then about a week later, I call the place she's staying at and they say she's in jail and [then they] hang up. No reason why, just my honey's in jail. So I get little partial messages from people who come in from county jail where she's at. I still don't know what happened. She gets here and they have her in receiving. We have no contact with anyone in receiving. The main yard is separated. So then they move her to the psych unit. Still no contact, can't find out what happened, how long she's here or anything. Then something happens in the psych unit, they move her to lock-up and the cops come and trash my room. That's how your last letter got lost. I still don't know what they were looking for. My poor bunkie was all upset. All they took were two felt pens. What's up with that? Anyway, picture 200 kids who are hyper-active, amped up on kool-aid, locked in your house for an hour or two with nothing to do. That's the condition they leave your room in when they search like that. They just tear everything apart, throw it all in the middle of the floor and walk around on it until they are done. So — all that for two felt pens. But, since they moved my honey I can at least see her from a distance and wave to her. Still can't talk to her. Don't even know how long she's here for.

Then a friend of mine got her case overturned and she's back in county fighting her double murder conviction. She's scared and not sure what to do and we're all encouraging her to not give up fighting, if not for herself then for her kids. In the middle of her court dates, her mother dies and she wants to just totally give up and come back here. So we've got a letter campaign going to try to keep her going and not give up.

Then last Friday, I called an old friend of mine and found out she had died. Drug overdose and heat exhaustion. I've known her for about eight years. She was one we called, "doing life on the installment plan." She would come in for a few months every year cause she was an alcoholic and a drug addict and just couldn't leave them alone. She was a really wonderful person, would cheer me up when I would get depressed. I'm really going to miss her a lot. I've put too many friends in the ground because of drugs.

And now I'm off work cause my boss got real sick and is in the hospital. The whole class is worried about him. He's really a very good teacher and tries to give the ladies a better chance when they get out by teaching them a trade they can use and earn a living at. He does a lot of volunteer work here also, helping women get their G.E.D.'s. It would be a shame to lose him. So we're all hoping he gets better. Where I work is in a trailer, half is a classroom, the other half is the repair shop where I work. He supervises both. So *that's* all that has been going on here. I'm still kind of in shock over my friend's death. I know you're a good mom, but please teach your kids about drugs so they never have to go through the Hell they put everyone through. I see what drugs do every day here and was a heroin addict myself for 17 years, from the age of ten to twenty-seven.

So, anyway, lets move on to other things. In here, there's always too much sadness, so you have to learn to look for good things. Even if all it is, is a nice, warm day with a light breeze. A lot of the lifers sometimes play the "what if" game, which can be a trap in itself. And we sit around and name the things we all want to do if we ever get a parole date. You'd be surprised, it's all stuff people take for granted out there and never think about. Things like being able to buy new shoelaces the same day you break them, not having to wait four months to get them. Being able to eat watermelon — we get it once a year, grapes, cherries, all kinds of different fruits. We get apples and oranges and one banana a week. A lot of women want to be able to do housework. Cook for their families. Be there when their kids come home from school or just tuck them in at night. Have sheets that fit the bed, be able to pull weeds in their own garden. Be able to go shopping. Talk on the phone longer than 15 minutes. Or just have a pair of shoes that they picked out and that fit. Just silly little everyday things most people don't think about. The reason the "what if" game is a trap is most of us know we'll never see or do any of those things because of how the parole board is.

Well, I'm going to close for now. I'm sorry I'm not in a cheerier mood. I'm afraid to think of what might happen next. But I try to always just hope for the best. Apparently my number's up on the bad news lately. But then, while it's all happening to me right now, then it's not happening to someone else. I'll be cheerier in my next letter, I promise. Until then, take care of yourself and hope everyone stays well.

Bye for now,
Brenda

Jenny,

I am so sorry I've left you hanging out in the wind. Let me catch you up on everything. Ready for Mr. Toad's Wild Ride? Here we go. First up, they let my honey out of lock-up, well, actually it was R.C. overflow. She was on the yard about two weeks, they endorsed her and shipped her up north. She's been gone almost a month and a half now. But at least I got to spend a little bit of time with her. Beats a blank as the saying goes. Then one of my fillings fell out. Then I came down with pneumonia. They almost sent me out to the hospital but the God-awful-tasting medicine they were pumping me full of started working. So, I didn't have to go.

Then they decided to take all of our personal property from us. It's not like we had a lot to begin with. We were allowed six cubic feet of personal property. I had four cubic feet, but I had to send it all out. So now I have one sweatsuit, three shirts, and about one each of the allotted hygiene items. Everyone was upset and fighting for their TV's. That didn't bother me, I haven't had a TV for 5 years now so it's not a big deal. The only thing that is a pain in the ass is in order to get decent-looking state clothes you have to buy them from the workers with canteen items, so I'm saving up for some now.

Oh, and before all this happened, my boss went out on sick-leave. So I was re-assigned to where? Of all places? Pre-Release! I passed my drivers test and graduated from Pre-Release then I was re-assigned to graphic arts — made this stationery in there. Do you like it? I like making this stuff cause it makes people laugh when they see it. Now my boss is back so I'm re-assigned back to my old job in electronics.

And I broke a tooth last night, but my dentist is still on vacation, so now I have a missing filling and a broken tooth. None of the other dentists will touch you if you're not their patient. So hopefully I'll be able to deal with it until Dec. 8th. I spent three hours on a bench in the clinic hall this morning waiting for the lady to find me an appointment time. She asked me if I could wait that long, I told her, "I have no choice but to, right?" Oh yeah, they put me back on my cane for another year. And the last thing is they put me on a low-cholesterol diet. OK, you're all caught up now. I'm sorry I left you hanging like that. But a lot has been happening. Chris is all right. She just hates it up north. She gets out at the end of Dec. They shouldn't have sent her cause she has enemies on the yard up there. Two girls that tried to stab her on the streets are up there. Per their own rules they are not supposed to endanger your life by housing you with your enemies. But they sent her anyway. Hopefully they'll keep her in lock-up or receiving till she paroles. It would be harder for those two to get to her. But it's the same there as it is here. It doesn't matter where you're housed — if someone wants you bad enough, they can get you. But my baby is a big girl, I hope she'll be all right.

Sorry I missed your birthday. So, *here* it is — HAPPY BIRTHDAY!!! Now give yourself a hug for me, OK? I hope you had a wonderful day. I'm a firm believer that you're as old as you feel.

The funny thing in here is the office of internal affairs is checking all the staff out because a bunch of the officers, from LTs. down to C.O.'s have been busted for having sex with inmates. If I can get any of the articles from the papers, I'll send them to you. It's a big, big scandal going on with staff being fired and going to jail on rape charges. I've been watching it for years. It's just not healthy to say anything.

So, write me back and tell me more of what you've been doing. I got real irritated at one point (and I was PMS'ing) and I wrote a letter to four senators, about the parole board — not that they'll answer me back. Well, I'm going to sign off for now and get this in the mail to you. Take care of yourself. I wish the best for you and your family. 32 is just still the beginning of life, not the end. You're not old yet. Take care and write soon.

Love,
Brenda

Dear Jennifer,

How are you? A lot has happened and been happening here. On top of everything I wrote you, they're still doing the investigation on staff here for sexual misconduct.

When I say "up there" or "up north" about where they shipped my honey, I forget that you don't know all the slang terms that are common, every day language here. I'm sorry. In California there are five prisons where women are housed. C.I.W. is the original prison, it's here in southern California. C.R.C. houses both men and women, it's just a few miles away from us here in southern Calif.. C.C.W.F. is further north in Chowchilla, by Fresno. V.S.P. is right across the street from C.C.W.F., and N.C.W.F. is further north in Stockton; usually when we refer to someone being "up north" we mean C.C.W.F. or V.S.P. If they went further, we just say Stockton. My honey is in C.C.W.F. She hates it and her parole date, Dec. 28th, this year, isn't coming quick enough for her. We have correspondence approval, so we get to write to each other. We're luckier than most. We have been through a lot together and I'm sure there's more on the way in the future. But the hard times seem to only pull us closer together. Our relationship is very strong in spite of everything. We're both very blessed to find each other and thank God every day. It's very hard to find any kind of "real" relationship in here. Especially one that stays strong and true.

I am mostly upbeat all the time. I have my moments of frustrations and despair. But then we all do. It doesn't much matter if you're in prison or the real world. We really don't have the luxury of sadness though. We have to be upbeat and strong all the time. We can't show the frustration and despair. Only when you're alone in the showers or in the dark, silently, before you fall asleep. Otherwise they say you are unstable and send you to the psychiatrists which knocks about 5 years off your chance for a parole date. A lot of my friends here are dying also. From AID's or hepatitis C or cancer. We have to be strong. If not for ourselves then for each other. Otherwise, no one of us would survive. All of the lifers here know we're in pretty much of a hopeless situation with the governor and the parole board. But we are all stubborn and won't give the state our dreams of someday going home.

I'm back. Didn't know I was gone, huh? I'm getting sleepy from my meds. I have *grand mal* seizures and they load me down on meds to try to keep me from having them. They've cut them down with the medication, but they can't get rid of them completely. So even with the meds I still have the seizures. They have a lot of different terms for seizures here. The flop and drop, the fish, the tuna, break dancing, the horizontal bop, etc.. Anyway, I had to make some coffee.

As to your question about "what the hell was up?" I was trying to escape the only way I could think of doing. My father had done everything a person could do to another person. The beatings, the touching, the emotional abuse, all from the one person I should have been able to trust the most or go to for safety. He was the one doing all the things you are supposed to protect your kids from. I got no help from counselors at school, no help from anyone. So I came to the conclusion that it would never stop. This was life. This was how things would always be. This was the hand I was dealt in life and there was only one way out: that would be death. I was using drugs, so I would push it to the limit. I would say, "Let me take this much and see if I wake up." I started putting myself in situations where I could have been killed. My friends then knew I had a death wish and just wrote it off as insanity. I had finally snapped because of the things that happened to me if I went home.

I got arrested for burglary in 1978. In Dec. of '78, my probation officer ordered that I be seen by a psychiatrist because of my obvious depression. They ordered my father to see the same psychiatrist because they wanted to evaluate why I was like I was. The result of the evaluation was they felt I should be placed in a hospital immediately because my depression made me a danger to myself and other people. Dad refused, he didn't want me telling anyone anything and said I lied and made up stories all the time.

He gave me a rifle and 700 rounds of ammo for Christmas a couple of weeks later. My probation officer almost had a heart attack. When she calmed down, she asked me how that made me feel. I told her, "like he's telling me to go ahead and do it." Every suicide attempt I had done in '78 had failed. I'd lived through them. I felt like such a loser I couldn't even kill myself right. He was telling me to get it right.

On the morning I did my crime, I sat there loaded and drinking. I kept thinking, "Can't even kill yourself right. What a loser." I thought if I ate the barrel of the gun and pulled the trigger I'd probably live, be a quadriplegic and be trapped even worse with dad than I already was. Then I'd be totally at his mercy, I wouldn't even be able to run. Then I thought if I shot in the air towards the school, the cops would show up. A couple more and they would shoot me. They'd been doing it all month in the news prior to that day — and they wouldn't miss. It would all be over, my nightmare would end. I'd have peace finally forever. I wrote a note and a will. Left them in my room. Dad found them and tore up the note. Put the will away in some papers. Things didn't happen like I had thought they would. All I ended up doing was hurting innocent people who didn't deserve it. Causing them pain and heartache that I can never repair or fix or make up for. Whether people believe me or not I do live with the sadness and remorse every day for what I have done to my victims, it's always right there in my heart and on my mind. I'm sorry I can't make things better.

The first month I was in custody it hit me. I hadn't been beaten for a whole month! It was a most amazing thing. It shouldn't have had to have such a high price for everyone. I still think sometimes that I should have just laid down and let dad beat me to death, instead of doing what I did. Fewer people would have been hurt. I wasn't acting out really. I was only trying to escape.

As for writing an article, I have to discuss that with Chris. Whatever gets written affects her as much as it does me. And I'd like to have her opinion first. So I can't give you my answer yet. For obvious reasons, I am scared of anything that might be written. The press has me made out to be such a monster, and I'm really not. I can't be what they want me to be, it's just not in my nature. But I have no way at all to defend myself from the press, Chris gets so upset also, because her initial response is to think whoever wants to write something wants to parade me around like a sideshow freak. She is very protective of me and gets so frustrated because she knows I'm not the "unfeeling creature" the press has made me out to be and there's nothing she can do to change it. So since we are a team, partners, a couple, whatever you want to call it, I'd like to get her opinion. I hope you don't mind. All I really would like in life is a chance to parole. A second chance at life. I'd like to be able to go home to Chris. A chance to prove to everyone that the time I've spent here and the money spent keeping me here hasn't been a waste. I don't think I ever will be allowed to parole though. Because of how the press depicts me. And I am very scared that Chris will give up and do something just so she will end up doing life in here with me.

Even my victims go solely on what the press says. I am not allowed to speak to them. Never have been. I wish California had a program where our victims could come here and see us face-to-face and speak their minds. Say what they have to say, ask questions that they probably have. Like "Why?" It's not much, but it's the only thing I could possibly do for them. Maybe give them some closure, allow them to heal. I don't know. I only wish the best for them and their families. I am truly sorry for what I did to them. And I know they are probably never going to believe me. No one probably will.

I don't know if any of what I have told you will help you understand me. You seem to be like me in a lot of ways. You seem to look at people with your heart and an open mind. I don't know if that's a blessing or a curse. Chris always says I'm too trusting because even after all I've been through, I still believe in the good in people. No matter what anyone has done, it's not my place to judge them. And everyone makes mistakes in life. I don't know that if I were in their shoes, who's to say I would do anything different. If I were in their situation, I would probably end up with the same results, and wind up being in prison for the same thing they are and the same amount of time. Does that make sense? Sometimes I'm not sure if I explain what I'm trying to say right. I don't know if you will ever be able to understand why you feel like you do about me. Sometimes it's just something you accept without question because there really is no answer. Given different circumstances, we'd probably have coffee together every morning and talk about the silly things our spouses did. And what big babies they are when they're sick.

I'm back, I had to go set an alarm on a lady's clock/radio she just got. She couldn't figure it out. I've got to go get my laundry out of the machine in a couple of minutes also. We get one load of wash a week. Or we have to do it by hand. Now I have wet clothes hanging all over the room. I am so lucky to have an understanding roommate. She's a very nice lady. The only thing she really doesn't like is my seizures. But she's getting better at them.

Well, wake up Jenny, I'm sure I've rambled on and put you to sleep by now. I'm going to close for now and get this in the mail to you. Take care and be safe. Write soon.

Your friend,
Brenda

CHRISTINA RIGGS

Born in 1972 and executed by the state of Arkansas in 2000, Christina Riggs viewed the violence and crime in her own life as especially tragic because it could have been prevented.

When Christina killed her own children during a 1997 triple suicide attempt, she had no idea of just how severe her depression, loneliness, and illness had become. Rather, she viewed her violence as a "way out" of a life that seemed to ruthlessly thwart her attempts at stability and happiness. Only after her imprisonment did she learn of the very real condition from which she suffered, and realize just how desperate and delusional she had become. Christina's life was filled with violence from beginning to end, and her letters reveal her longing for the peace of death.

The patterns of violence and abuse in her life create a complex picture. Christina wrote her story and her letters more as a way to expose the dangers of undiagnosed psychological disorders than in search of exoneration. She referred to her childhood as "normal," and throughout our correspondence she hesitated to speak of the stepbrother who molested her from ages seven to thirteen. She was also reluctant to discuss the neighbor who raped her at age thirteen. Christina felt that her own acts of murder had already caused enough grief and that she had no right to point fingers. Ironically, it is only with a close exploration of

Christina's childhood experiences that we might be offered insights into her reckless and horrific actions as an adult.

As is generally the case in childhood sexual abuse, Christina kept her molestation a secret. Later, the demons of silenced pain and repressed rage rendered her insecure and even dangerous. As a child and young adult, however, no one in her world paid much attention to her. Her parents seemed to be constantly divorcing and re-marrying, leaving Christina struggling to keep up with changing siblings and to acclimate to new step-parents. When a step-brother raped her at age thirteen and her parents refused to believe her, she lost trust in her family and began to create an independent support system of friends and lovers. The crowd accepted her for who she was, but was also heavily involved in drugs, alcohol, and sex. Christina would do anything to feel loved and needed, and she found partying to be fun and an ideal escape from her problems at home.

Christina wanted someone to give her attention, someone she could love, and someone who would love her back. She confused her first consensual intimate encounter with love. Rejected shortly after (her partner would sleep with her, but not date her), she soon sought new partners to fill her emptiness. Overweight, Christina felt insecure and perceived herself as too unattractive for a man to be truly committed to. She began to anticipate rejection. She also began to drink heavily to cope with the accompanying depression.

By age fourteen, Christina was using drugs and drinking regularly. She became increasingly promiscuous — physical connection satisfied her natural craving for affection. Her lifestyle led to pregnancy and, at age sixteen, she gave birth to a bi-racial son. Knowing what a scandal her son would be to her family (because of her age and his mixed ethnicity), she hid her pregnancy until her seventh month. On January 26, 1988, Christina gave the baby up for adoption.

In spite of such disruptions and challenges in her personal life, Christina still managed to graduate from high school. Though barely scraping by, her graduation was a personal success and motivated her to attend nursing school. As Christina accomplished her goals, her professional confidence slowly began to grow. Yet, though her success continued — she earned a nursing license in Arkansas and excelled in her occupation — her personal life remained in shambles.

No matter how hard she seemed to try, Christina's relationships continued to fail. In 1992 she gave birth to a son, Justin Dalton, and in 1994 a daughter, Shelby Alexis, in 1994. Her partners dismissed their parental roles and provided neither financial nor emotional support for their children.

Despite everything, Christina still fantasized that a man would enter her life and offer her an undying, unconditional love. In the meantime, Christina continued her work as a single mother and the sole source of emotional and financial security for herself and her children.

Christina's days consisted of ten-hour work shifts, daycare, transportation, meal preparation, laundry, and housework. She would stand in her kitchen at 1:00AM making lunches for her children's next day, thinking about how she needed to be up and going again in four hours. She pushed herself to the limit, just to survive.

To complicate her hardships, Shelby was often ill. High fevers and hospitalizations for blood infections, bronchial infections, pneumonia, even E-Coli infections, were disturbingly regular. She feared for her child's life and for a way to pay the medical bills. When she looked for help and was denied by everyone, including Shelby's father, she suddenly realized just how alone she and her children really were.

Nevertheless, Christina trudged along, creatively stretching her dollars. On the surface, she appeared to be keeping her life together. In truth, no matter how many hours she worked, she still could not "make it." With few options left, she moved in with her mother, who had recently been divorced for a second time. The familiarity of old furniture, even her mother's perfume brought back difficult memories of her stepfather, the siblings that came with him, and her childhood abuse. Christina became determined to enlist the aid of her children's fathers and to get her own place again.

Securing paternal aid turned out to be a vain effort, but at least, while living with her mother, she was able to save money. Christina eventually found an affordable place to live. She seemed to be pulling her life together once again.

Beneath the surface, however, Christina was, as yet undetectably, emotionally unstable. She had spent her entire life in crisis mode.

Christina's unhealed past traumas, her ongoing stresses, and her unstable future all combined to jeopardize her mental health. Christina could be described as a time-bomb waiting to go off.

In fact, it was a bomb — the 1997 Oklahoma Bombing — that finally detonated Christina. As a nurse, Christina was asked to participate in the aftermath; she witnessed the horror of lost lives all around her. Christina was not equipped for this sort of mass tragedy, and the experience proved to be her breaking point.

Shocked that something so horrific could happen, the young woman fell into a deep depression after the bombing. She wondered what kind of a world she had brought her children into — first, their fathers had proved to be worthless, now, on a larger scale, the world was proving to be an incredibly unsafe place. Her thoughts focused on the fragility of life and the evil that could so thoughtlessly take it away. Christina felt increasingly frightened and isolated as it became more apparent than ever that she was alone in a dangerous world with two babies to protect.

Christina thought of suicide. After reflection, however, she realized that if anything happened to her, Justin and Shelby would be left completely alone in the world. They would have no one to turn to and no one to protect them. Christina decided she was not "woman enough" to cope.

In November of 1997, Christina Riggs decided to "save" Justin, Shelby and herself from the atrocities of the world. She believed they would all be safer and better off in heaven. Using potassium chloride and morphine, she injected her children with lethal dosages, then injected herself. In her suicide note she stated her intention to commit a triple suicide. Her words expressed her hope that "one day you can forgive me for taking my life and the life of my children. . . "

As she lay on the floor beside her dying children, Christina regained consciousness. Shaken out of her depression and confusion, Christina suddenly realized what she had done. In a moment of lucidity, as her own body moved towards death, she realized that she would never see her children again. By the time she called 911 and the three were taken to the hospital, Justin and Shelby had already passed on. Christina alone survived.

Christina's trial was as fast and deadly as her crime. Prosecutors argued the note was a sham. The jury agreed. Christina Riggs was charged with two counts of capital murder and given the death penalty.

Christina's story does not end with her sentence. Her case is, in fact, a perfect example of what has come to be known in the field of psychology as *maternal filicide*. Maternal filicide is a condition that renders a mother capable of murdering her children in order to provide them with a safety in death that she feels she cannot provide them in life (please see a list of related sources on this topic, following Christina's letters). Christina's case has gained further attention through her association with this disorder, and her letters reveal her personal dedication to making the general public aware of how to identify and support women suffering alone. She even went so far as to speak on national television, from death row, in order to bring the issue to the public's attention.

The definition and description of maternal filicide provide that criminal behavior generally results from underlying disorders and environmental stresses, rather than from innate criminality. Disorders associated with maternal filicide include anxiety, paranoia, and suicidal tendencies. Defining the significance of Christina's crime in terms of maternal filicide, rather than accepting the explanations proffered by the prosecution in her case, means suggesting that her motive was born of pathology — a personal history of violence and deviance.

Christina's letters reveal that she suffered, before and after killing her own children, and that she was not only prepared to face the legal consequences, but that, in a way, the state did what she could not do: take her own life.

On May 2, 2000 Christina Riggs was executed. The last months before her death were lonely and filled with grief and regret. In one letter she confessed that, "Every day I smell something that reminds me of [my children]. . . I am overwhelmed with grief and loneliness. . . I don't know how I could have thought death was reasonable. . . "

With only pencil and paper to occupy her time, Christina contemplated her actions from a dank death row cell. In retrospect, she found what she had done unbearable to live with and welcomed the coming relief from the mental and emotional pain that haunted her. Her last appeal for life was denied on November 4, 1999. As her execution approached, her letters gained a lucidity and a clarity of focus that had been absent in our earlier correspondence. It was almost as if she were finally at peace, and for a brief moment found the strength to put the power of her story and her life into words. In her last letters, Christina pleaded with those who cared for her to let her pass in peace. "Please do not try to change my mind. I do not wish to fight for my life. The only solace I will find is through death. I can't live with this memory, this guilt. I just want to meet my babies in Heaven."

Hi, Ms. Riggs,

I am writing you after hearing about your case from another female inmate housed there in Arkansas for the same crime, murdering her children. I'll get to that. . . more specifically, I began to research your case, and have become very interested in knowing you. I realize journalists and authors write to you, wanting to "tabloid" your crime, the horrific tragedy of lost lives. I am not trying to exploit you or your children. I would like to understand better what drove you to act in such a terrifying way, and with some luck, that same glimpse of reason can be passed along to other people, less interested in "rubber-necking" your pain and more interested in seeing that such things cease to occur.

I refuse to think that a mother would overdose her kids during a moment of sanity. I think there is much to your story. I understand you had no significant partner, no significant help, and though you worked overtime, it did not quite cover the bills, which included your very ill daughter's hospital expenses. These are not reasons for murder, but I have the feeling that if explored further, I would find that behind your work and your fears of supporting your children and your aloneness was a terribly frightened woman. I wonder, over time, what would such fear do to a person?

You will probably be executed, as that is the way of the world. Before this should occur, how would you feel about providing your circumstance, using your own voice? My promise to you is to see to it that, should your words be published, it would not be with the intent to distort you, cause further pain to your family members or harm to the memory of your children.

As a mother, I think I can say there is not a one of us who has not touched on a sense of isolation. We have all peeked in and looked at our own souls at their worst hours. I want to listen, and not to perpetuate the hate you've become all too familiar with. I want you to be heard, because in the end, you can leave this world with the satisfaction that you gave knowledge and insights to women who may not be in a very different place than you once were. And as you know, it's an extremely dangerous area.

My name is Jennifer Furio. You can use the address and/or phone to respond.

With all sincerity,

Jenny

P.S. The woman I spoke of is Shirley Curry. I guess she flipped out one day, toward you. She is involved in research I am doing for a book. She mentioned her guilt over the incident. She asked that I pass along her apologies. Her medications create wild mood swings. She tries to keep herself "controlled," but she can. . . flip.

Jenny,

Hi! I got your letter — sorry it took a long time to get back — your letter expressed a lot of compassion and sincerity. You must have a big heart to reach out to women like Shirley and myself when everyone else considers us heartless monsters. Thank you. I am a bit frightened about strangers writing out of the blue. You're right: I'm hated. But if this is a trick, maybe I deserve it. If it isn't, well, I owe it to other people to talk. I can't get emotional, I still get frightened of losing control. . . once I start to cry, it's terrible. No one does anything. I have known alone before, but I always had my children. Now I deserve this. I can't believe there was a time I thought life could not be worse.

If you would like to learn more and you have a computer, look up keyword "Maternal Filicide" or there is info on my website. The address is on my return address label. This is just becoming public, that there is more than "murder" to cases such as ours.

Yes, Ms. Curry was rather rude on one occasion. But I didn't take it personally as she was not herself (those drugs). So tell her that there was nothing to forgive. In fact, I admire her courage and strength for surviving in the place. I look at her as a model on how to survive. She's been through Hell here, yet she manages. Hell, before. The things she must have had to endure I can only imagine. She has lived here for 20 plus yrs. To me it is just amazing. I fear living here for that long, it is so hard to get through each day, knowing what I did. So tell her please that we are "friends." I think she can be frightening, her moods, but I know it's not really her fault. I don't know what you know about her. Please don't mention this to her. Anyhow, this place, the personalities. I can't take being hated in here, knowing what's out there. If you knew me, you'd think this was all wrong, but I know it's not. It's just punish- ment. It's hard, though, because it's like I stepped outside myself, and when I came back I had lost my children, I was a "monster," and I was convicted to die. Yet I know it was me. . .

I am not allowed any contact with anyone except staff. I am on Death Row. Which is the Segregation and Disciplinary Unit. I can see the other inmates and maybe exchange greetings, as they pass my area. . . or if they are in cells that I can see from the Dorm of D/R. My room has a tiny window, nothing else. I go crazy, nothing to keep my mind busy. Hell on earth. I think of them every minute. I think how much I hate what I did, there is just no describing it to anyone.

We are not allowed to write other inmates in the system. So please tell Shirley I got the info on "Women on the Row" by O'Shea (you sent that to her). I have been writing Kathleen since Feb 99. She puts out a monthly newsletter for and about Women on Death Row. Thanks for thinking of me.

I will close for now. I hope you continue to write.

God Bless,
Christy

Jenny,

Hi. I got your letter today. It was good to hear from you and to hear that you feel the way you do.

M.F. (Maternal Filicide) is new but is gaining more and more at- tention. Just since my crime (2 years ago) there have been 6 new cases just in the murder-suicide where the mother survived. Every one was a white, single mother w/ more than one child, between twenty-five and forty. Not to count the ones that didn't survive their suicide attempts. Because then people say, "Oh, how tragic," but if you survive people believe you never intended to die, you are just a heartless murderer. There are several different categories of Maternal Filicide. You can read an excerpt of a paper done on it on the web. Plus on the Internet there are several websites where you can get involved and get more info.

If I had had the info on the disorder, during my trial, maybe it would have helped. I know in some of the cases the prosecutors have been lighter when they had the info on it.

Did you see the story a few weeks back by Geraldo about women and prison? It was really good. It spoke of the mistreatment, rape and abuse of women in prisons that are run by men. Luckily, here it is 95% women.

How did you get to know Mrs. Curry? She is a really unique lady, from what I hear from others. I have nothing but respect for her strength and courage to survive in this place. I fear it. I could never turn my back on her. Because we may be years apart, but we are so similar *no one* can ever really understand us or our crime. Only those of us who have been there. If I was to get my sentence reduced I would want to ask her to help me to cope and survive, because she has been there.

It is hard to talk about, without becoming upset. I survive each day with the grace of God and trying not to think about that night, waking up everyday, with the burden of the lives I took, the people I've hurt is so hard. I miss my babies, they were all I had. They were the only things I did right. Even here in prison so much reminds me of them. Daily. It is rough. I don't know how I would cope in the free world. Especially when I would see another child resembling mine. But here all it takes is a phrase, a smell, even a TV show to trigger a memory that catches me off guard and I fall apart. I try to cope the best I can. I don't get any help here. Keeping my mind occupied is what works the best.

I feel fortunate to have the love and support of my family. Especially when I have hurt them so.

Facing death doesn't scare me. I'm ready. I'm ready to be with my lord and savior and my babies, eternal life. No pain, heartache or anger.

To live is Christ, to die is to gain. My favorite verse is Romans 10:8 "Yet even though Christ lives within you, your body will die for sin, but your spirit will live — for Jesus has pardoned it." I'm ready to accept whatever he decides. My appeal was heard last Thursday and is in his hands. I believe and have faith that whatever the decision is His will.

Give Shirley my best, and take care of yourself

God Bless,

Christi

Jenny,

How are you? Things here are the same.

Things here have been crazy. Just last week I did an interview with the Leeza Show. It is to air this month (the date hasn't been set yet). The topic is SSRI drugs (antidepressants) like prozac, zoloft, paxil, ceratone, etc. And the violent side of the ex of Phil Hartman. . . "News Radio, Sat Nite Live". . . His wife shot him, while she was on zoloft. Eric Harris from Columbine was on prozac. Elavil is one of that sort of drugs — it was one of the meds I was on, and overdosed. This lady, A. Tracy, Ph.D., has studied for 10 years murder/suicides involving mothers and kids and found: out of 32 cases, 24 of them — 88% — were on these drugs! I'm having my mom send you some info on it. Please pass it on to Shirley.

I'm sure Shirley told you by now, my appeal was denied. I'm not surprised. It just wasn't His will. I'm OK!

I know this is short, forgive me but I'm so far behind on my mail. Take care and send Shirley my thoughts and prayers.

Sincerely,

Christy

Jenny

Hi, I got your letter. Sorry for not writing. But I haven't been writing much.

My appeal was officially denied on Nov 4th and I have decided to drop all future appeals: I don't expect people to understand or agree. I do ask that you please stop trying to change my opinion. You don't know. Thank you for the change in my own life — your sincerity made me feel cared for — but we can't dismiss the ceaseless pain.

But this is a personal choice, I'm tired, I'm ready to be with my babies and savior. The pain, guilt and remorse I live with daily is too much. I am at peace now more than ever in 26 months. I'm sorry. But please respect my choice. Send my love to Shirley!

Thank you,
Christy

Note: I received the following letter on May 4, 2000. Christina Riggs was executed on May 2, 2000 by the State of Arkansas.

Jenny,

If you can show anything to anyone, show people that evil and illness are not the same thing. I am not evil, though I feel like it when I think of what I did. We aren't set up to help, just to make sick people sicker. . . because it's bad to have illnesses like mine. This is so much about my children and how much I miss them, and how much I want to be with them, but certain things need to be known.

I was abused as a child, I was overweight and not wanted. The fact that I had a child with a black man caused more. . . aggravation. Then the child was taken away. Drinking and using drugs masked my pain. Pain turned to illness; as anything will when it's chronic.

Then I gave my love to men, and rejection after rejection. I was not pretty, typically, but I was at the least a vagina. Thank God, I guess, because it meant my children. But then the daily reality of no support system. Not a tool I could think of to make it easier. I was a nurse, good pay, but never enough. I wasn't a lavish person. But the grind, daycare, getting up before the sun to pack not just lunches, but everything toddlers need for the day. . . then ten hour shifts with sick people; I was too shy and inhibited to make friends. Maybe too much rejection. . . then pick up my babies and home to take care some more. If I could have gotten a back rub, someone to touch me, anything. . . but we aren't set up like that; and to show a need is weakness. Children are even taken from us if we expose our depression, illnesses. We aren't "fit." It is all so scary, and so illness progresses.

There is no way to know why I survived and my children did not. I was insane, when I reached that point. I have to look at it second by second with a sane mind, since that was my momentary snap. I'm not blessed with chronic insanity, freeing me from the endless remorse. Every smell, even here — macaroni, bleach. . . it's them. They're inside those smells.

I honestly can't wait to be dead. I can't take this pain. I just hope that your book gets out there, and that people might at least try to stop hating for even a second and maybe another mother, alone and frightened and ill can seek help without fear of loss. Because it's inevitable — one way or the next, that mother will lose either her children or her sanity, or both. . . thanks for our communication, your patience and tolerance. I'm scheduled for the 2nd, if nothing else comes up. . .

Christy.

You can talk to my mother, if you need to, but honestly, I'm fine. Better, knowing I'll be with my children very soon, God willing.

BETTY BRODERICK

Probably the most talked-about, most controversial female murderer in recent history is Betty Broderick. Her life has been played out on television and in best-selling books. Betty's crime is, in many ways, surprisingly simple. When her husband Dan left her to marry a younger woman, ending their 20-year marriage, Betty retaliated by shooting Dan and his new wife in their sleep, at their San Diego, California, home.

In the wake of the murders, one question has lingered: did Betty Broderick act in a single moment of panic or out of scornful, premeditated revenge? This infamous debate, raging for over a decade, has garnered the attention of judicial reform activists and feminists who assert that Betty had a horrific but momentary response to years of Dan's mental abuse. On the other side, prosecutors and their supporters argue that Betty Broderick was a sociopath, capable of murdering anyone who stood in the way of the lifestyle she had worked for so arduously. Whatever the interpretation, the story began years before, with a mutual love.

Elisabeth Anne Bisceglia met Daniel Broderick in 1965 at a University of Notre Dame football game. "Betty" was a college freshman, only seventeen. Dan was a pre-med senior. Eventually, he switched to law and graduated from the Harvard School of Law.

The couple married in 1969. In the first ten years of marriage,

Betty became pregnant fourteen times, but had multiple miscarriages. Though some assumed that Betty's life was enchanted, even from the earliest years of marriage she faced unforeseen sorrows.

Knowing firsthand the fragility of life, family meant everything. Betty cherished her four children, and her Catholic background reinforced her commitment. Betty's first priority was family, yet she learned to find a balance between her life at home and the need to work to support Dan's education. She took on several jobs while raising the babies, and Dan continued his schooling. Years later, in divorce court, the one truth both shared was an earlier devotion and commitment to family and success. Dan had relied heavily on Betty for nurturing and income while he continued school.

With Betty's support, Dan was able to graduate and begin a career in medical malpractice law. He became president of the San Diego County chapter of the American Bar Association. After years of work, Dan finally found financial success in his career, and his influence and his bank account became substantial. Despite her family's newfound status as millionaires, Betty did what she had always done — she cared for her children, her home, and her husband. Day-to-day life was the same, just on a grander scale. Rich or poor, Betty Broderick was a model wife and mother.

Betty and Dan's relationship was as complex as it was common. While she worked endlessly to keep the family and their home in order, Dan seemed to demand more and more of her. Despite his dominating presence, Betty strove to make their life "work out", no matter what the personal cost. Though seemingly small, his silent disregard for Betty's needs took its toll. For example, in one instance, Dan signed on to be a Boy Scout Troop leader, only to force Betty to take over the position to "cover" for him. On other occasions, he would make decisions — such as where and when to buy a new house and move — or plan a vacation with his friends (announcing that Betty, but not the children, would come along), and then expect Betty to carry out his plans unquestioningly. Betty strove to fulfill Dan's expectations and to meet the needs of her family. Some argue that she was compulsive in her need to please, while others believe Betty was just truly in love with her life and her family. Regardless, while Betty was at home holding the family together, Dan was out enjoying newfound attention from women.

In 1983 Dan began an affair with Linda Kolkena, a 21-year-old who worked at his office. Linda and Dan lived a secret life for three years before Dan finally felt ready to ask Betty for a divorce. When Dan began to move his things from the family home in 1985, no one was more surprised than his wife. Betty had recognized Dan's flirtations but had brushed them off as "sowing his oats. . . " Dan had been an awkward youngster, but later success had women falling all over him with romantic offers. Naively, Betty thought it harmless. Just forty, she was a good-looking woman. Accustomed to men's attention, she never thought to reciprocate, and she assumed her husband would respond similarly should the roles be reversed.

It was difficult for Betty and her children to deal with Dan's emotional abandonment, but the legal battle was worse. Betty did not have time to digest that her husband had been cheating for three years — she had to prepare for court: a daunting task if your husband *is* the court. As Betty explains, "Dan was "in bed" with every attorney in town. . . he got everything in the end. . . the house, the money, our friends, even my children. . . "

Dan's notoriety within San Diego law firms made it impossible for Betty to find representation. In January 1989, after an eight-day closed trial, the Brodericks were officially divorced. Three months later, Dan married Linda.

Betty and Dan still argued over custody. Dan recorded a phone message from Betty, exposing her temper, then had her arrested for harassment. Dan's legal powers appeared infinite. Betty became more and more aware of his influence. The incident happened before the divorce, but Dan continued to use her "jail record" to gain full custody, threatening to have her thrown in jail again if she did not comply with his custodial requests. He sent Betty a certified letter in which he stated that: "I firmly believe. . . another jail sentence will be imposed." Betty could not take his threats. She was scared to death of losing her children. She knew Dan had the power and will to take them; after all, he'd betrayed her in every other way.

In a panic late one night, Betty took a gun from her home and went to Dan and Linda's house where the couple was asleep. Betty shot them, then called the police from a nearby phone booth. She was later charged with a double homicide.

Betty Broderick's first trial for murder ended in a hung jury. Was she cold-blooded or driven mad by Dan's own cold-blooded control? One juror voiced his opinion when he said to reporters, "We only wondered what took her so long to kill him."

When Betty went to trial the second time, she was sentenced to thirty-two years to life in prison. She is currently serving her sentence at a California facility and her first parole hearing will be in 2011.

Betty's supporters believe that she deserves to be let out sooner. Betty herself remains unapologetic about her crimes, insisting that she simply reacted to the intensive and ongoing stress in her life, and that she had no plans to kill or even injure either Dan or Linda. Her confidence is at times shocking. For example, in one letter she argues that: "My case is *more* than a murder case. There are two deceased people, but they were not 'murdered.' . . . God put those bullets exactly where He wanted them, . . . I couldn't possibly take the credit for such a *miracle*!!"

Though Betty acknowledges that such a perspective might "sound nuts" to some people, she does not allow outside judgments to impact her words. She knows that those who truly know and love her — her children — will understand, and that is all that matters. As we corresponded, it was through our shared experiences as mothers that Betty and I were able to find common ground. Her love for her children and her dedication to their well-being is apparent. In her perspective, she put her freedom and her future on the line to be with them and, though for now she seems to have lost both, she hopes that someday, with the help of supporters who find her case compelling, she will gain release.

Betty's letters themselves partially validate the arguments of both sides of her case. On the one hand, she is unapologetic about her crime. She sees no need for rehabilitation or reconciliation and refuses to express sorrow for either of her victims. Based on such responses, it seems completely possible that Betty is a cold-blooded killer. At the same time, with every word Betty reinforces her commitment to her children. They are at the center of her thoughts, her world, and her actions. She feels that everything she has done in her life has been, with the grace of God, for them. She sacrificed years to give them life, a home, emotional and financial security, and a mother who was there for them when they needed her. Betty's children recognize her dedication to them, and have responded by supporting her while in prison. In addition, Betty claims that her crime was in no way pre-meditated, but that her actions took place in a moment of panic. From this perspective, Betty seems to be simply a woman looking for a way out of a nightmare that threatened to steal her children permanently.

Regardless of the opinion adopted, Betty's final letter, which summarizes her interpretation of the past and her hopes for the future, should be read closely. In a moment of reflection, Betty recalls that: "I thank God that my children and I can be close, . . . Dan can't take that."

Betty,

I wrote to you once before, a long, drawn-out letter. I never heard back, and perhaps that's because it's sort of creepy to get a letter from a complete stranger; I do wish you'd write back, even to tell me what it is that makes you not want to respond. I'd like to share more with you why it is I'm so interested in you.

Your life, the way that you think, what you did — it is important. Through your victimization, you shed light on what happens to some women, when emotionally abused. You took action, after Dan spent years ignoring and using you.

Given the right light, your experience could be used to help other women. The judicial system, the treatment of women, the power men still have. I'm not a crazy, letter-writing stalker out here; I'm an educated woman. I feel intrigued by your story. There are women out there who have similar experiences, who can draw from you.

I grieve for any murder case but society must learn to detach the definition of a criminal mind from a criminal act. An act doesn't make one pathological, insane, etc. There was just that moment in time, based on so many manic moments created by an affair (and abuse), and you acted. And I feel this isolated incident should be treated as such. Not to be ignored but to be acknowledged for what it was.

A system that can turn our children away from us, put us away forever, this is so wrong. You were such a monument to your children — to your community. And then the attempt to sweep you under the rug.

I hope my continued efforts to communicate with you aren't a bother. I'm sure you have people who care about you. I would just like to know you as well.

Sincerely,

Jennifer Furio

Dear Ms. Furio -

There is no way I can possibly answer all the mail I receive. I work very hard at my job and the weekends are spent just keeping up with my regular correspondence — mostly to my children. Lot's of people are "impassioned" by the injustices of my case. I was the sort of person, citizen, wife, mother that everyone is supposed to be! I worked *very hard* all my life at doing the right thing. My children are my work product — they are lovely!

The "affair" was not my case — the callousness and corruption of the courts that were supposed to protect us, is! I wasn't "swept under a rug," that would have been easy compared to the endless litigious assaults that were waged upon me for the years *after* the split. I understand the confusion regarding the killings, but they resulted from years of his taunting, his torment. When I actually went that night with the gun, it was as if it wasn't in my hand. I refuse to take responsibility for something so outside of myself as anything more than that — Dan created this "altered state" with his lies and deception, and in an "altered state" the gun went off.

Sure you can come visit. I'd like that. I've had lots of visitors that have come from all over the country. I am very blessed.

Where are you lecturing? And what topic?

My case is *more* than a murder case. There are two deceased people, but they were not "murdered." There was no premeditation and no intent to shoot them. I was not calculating. It was a fluke that could never be repeated — God put those bullets exactly where He wanted them, in a moment of panic and movement. I couldn't possibly take the credit for such a *miracle*!! That sounds nuts, but if you were there, and could have witnessed me during that event, I was not thinking death, or anything else. I suppose it was a rage, a need to say, "See? This is fear, you son of a bitch!" But I leave everything after to God.

Here is a visiting application. Visits are on Thurs — Fri — Sat — Sun only. I'll provide more details as the date comes closer.

Have you read "Until the 12th of Never?" If you read that, I won't have to start from the beginning —

Sincerely,
Betty Broderick
"Radical Mom"

Betty,

Just thought I'd let you know that I called today about visitation. . . I'm still pending. . . the man explained to me that they are still sorting through March!!! So, my plans to come down as soon as I had hoped have been delayed, sadly.

I had no idea how "famous" you are. I mean, I know women, specifically women who are involved in organizations re: the legal system and so on, who are very aware of your case. Women who feel you did what many women may do after years of neglect, separation from children, spousal abandonment for another woman. I also know that the media is still interested in you, after all these years, but I had no idea that people still think of you as the "housewife turned rebel" — I'll explain.

What I find "humorous" is that our society makes it out like what happened to you is not only unspeakable, but unheard of, as if this has never happened before!! I just hung up the phone with a woman who works for the Prison Resource Center in Berkeley. She was not at all surprised at how shocked people are when a women, intelligent like yourself, with a Hell of a lot to lose, and no help from the system, has her "moment."

I believe the reason people are interested in you is that in the deepest parts of themselves, they know what you did isn't so surprising (I wonder how many women in such circumstances have entertained similar thoughts). Murder is a horrible result, but it is a result of something else. No one comes right out and says so, but basically you took an action — you were panicked, but you still reacted, and men and women privately have to ask themselves if honestly it is so alien to their own human capacity. It's like "The Emperor's New Clothes."

There are women all over the world who have done what you finally felt backed into. And so what is there to do? I do know people want very much to see women like you released. I am going to a function in San Francisco this Sunday night to discuss such issues. Should be interesting. It's kind of funny: Frances had a "playtime" at her friend's house today, we have a birthday party to attend tonight in the park for one of Dennis' friends, and then it's off to hang out with prison activists this weekend. It's the only thing I do outside of family but it's so important to me because I want my kids to understand that by the time they have grown, society will have had to have made some changes. It's too barbaric, putting women away, even killing them, after all the suffering the courts won't acknowledge the women endured.

Anyway, how did I figure you were so "famous?" 20/20 called me. I guess someone who had read another book I had written had called them, so they are talking about doing a segment on these issues (legal reform), blah, blah, blah, and they mentioned to me that they'd "even had Betty Broderick on the show!" The guy didn't seem nearly as interested in the fact that murder had occurred, or your abuse, but more, in a very unsettling way, that they were proud of having met a "celebrity." An incredibly scary footnote about our world.

Anyhow, I hope to hear from you soon. I know you have work, and kids, not to mention Mother's Day (I hope I remembered to wish you the best)... so I can't expect to be a mail priority, but when you can... Sorry, gotta go — the kids are tugging at me: Dinner!!!!!

Jennifer

Dear Jennifer -

I loved the photo!! So you know how much a mother loves her children and how difficult it is to be Super Mom! Difficult but well worth it. I loved being a busy, involved mom — I made my choices happily. I always wonder if I was a good enough mom, and if I could have done a better job. I tried really hard, but to a person like me, there is no such thing as *good enough*!!

I get very very sick and upset even now, whenever I think of all I endured. It was all so cruel, inhumane, and *illegal*! So I do not look forward to meeting with you [and rehashing this]. If you can get *Until the 12th* it will save me telling you the gory details. That author had no children and was a kick-butt working-gal feminist — she really couldn't understand what a mother does for her children or why. She was very good at legal researching. The other *two* books just do a surface/emotional job of the story. The DA's only version is: he left her for a younger woman and she went there and shot them. *Duh*!! There is a 6+ year time span to cover, here!! 1983 — 1989!! The "affair" was over in 1985. This is a story of litigious assault by an armed and dangerous terrorist. The children were P.O.W.'s of the war he started and he kept going for 6 yrs!! I never stood a chance as the "defendant" he forced me to be — it was so sad and there was nothing anyone could do to make him stop. He was determined to eradicate me from the face of the earth by one means or the other!

. . . Your kids are adorable — It's great you work and mother both at the same time. Very difficult, I know. I always worked and had *four* kids to spoil!! Pretty busy gal, I was!! I also kept a beautiful, clean and orderly home and did 99.9% of the housework myself. We had Maria, who worked 8 – 3:00, one day a week, mostly helping with laundry. We were never "rich" while married. We didn't get "rich" until 1983 — the first thing he did was get a red Corvette and a bimbo. We spent an entire marriage in our first and only tract home with little to *no* furniture! As soon as he was ready to take the leap *we* had worked so hard to attain, I got nothing but the big middle finger as "thanks" for everything!

Sorry I have to write like this. Things as mundane as paper, cheap pen, envelope and stamps are hard to come by in here — Life is very difficult in here but I find myself doing as I did before: putting on a happy face and coping the best I can.

If I bitched, screamed, and complained more, maybe people would be in more of a hurry to get me out of here!

Here's another form. Visiting here is no fun as you probably know from your other prison forays — Many rules and restrictions which I will send along when the date is nearer.

Glad you liked our "prison" photos —

See you soon,

Betty

Jennifer,

What Dan did, he did to himself, when he decided to give up on family and everything I had given to him for a younger model of me. Pretty easy to step in and try to play mom at that point. But that's not the point. It was the literal war he enforced. Lots of money, the kids older — I was left with nothing. It was so hard on everyone. Dan wanted me to look crazy. I admit I was pissed. But I was not wrong for my feelings. I was betrayed in a way *you cannot know*!!!! Murder is not wrong for my feelings. I was panicked. Out of my head. I had to get myself out of that whole, long-lived nightmare. I wasn't thinking about murder, I was just out of my head that night. I had a gun. I wanted to scare someone, maybe kill myself, I don't know. Who knows but God? Like I said, *you cannot know*. Everyone was being turned against me. I was kept in the dark about all of our finances. Dan gave me up, and he thought he had the right to walk away from all of his experiences, built up over twenty years of *our* lives!!! I don't know what happened that night. I thank God that my children and I can be close, that we have that. I worked all my life to have a relationship with my kids. I'll have it from wherever necessary. Dan can't take that.

Betty

CAROL BUNDY

Of all the women and crimes profiled in these pages, Carol Bundy's story is perhaps the most difficult to understand and is nearly impossible to empathize with. In the early 1980s, Carol Bundy helped commit almost a dozen brutal murders, involving not only killing, but rape, sexual abuse, necrophilia, and molestation. On the backdrop of such shocking and repulsive crimes, Carol describes her life as one "of hardships, abuse and low self-image." In fact, it seems that her roles as a victim and as a perpetrator are equally true, and inextricably linked.

In great part because of societal expectations of women, Carol's health problems, her bland features and obesity limited her employment options. Nevertheless, it is irresponsible to suggest that her poor health and insecurity alone could lead to the atrocious murders she committed. Possibly, within her relationship with her lover, Douglas Clark (later dubbed the "Sunset Slayer") and her past experiences of abuse, the reasons for her crimes can be uncovered. In the end, however, only Carol knows what went on inside her head as she transitioned from a lonely, insecure mother of two into a brutal murderer. Eventually, her transformation climaxed in her participation in acts of necrophilia (sex with the dead), and, ultimately, the initiation of kidnappings and mutilations.

Carol claims that she spiraled into a cycle of victimization in order to keep her lover. She has explained that not only did she have no sense of who she was, but she had also been jilted by the true love of her life — a man she ultimately added to her list of victims.

The scene begins when Carol, a 36-year-old single mother, an ex-battered wife and a needy woman lacking care and attention, moved into a small apartment complex in Los Angeles with her two sons, who were five and eight years old, in January of 1979. After finally leaving her abusive husband, it seemed that the threesome were beginning a new life. Though she was a diabetic, suffering from cataracts and obesity, she had a future with her children and a new, supportive man in her life: John Murray.

Murray, an immigrant from Australia, took pity on Carol and began a one-man crusade to help her improve her life. He ran errands for her, helped her to receive Social Security benefits (which added $620 per month to her income), took her to a doctor to be fitted for a cane, and even paid for her new contact lenses.

Ten months after moving into her apartment, John Murray became her lover and, while he went to great lengths to help her, he already had a wife and children whom he was not willing to completely abandon. Infuriated, Carol confronted his wife and threatened her safety, but the marriage continued nonetheless. In desperation, Carol then attempted to buy Murray out of his marriage, offering his wife $1,500 to "go away." Finally, he chose to stay with his family, ending his affair with Carol.

While devastated, Carol did not let the breakup stop her from going out and trying to either reclaim her lover or meet a new man. She regularly hung around the Country & Western nightclub, "Little Nashville," in North Hollywood, where Murray was a part-time singer at the bar. Carol's attempts to approach Murray there and to re-ignite their relationship failed. Despite her disappointment, something monumental did happen to Carol at the club: she met Douglas Clark, a charming man five years her junior and well-known for his wild lifestyle. Doug was not choosy about his sex-mates, often receiving money for his escapades with lonely women like Carol Bundy. Though her appearance did not match his "ideal," Carol's needy nature and willingness to turn her life over to her lovers proved to be the fulfillment of Doug's darkest fantasies — fantasies which included rape, torture, and murder.

Carol fed off of Doug's attentions; he made her feel attractive, and their torrid affair made her giddy. Their sex life also increased her self-esteem. In Doug's world, Carol felt more powerful and special. He had good looks and during his childhood had traveled all over the world as the son of a Navy admiral. Despite his thrilling past, Doug was a mechanic by trade; Carol would not have cared if he was a vagrant, as long as he was passionate about her. Before long, the slick younger man had convinced the "older" woman that he was smitten, and for a few weeks Carol would remain blissfully unaware of Doug's dark intentions.

When Doug began to discuss his desire to bring home young girls, Carol tried not to lose the fragile sense of self she had only recently developed. After the heart-breakingly slow demise of her relationship with Murray, Carol believed that if she could hold her tongue and go along with Doug's yearnings, she would not have to lose another man. Secretly enraged and jealous, Carol contained her feelings, eventually taking them out on her victims.

As their relationship intensified, Doug continued to maintain a job in a boiler room, while Carol worked occasionally as a vocational nurse, still receiving her social security income. When Doug asked Carol if he could live with her, she accepted. Not only would it give her more control over his daily life, Carol also hoped to make her past lover, John Murray, jealous. The plan backfired. Carol may have known her live-in lover's movements on a daily basis, but once he moved in, he was in complete control of their world. From doing all household chores to living as a sex slave, Carol became Doug's puppet.

Even her children and her responsibilities as a single mother fell by the wayside. Doug paid little attention to her children, who stood as tiny witnesses to his sick appetite. Doug used fear as one method of controlling the boys and Carol: disobedience was met with terrifying threats or physical violence. When Doug slashed Carol for disobeying him, the boys became frightened for their own safety.

Since Doug displayed no interest in homosexuality, Carol felt her sons were safe from Doug's sexual urges (though in nationally televised appearances, her sons have told a far different story). Other children, however, were not. One eleven-year-old girl, a neighbor who played near their small apartment, was perfect prey for Doug. He eventually lured the child into their apartment and persuaded her to shower with him, at the same time convincing Carol to join in. In order to maintain the facade of their lives, all involved discounted Doug and Carol's pedophilic acts as a sort of "game." This was, of course, only the beginning of the couple's string of violent crimes and sexual abuse.

The first victims to actually vanish were two teenage girls, whose murders would later be linked to a series of killings dubbed the work of the "Sunset Slayer," a psycho roaming Sunset Boulevard and surrounding areas. Gina Narano, fifteen, and her sixteen-year-old half-sister, Cynthia Chandler, were abducted in Huntington Beach on June 11, 1980. A day later, their bodies were dumped near Griffith Park, an area of Los Angeles that runs along the Ventura Freeway not far from Sunset Boulevard. The crimes appeared to be the work of a solo serial killer. Doug reportedly bragged to Carol about forcing the girls to perform oral sex, and while doing so, shooting them each through the head with a pistol.

Less than a month later, on June 24, Karen Jones, a prostitute in her early twenties, was found dead behind a restaurant, also shot through the head. That same day, a headless corpse was found in Studio City, later determined to be twenty-year-old Exxie Wilson, also a prostitute.

Throughout this calculated killing spree, Carol's children were spending more and more time with relatives, facilitating Doug and Carol's expansion to more atrocious activities. At one point, Doug brought home Exxie Wilson's head and kept it in the freezer. Carol has confessed to "putting make-up on (Exxie) for Doug and me," while Doug would reportedly shower with the head, performing acts of necrophillic fellatio. Carol later tossed the head into a ditch.

As the couple's violence increased, the media was making the public aware of a lunatic madman on the loose. No one had survived to report that a woman had participated, though in reality it was Carol, with her Plain Jane features and quiet composure, who succeeded in luring many of the victims.

Despite the media attention, the murders continued. A young, unidentified woman was found on Sunset Boulevard, also killed by a single shot to the head. Other bodies and other body parts were found: Exxie Wilson's head was put in a wooden box and left in a Hollywood alley. Then two hitchhikers found various body parts in an area near Malibu, including a skull bearing the signature single bullet from a .38 pistol.

As the murderous activity escalated, Carol was weakening. On August 5, 1980 she went to "Little Nashville" and confessed her involvement in the crimes to John Murray, who was repulsed. Nervous about his response and regretting her confession, Carol asked Murray to meet her at his van and he agreed. In fear and anger she stabbed her former lover and supporter nine times, slicing through his buttocks, and finally decapitating him.

Carol was losing control. On August 11, during her shift at the hospital where she worked part-time as a nurse's assistant, she broke down and sobbed that she was taking lives rather than saving them. Another nurse called the police, who searched her apartment and found not only victims' garments but also photographs of the nude eleven-year-old in varying positions, both alone and with Doug and Carol. The many "trophies" they kept of their crimes gave them away.

In addition, tests revealed that the gun found in the apartment was the same gun used on all of the "Sunset" victims. The police picked up Doug at his workplace. Upon arrest, the two lovers became instant adversaries — while Carol made a complete confession, Doug claimed and continues to insist that Carol Bundy and John Murray were the killers, and that Carol was a "lesbian whore who continued to kill even after she took out John."

As evidenced in her letters, Carol continues to construct herself as a woman in need. My invitations for correspondence were met by cold calculation and dismissal, until I sent her money "to pay for her glasses", at which point her letters softened and she opened up in a "friendly" and "familiar" tone. Unlike many of the other women in the book, Carol speaks little of her regret, changes in attitude or outlook, or desires to be with her children. She expresses more fear for her own sanity than for the pain of the families and friends of her victims. Her fear/love of Doug is evident in her letters. Though she says she once was weak, she does not seem to have found the strength that she needs to

heal or to begin to make amends. Her story is more than a double tragedy, and it appears that, through Carol and Doug's relationship, more
lives were lost than have been accounted for.

Carol presents herself as Doug's victim, yet her letters reveal a
woman who is determined to be her own victim as well. Any semblance
of grief that she might feel is hidden behind an impenetrable exterior.
She mentions her children only as characters from the past, and refuses
to discuss any impact her actions might have had on their lives. Unlike
most of the women in this book, Carol Bundy has done little with her
time in prison and it appears that she may continue to perceive herself
as a victim — while failing to acknowledge her own very real victims — for the rest of her life. Carol's staunch refusal to confront the
damage she caused is another form of violation to her victims and their
families and is, for her and her family, a tragic and destructive way to
live.

Carol,

I have tried to write to you before. I wish you would return my
attempts. My name is Jennifer — in case you've forgotten. I am a writer.
I speak to women all over the country who have been abused, brain-
washed and horrifically manipulated by men they love(d).

I have also written to men. Many never confess — or they blame
the woman, but I feel men have so much power — especially over how
we see ourselves and how far we will go for them.

I know you were a young woman — my age — when life spun out
of control for you. Like you I also have children. I can't imagine not being able to touch them everyday, yet I see how swiftly a man can make
us lose our priorities — do things we never thought we'd do.

I don't want to correspond with you in a way that's painful but
enlightening. I am sure God forgives. I'm not here to judge. I'm hoping
that by gathering important messages such as your own, about what
happened, how you feel today, and allowing you your voice rather than
writing about you, people can see a very clear picture of what can happen.

A society can change when those who have been misjudged by

their actions begin to educate. That is my intent, to ask you to write and let me share your feelings. I hope by being honest, we can know one another, and you'll open up to me.

Jennifer

PS: I must admit, I know least how to approach you, of all the women imprisoned for murder whom I do approach. Truthfully, I am frightened.

Dear Madam,

Your letter is 100% manipulative horseshit designed to hit all the emotional buttons. Sorry, I'm not available for interviews. Save your Postage.#

Hi, Carol.

Nice backlash letter. I think I understand your defensiveness, but I'm not out to get you. You are right: Most people who write like I did are trying to provoke you. That's not true here. I have seen you speak , and I know you're not just a one-dimensional person. I believe it was your incredible dependency that got you where you are. That was probably your biggest "flaw" and what scares you most now. . . maybe I pushed some buttons you aren't ready to have pushed — at least by a stranger. Sorry for that. I guess I could try being more of a hard ass (ha). I imagine you have many sides. You can't be all "evil" or as tough as you tried to come off with me. I'm not out to harm you. If you'd give me a chance, there's much I want to talk to you about. I am definitely NOT trying to manipulate you in any way. Not knowing me doesn't mean you can't at least give me the shot at trying out TRUST.

If you knew the stories I have studied about serial crimes, about the way I feel about it; I want to know not the sensational details, but the person behind the cell wall. I think you are bright but easily manipulated by men. I realize you think I'm overstepping boundaries by saying even that much.

I have things to talk to you about, if you'd be willing. You might find a correspondence healing — beneficial. We are women. And just like women and their children, there exists something between women which, at least with me, makes me want to understand how we can be screwed so cunningly — and when we please a man, we can even talk ourselves into believing we like our lives. I think I'm beginning to speak in the abstract, but I don't feel comfortable being more than vague on that topic until you agree to talk to me. Who knows? Maybe you'll end up using me in some way. . . I hope you don't play games. I just want to share letters with you. And I know if you choose to write, you would be interested by some of what I want to talk with you about.

> Sincerely,
> Jennifer, AGAIN!!

Dear Jennifer;

There are many things you don't seem to grasp. You must. You are not going to "get the story" from me. Please understand that I get 3 or 4 letters a year from writers who want to tell "my" side of things. They all are caring, compassionate souls who know I was also victimized. These letters all sound so much alike they could be mimeographed from some ancient master copy. I have been at various times polite to you, rude to you, ignoring you, BUT NEVER ENCOURAGING. I don't want another word about me. I'm old now and ILL! I'm going blind. Please stop bothering me. I owe you nothing. I don't even know you. You want something from me, yet you never once even thought to ask me if there was anything you could do for me. Do you know that I am unable to work, have absolutely no income, and live in abject poverty? You plan or want to write a story about me that you'd like to sell. I can't give you that. I want to live the rest of my life in quiet obscurity, unbothered with, or by, the curiosity of a world who will read your piece and throw it away. No one remembers, so why wake it up?

As I said, I owe you nothing and that's all I can give you. Please stop bothering me. I won't change my mind.

> Best Regards,
> Mrs. Bundy

Carol,

Having just gotten your letter I can only say I'm sorry. It was stupid on my part to assume I could offer you "emotional solace." That would take time. I'm sure your concerns are more about your survival, your needs for today. I would like to feel that I could help you out in some way. It would not be much, but you need to understand I am not just interested in the gory details of your crime, but who you were and who you have become, part of that is realizing many years have passed, and with time, ailments. Blindness would be among my worst fears. Activism is a cliché word, but it defines an understanding of alternative lives, a desire to understand, anyway, and perhaps help. A woman like yourself has lived forever a life of trade. Tit for tat. That's your world. I accept it.

I hear the requests between teh lines. I wonder what I was thinking, how far back to the world of the emotionally intact, from a place of dismemberment and sodomy, could you have come? A woman taught to lure and coerse, to kill. I wonder, Carol, will you ever de-program?

Jennifer

Dear Jennifer;

Hi, there! This little sloppy note is written through the courtesy of modern electronics - my library's closed-circuit T.V. unit. It's not easy to write with, but is a joy for reading with. It does, however, let me follow on the lines.

I saw the clerk who orders the eye glasses and he gave me an estimate of prison charges: Frames $20, Lenses $50, for the pair; scratch proof coating $18; total apprx $130 with the photo gray tinting (Lots less than I had guessed).

I made an appt to see the optometrist on Nov 22. I'll probably order my glasses then but I will not be given them until paid for.

It is true that the prison must provide me with glasses (no frills like the coating) whether or not I can pay for them at the time — but if I'm indigent a "hold" is put on my account until every dime is paid, no matter how long it takes. I could not ever shop for anything, not even soap and toothpaste.

I tell you these things so you will know that I'm not trying to "take advantage" of you (against your will).

Whether or not you are able to help me, it is very nice of you to make the offer. I just wish I could afford not to have to accept it — I never expected such a meaningful offer of friendship. Usually it's about getting my story — never my life today, just the gory past.

Aside from my health issues, what would you like to talk about? I'm enclosing a photo taken two years ago. I haven't changed much over the years. We no longer are permitted access to a camera so this may be the only photo I can send you. Do you want me to look over your questionnaire? No promises about what I may or may not answer, but I'm curious now. Perhaps you DO understand!

Okay, I'm waiting to hear from you. I can't believe I'm saying it, but write soon!

> Best,
> Carol

Jenny,

You have been a warm friend to me. I thank you from the bottom of my heart for your help with my glasses. I am sorry I have been almost cruel at times but how could anyone write to me without a need to hurt me, after the things I have done?

I know that you are writing to Veronica Compton. When she served time in Los Angeles for helping the Hillside Stranglers, ironically, we were celled together. I know that she had an affair with Doug. As bizarre as this may sound, he was able to charm women. You know. . . from writing to him, yourself. You should include his letters to you with this part of your book, if you want people to understand how cunning he could be. I'm not blaming him completely, but I never knew anything about sadism. I never thought about such things. I was very lonely. You must be strong and educated to see him as he is. First, I let him have me, then I helped him TAKE others. I lived because I was more helpful as a server than as a sex fantasy. And that had to mean

murder, after what he'd do. I was so frightened. For the boys. For everyone, but I kept doing it.

Carol

*The following is a letter from Doug Clark, with whom I briefly corresponded
while researching my first book,* The Serial Killer Letters.

1998
Hey Sexy-Jen,

    I can just tell by the way you write you probably are a babe. You
can tell me anything. I love to help women out with their sexual needs.
I'm glad you wrote. You seem really smart — that's a total turn-on.
Your husband better be careful. Does he mind, men out here, lonely
men, fantasizing about you?

    Okay, enough before I get myself too turned on. But I'm smiling,
because I know you probably love knowing there's a guy out here,
wanting to get down, between your legs and. . . OKAY!! Enough,
enough, enough!!!

    I let you use my letters, so I guess I need to say something impor-
tant. But just like, what I wrote, you can't jail a person on their fantasies. . . and that's all it was. I love women and sex and we all have fantasy, but Carol. . . .she was the one who was the lesbo-murderer. She
took gals in and did sick things. I was not the one. I have hundreds of
friends who know I was set up by her!!! You could ask her boyfriend,
Murray, but that's right: she killed him too!!!!! Just whacked him up and
cut off his head. Do I sound like the kind of guy who goes beyond a little kidding? She was crazy about me. She was rent, and for a while, I
guess I cared. Shit, she was a lonely bitch. But I'm no killer. I had no
clue about most of this shit, until she set me up. My transcripts prove
it!! We've been writing from OSP to my move to San Quentin. They
think they can kill me but no way. I'll be out some day, and she doesn't
have that luxury. . . they have too much on her. Cutting up heads, fuck-
ing women, I know for a fact she had a lesbo partner helping her when
she wasn't getting laid by her married LOVER!!!

171

I might have sexual needs, but I can get off with a Playboy. I am no way like her, but she has ruined me!!! I'm getting pissed off. Let's talk later.

Doug

Dear Jenny;

Merry Christmas, my new friend. And (belated) Happy Birthday wishes, too.

I wrote you a letter yesterday while I was in my unit's day room. I didn't have your letter with me nor could I have read it anyway. I responded to your letter as well as I could remember. Today is better, though. Your letter is with me and I'm sitting at my favorite c.c.T.V. where I can read and write in comfort.

Tell me about the organizations you are involved with. If it is a newsletter, I used to get it. How can subscribers alone do much to help me? I don't like the idea that Doug will read anything about me. He still scares me even though he can't reach me I am aware of his Internet efforts but about all he can succeed in doing with it is frustrate himself It's really a form of mental masturbation. I won't even read the printouts his friends create for him. They are spending a lot of money that is just wasted. Truthfully? I have never followed his case. I don't even read the case law in books. You asked if I'm a happy person. Yes. Even in here there is much joy in life. There is the pleasure of shared friendships, shared music, TV, movies, etc. Sharing food with friends the fun of crowd, or the peace of being alone. There is pride in achieving what you never knew you could accomplish. There is an almost savage pride in fighting the prison on a meaningful issue and winning. And there is the knowledge that if you get knocked down on some issue you'll bounce back next time.

What are your kids like? How old? It's been hard without my boys, it's true. But they have been exposed to too much bad stuff about me and are closed to any possibility that I'm a nice person. They chose to let me go so they could live ordinary lives out of my shadow. It's best for them. I hope someday they'll want to see me, but they have to heal a lot. What kind of work do you do now? I'm getting tired now so I'll close for now and take care and stay well.

Carol

Dear Jennifer,

Please forgive this sloppy writing but it can't be helped. I'm at home right now and don't have the tv to use so you are getting this "au naturale."

I have a complication of my eye. I've gotten an ulcer on the cornea and I'm mad. I was supposed to go to my doctor 30 days after surgery and make sure the right prison employee knew about it in time to get it scheduled in time. It wasn't and the ulcer developed. . . 30 extra days passed and I started to raise hell about it after the prison optometrist told me something was wrong but wouldn't say just what it was. It could have just been taken care of early on. Well, I'm on anti-biotic eye drops now. So I finally saw the opthomologist. He put a "bandage con-tact lens" in and told me to come back in two days. Of course I was not brought back for that appointment, either. I had to switch to an ordi-nary pen but I can't read what I write so if I screw this up I'm sorry.

I get by okay, I guess. Jenny, Thank You for your help. It will make the difference.

Best,
Carol

Carol

Your latest letters are more. . . approachable. Thank you. I felt like you shared some things about yourself that make it easier for me to know you, at least a little. I'm so sorry about your condition. And the neglect you feel. I think there will always exist an unconscious bias in your sub-culture. Everyone experiences it in their own way — or so I'm told. But it's unto itself, in prison. The judgments. I'm trying to look beyond that and simply listen to your thoughts. Your take on Doug, your connection and part in the crimes.

I understand your fear of Doug. It will probably stick with you the rest of your life. He had you completely. I know him, so I can get a strong feel for that process. He is so charming, so credible. I know you think he and Veronica Compton had a "thing," but it was just more misconstrued lies. He claimed to be a navy admiral or something (as was his father — an easy persona for him). He wrote to her claiming his sincere angst regarding her situation. He was never more than a "friend," and when she realized — through the media — that he was claiming her as his "lover," she was more shocked than anyone. The letters were sent to his friend's house, and mailed from a street address. She had no clue they originated from a prison. He is clever. He "opened up" some in my last book. When I was interviewed, the gal questioned him about our correspondence. He called me a "bored housewife who needed attention." That's Doug.

Still, it's smart to be leery. And I understand about your boys. Not wanting them to be hurt by things that are written. I agree. You and your children have been pushed apart enough.

Anyhow, I hope you have a wonderful holiday. I think we will. The kids still believe in Santa — it's getting harder with my eldest. 'Have to be pretty crafty to beat her at that game!

Jen

Dear Jenny,

Thank you for the letters received about a week apart. There is much you say that I can relate to and much that sounds off alarm bells.

My eye has entered a phase of rapid healing and my doctor finally told me he doesn't think I'll lose its sight. Major relief! He said we'll talk about new glasses when I return in two weeks.

I'm doing too much stressing. I can't pay for the glasses so I can't order them.

I can't believe he did this, but Doug sent me a "nice" Christmas card where he refers to something from when we lived together, a teddy bear I had long since forgotten. Yes, I know he can't hurt me, physically, I'm not concerned about that. Rather, I'm scared he may still be able to affect my state of mind. Until you've been in his control you cannot begin to appreciate it. I was too fragile mentally back then and I don't

want to go back. I am not that fragile now, but I remember. . . all of it.
I'm tired today so I'll keep this short.

> Take care,
> Carol Bundy

Carol,

You speak of Doug like it was yesterday. Would you still kill for him? I wrote in hopes you could explain life with him, what it did to you, the subtle tactics he used which rendered you a kind of hostage. But we don't seem to make it there. I am not versed enough in criminology to know how to label you, diagnostically, but in layman's terms, it's not helpful. You are not helpful. A school girl giddy over a teddy bear, no show of grief over the boys, and feigned interest in this project when you are in financial need.

Take care of yourself. I suppose some stories do just dead-end. Maybe there's a message within that. I was so scared to write you. But I think it's you still held hostage, still afraid.

> Jen

SHIRLEY CURRY

Sometimes, when children are born, a woman's instinct to leave an abusive spouse is outweighed by her fear. A mother is spiritually linked to her offspring. Knowing the strength of that bond, her violent partner will often threaten this relationship through manipulation and legal attacks if she decides to leave. Frightened by the possibility of separation from her children, the battered woman can become subservient; beatings are more tolerable than losing custody. Shirley Marie Curry lived with this type of intense fear and suppression. Though not all battered women respond with Shirley's degree of violence, many do strike back. Shirley's case is an extreme example of what many women suffer and survive on a daily basis, but it illustrates the very real dangers posed by women who sacrifice their sanity to protect those they love.

Shirley is imprisoned for life without parole, for two counts of murder. In fact, her victims were five (one of the six people she attacked survived). Shirley's crime would shock anyone: she killed her three children, her ex-husband, and her ex-sister-in-law, and injured her sister's ex-husband. Her story raises many questions, including how those with mental illnesses are treated within the criminal justice system, and how battered women can be supported by the court system in their healing process.

Shirley's first experiences with fear and repression began when she was a young girl. Throughout Shirley's childhood, her father ruled the family with an iron fist. Her family and community accepted male dominance and regarded it as a cultural strait. Without questioning such communal values, Shirley moved into a union that perpetuated the dominant male and subordinate female roles that formed the core of her early world.

By age thirty, Shirley had succeeded in mirroring both childhood familial models and societal beliefs. In 1967, she was the mother of three and had almost completely satisfied her family's expectations. Underneath her happy facade, however, her husband's stringent rules and abusive manner secretly fed Shirley's rage. She detested the strict gender roles and his heavy-handed authority, yet waited years before taking action. When she finally told her husband that she wanted a divorce, he flew into a fury, hitting, threatening, and yelling at her in front of the kids. His humiliation pained him as much as what he perceived to be her betrayal. In the midst of his increasingly violent rage, Shirley feared that he might kill her. Focusing on her commitment to "save" her children from the man's temperament, she endured his attacks.

In the following months, Shirley struggled to present a strong role model for her children. She stayed firm in her commitment to leave her husband and create a violence-free life for herself, her daughter, and her two sons. Her choice was not, however, without consequences. People gossiped; she lost friends and family. Shirley recalls, "My stance took its toll. I didn't have the stamina to fight the gossip or the system." Yet she did try to fight the system and deflect the gossip that plagued her life.

Shirley won a partial victory from the courts: she was awarded custody of her children until their fourteenth year; then each child would choose whether they wanted to live with their mother or their father, and the court would respect that decision. While the court felt it was important that Shirley perform her duties rearing her youngsters, it also emphasized that as young adults they were entitled to be exposed to their "heritage" — something their father emphasized that he valued. Shirley was viewed as a liberal woman, mocking her state's family values, while her husband represented himself as deeply committed to preserving his children's connections to their biological and cultural roots.

Shirley had been weakened by vicious gossip, but nothing upset her as much as the possibility of losing a child. The idea that the children could leave her at any time created a continual feeling of paranoia. Shirley felt that every action she took carried unknown and unforeseeable consequences: "Every kid goes through rebellion. I always felt that someday, their dad would seem perfect. He wasn't around. That makes it easy to look good. I had to be mom, and I was furious that the men in those courts could make a choice that gives kids power. Of course they hate some of the decisions a mom makes." Such thoughts burdened Shirley to the point where simple arguments over grades, household responsibilities, even conflicts over clothing allowances frightened her. Shirley feared abandonment, 24 hours a day.

Sabrina, Shirley's eldest, was first to pass through what her father described as the "forever-open door." Despite having dreaded this moment for years, Shirley was unprepared for the gravity of Sabrina's betrayal. Shirley and Sabrina stopped communicating for three years. Shirley felt she had sacrificed herself to ensure no man would have his thumb on her kids. After the divorce, she had worked a full-time job and struggled to raise three children, all the while knowing that by the time they reached adolescence they would almost surely leave her. Shirley knew that, emotionally and financially, the life she could offer her children would be one of struggle and hard work. At the same time, she realized that her husband and his new wife could give them a comparative life of ease, with a full-time mother and financial security. Shirley wanted to teach her children how to treat others with respect and how to support strong women, but despite her noble intentions her anger began to affect her relationships with them. Enraged, Shirley's paranoia increased. *Who would leave next?* she wondered, *and when?* Possessed, she became a tyrant, demanding constant attention and assurances from her children. Her whole world was wrapped up in their small bodies, and as they grew further from her, she relied more and more on their presence for her sense of self-worth. Without the children, into whom she had poured all her time and effort, heart and soul, she had nothing.

Shirley's fears were realized in a painful slow-motion sequence. On July 19, 1974 Shirley was called back to court for a humiliating appearance when Richard, her middle child, finally became tired of living with her madness. Curious to know his father, and missing his sister, he believed that moving might mean a normal, less emotionally-draining lifestyle. Richard made a successful his plea to leave, and his father came for his things on July 21; and Richard planned to leave that weekend.

Crazed, Shirley felt rejected by everyone. She blamed her husband and she blamed the court, but in her anger she wanted the entire family to suffer. Shirley paced their home and ranted about the dishonors that had been dumped on her. Eleven-year-old Jessie was terrified. Tragically, only those closest to her and most vulnerable to her rage knew that Shirley posed a serious danger.

In many ways, Shirley was not truly "lost" until this moment. Imagining her life alone, her children despising her, and her community shunning her, Shirley snapped. She went into action, and the action she chose to take reveals that she was delusional and dangerous, in fact — insane. Weighing her options, in a growing panic, Shirley concluded that death was the answer: death to men that ruined women's lives and thieved children; and death to children who allowed it. Shirley's motives are complex and difficult to contemplate or understand. She felt that she was killing partly out of rage, yet she also maintained that, without her, the kids were better off in Heaven. Shirley, perhaps more than any of the other women in this book, truly lost her soul to her own violence.

That Friday, before Richard's departure, Shirley initiated her rampage. Even now, she doubts her crime could have been prevented at that point. She confesses that, "I think if I could have hidden away, one of two things would have happened. I would have calmed down and gone home, and faced them leaving, or I would have done what I did anyway." Realizing that she was in a fury, Shirley did in fact attempt to "hide away" by driving to a piece of property in the countryside, left to her by her father. However, traffic on the freeway was stop-and-go, for miles; she pulled over onto the shoulder, ran up a nearby hill, and screamed at the top of her lungs. She was trying to get her rage out, to expel her anger, and to find the strength to let her children go. . . even though it would destroy her. Instead, when she returned to the car and her frightened children, she found that a man on a motorcycle had stopped to help them; he berated her for leaving her children alone and insisted that she return home with them immediately. Shirley went home, and began pacing frantically, again. Her sons were scared but had no idea what to do. Shirley acted, before anyone had the insight to recognize her need for help.

Shirley began the killings at her own home in Lowell, where she shot and killed Richard and Jessie. Then she got in her car and drove to her ex-husband's home in Fayetteville. She knocked on the door and when he answered, she greeted him with a round of bullets. Shirley pushed her way into the house, over the body, and headed to her daughter's room. Shirley shot her only daughter, Sabrina, in the head.

With her children and their father dead, Shirley headed toward another community, Springdale. She surprised her ex-husband's half-sister Jo Ann Brophy at home, and shot the 27-year-old in the chest. Shirley felt betrayed by Jo Ann, who had discontinued her relationship with Shirley after the divorce. Shirley then drove to Farmington where she shot her sister's ex-husband, James Dodson, twice. She wanted him to pay for the grief he had caused when he left her sister. Shirley despised him for initiating the painful divorce her sister had suffered through. As the final victim, Dodson was the sole survivor of Shirley's rampage.

The following Monday, July 22, murder charges were filed against Shirley Marie Curry. The first concern of investigators, prosecutors, and defenders alike was to establish a motive for the killings and to investigate Shirley's mental state. Her statement, during psychiatric examination, that "at least the children were safe", triggered further psychological testing. Shirley was found incompetent to stand trial by reason of insanity.

Over the four years that Shirley lived at the state hospital, doctors continued their psychological testing, and later, four of her primary doctors testified that during the shootings, Shirley Curry was legally insane. Throughout the early 1970s psychologists argued against having Shirley stand trial, but after listening to the prosecutors' arguments, an Arkansas court saw no reason to keep her institutionalized. The State of Arkansas announced that "Ms. Curry might be evil, but she is sane," and ordered her to stand trial. Shirley was convicted on two counts of murder, and sentenced to life without parole (jurors were never asked to reach a decision in the shootings of her two sons or Jo Ann Brophy).

Shirley and her lawyer decided to contest the decision, and her appeal played its way through the system for three years. Some Arkansas Supreme Court justices even agreed that "psychiatric behaviors influential to her actions on the night of the shooting should have played a role in Ms. Curry's sentence." In fact, one dissenting justice claimed that the evidence of insanity was "overwhelming." Despite such opinions, in the end Shirley was ordered back to a state penitentiary. The judgment of sanity stands, and Shirley will spend her life in the prison system, receiving no psychiatric support, only psychotropic drugs.

Today, Shirley is kept on mandatory tranquilizers. She often acts inappropriately, and bouts of physical misconduct and paranoia control her. Rather than being viewed as manifestations of a diagnosed psychiatric disorder, Shirley's behavior is punished as disciplinary infractions. As punishment, she spends a great deal of her time "in the hole", where she is isolated from the other prisoners and denied any semblance of routine. Such extreme isolation only further aggravates Shirley's condition. Her ability to maintain sanity is her greatest fight and also her greatest fear. If she fails, she will spend most of her time living out her nightmare: isolation.

Shirley's letters demonstrate the ambiguity of her mental state, though she writes with only the best intentions. When she reports that she has been let out of the hole, the effects of sensory deprivation (poor handwriting, confused thoughts, lack of grammatical structure) are clearly exposed. Still, her letters to me belie her soft, thoughtful nature, and her strong faith. Shirley opens and ends her letters with prayers for the safety and happiness of me and my family. At the same time, her words betray her continuing belief in her need to "save" her children. In one letter, she confesses her hope that her letters "will aid someone else in avoiding fear so great that one kills to protect those they love the most in this world. . ." In her final letter, she admits that "I can't say now they are 'better off' in Heaven, but I know they are okay." The need to believe that her children are finally safe fills her thoughts, while her efforts to come to terms with her actions seem incomplete.

Shirley's story is about more than punishment or redemption; Shirley suffers from a mental disorder that renders her incompetent and frequently violent. With little control over her own life or routine, she has almost nothing to connect her to the world of the living. Surprisingly, if Shirley is aware of anything, it is of her need for further psychological support. She writes lucidly about her desire and inability to find help for her condition. Her ability to deal with and confront her crime has been limited by her lack of psychological support; healing and rehabilitation seem to be nowhere in sight.

Hi, Ms. Curry,

After researching your history and conviction, I wanted to write. I understand that you were the mother of three, unhappily married then divorced. The courts allowed an odd custody decision. The children were awarded a choice to leave you at the age of fourteen. One by one, they began to head to their father's home, and basically, a sense of betrayal consumed you to the point of becoming a murderer.

I am a mother. I love my children more than life itself. But like my mother used to say to me, "no one wants to love them like their mother, but no one wants to kill them like their mother!" Of course, it was just a joke, but is there some twisted "truth" to this? Though most of us can't fathom murder, I wonder what kind of anguish such desertion would provoke? We love our kids so much, if they should abandon us, at least in my own case, especially for some ex-husband, I would freak! Not murder, but lose it, somehow. I wonder what it felt like to know such fury and abandonment; I wonder how you live with their murders.

I can remember the days when I had time to put on lipstick. Now my kids keep me running so fast, I'm lucky to get in a quick shower before lunch! If they should flippantly "move in with dad," after all my love, God knows it would come close to killing me.

Again, I'm writing this based on research. I want to hear your side. I hope you don't think I'm a nut. I am the first to say that a lost life is unimaginable. I am so sorry and I pray about that, but you are still here and I can't help but see a victim, in a sense, when I read — between the lines — about what happened in your own life. What did happen is now between you and God and I'm sure you have made your penance to Him. It is not my job to stand here and judge you.

I do pray that this sort of heinous rage would stop. I don't think it will, until we hear from women like you, who have acted out your rage — not psychobabble from a circus-sideshow talk-show host, but from the women who really know. I meet many people, active in prison reform, who agree.

Your life isn't over and you still have a very incredible purpose. You can help women all over the world trying to cope, alone, with your very situation. You aren't alone, and women need to know they aren't the only ones losing control. You have that to offer. Please begin with me? I want to learn more about you, what you feel like, how well you fare now.

Please write to me,

Jennifer Furio

My Dear Jenny,

Thank you for writing and forgive me for not replying sooner or completely today. As soon as I get better caught up I shall write and reply to your letters in depth. I haven't been out of the *hole* very long and am replying to not only the ones received that I couldn't have until my time was over but also each day's mail.

I most definitely decided this morning I would reply even tho not much. I wanted you to know how much your letter meant as it came the evening of the anniversary of 25 years and the only letter that I got — got them later, 21 plus probably more today, so for that reason and that God and Jesus put in your heart not to give up on my replying I feel close to you.

Bye for now. God bless, keep, guide, lead you and give you health, wealth, joy, peace, happiness, patience and keep you in wonderful spirits. Me too.

Love Shirley

PS. Lovely stamp — I sent them to Stamps for Children from myself and all in this pod. Pester til they do. Ha!

Dearest Jenny,

I trust God this finds you healthy, coping and in excellent spirits. I am.

Recently, April 16th and the following week *NW Arkansas Times* published front page and inside their version. I told you a little of what occurred May 5 (SEG) [*author's note*: that is, isolation]. Now, *Arkansas Democrat/Gazette* ran another but not nearly as much horror printed — neither one know the true facts. It was July 18, 1999 For *Ar Dem/Gazette*. The women in this unit are very supportive — just the opposite of H2-B and I truly Thank God, yes indeed for I did put on a cold, hard front when quizzed with remarks in H2 and my stuff, moved and some completely missing or torn up — Not so in here. More another morning (2:00 am now) A couple was taken to SEG earlier tonight and I got interrupted (oops). Would you like to hear about my out of body experiences? It has occurred twice, the last time in 1963 after Kennedy was shot. It is now 4:15 am and just announced, time to get up and go to pill call. I take the mandatory prolixum shot every two weeks. The next shot is due Thursday so at this time I am not exceedingly doped up or down.

How many children do *you* have? Ages? Boys, girls? My girl who was my first born got on the stand on the 19th and told that as far as she was concerned her mother was Sandy, the wife. The only thing I ever did to Sabrina was whip her in order to correct her. My husband told me once that she wasn't suppose to help do anything that I was suppose to take care of, prior to the divorce. I guess Sandy did obey but I refused to and thus she was turned against me by both of them. None of my children had been in any trouble, nor had I until that night after much weeping — click — I recall very well. Can't go there now. So if you are married and considering a divorce, Don't! For men can be very cruel and vindictive. I was going to write you a longer letter but guess this will have to do for now. I'll answer as able. God bless and keep you and yours in love, peace and happiness and in excellent spirits. Me, too.

Peace,

Shirley

My Dear Jenny,

I trust God that this letter finds you and your loved ones feeling mighty fine and dandy. I am. Well, I put off writing you until the mood struck. I am able to just flow when this way. My mind feels pretty good. I guess you understand about my moods? I think the drugs make it worse — I have no choice or I go to the hole for being "incorrigible."

Here in Arkansas women have to do more time on the same sentences as the men. This has been true since I was brought to prison on October 1979. Before that I was in the State Mental Hospital with freedom of the grounds, no fences or guards watching me. At that time there was no place to keep me locked up for the hospital wing I was in for 9 months was condemned along with the remainder of the hospital. In it there were both women and men who had a common social area. These men and women were from prisons in Arkansas, plus a program for dope addicts trying to "kick" the habit (these were hated by the staff) some of these just came to get the substitute non-habit forming drug used to taper off the effects of the addiction; some were patients from the permanent mental institution (plenty of stories here). Anyway, Dr. Taylor told me he would put me "on the Hill" (term used as mental hospital sits on a hill) if I would promise him I would *not* run away. I told him I could not promise such as I did *not* know; he let me go anyway and I never succumbed to several offers from patients leaving to go with them as I hurt my mother enough without adding any more. When a section was made in the Men's Mental Hospital lock-up for the women I was left "on the Hill." The nurses would take me to town to shop, eat etc. until my first trial in 1978 but I wasn't moved to lock-down for women and even though I told Judge Cumming I wanted to sit in jail until my second trial he ignored me so I spend almost 9 more months "on the Hill" (enough of this) If you want the remainder in segments, let me know. Strange though because we were all bad, but had room to move and there was less trouble than there is here.

You say your children are 6 and 4. Boys, girls? You didn't state names by the way, when is your birthday — mine is October and I will be 63 years young. Ha. Would you please, please tell the mother of the child who lied on her that she is extremely lucky — why? One of my former roommates spent about five years in here, over the very same thing. Here in this state there is a prison sentence given by the Judge plus removal of any other children she has — permanent removal of the children. Those children of hers who were old enough visited her as the Judge could not control or keep them away. Probably would if possible and within his powers. That in itself should have shown the child 16 years old, I think, was a liar. She was lucky as there are some here, now, on child abuse who swear that they are innocent yet, if they want out they are going to have to have certificates of completing the several programs dealing with abuse and admit to the parole board they will never repeat in order to be on paper, all to get out of prison on parole. Just have the neighbor read this then get down on her knees or in her closet and fervently *thank God* for His great mercy toward her in this manner. And I'm the nut?

What made me "*click*?" Well, I was so upset I wept and wept for hours — my boy calmly watching TV; I could not stop. I even put them in my pick-up to run away with them to Florida — no clothes, no packing — just run but when I got to the highway, the traffic was bumper to bumpers in that direction due to road construction — so I proceeded to drive to my property in the county where I was born that my daddy had given me — I got a ticket for going 25 miles per hour in a 15 mph zone. Weeping most of the time. Finally approximately 30 miles to what I called my Hollering Mountain I left the kids in the picnic area and climbed the steps to the top of the rock cliff. There I screamed many times and meanwhile a teenager on a motorcycle had stopped and was talking with Richard and Jesse but when I let out my scream he got the hell away. Enough for now, OK? Except news says I killed from home and I did, but I was weeping as I was already thinking of it. I wonder if I would have controlled my sadness and anger away from my ex, and not be here today? It's my cross.

I sent the Article you sent to Christina Riggs 000949, RMCF admin SEG who has been on death row since the summer of 1998 separated from those in SEG either who may be in the "*Hole*", protective custody or investigation status. Many of the officers allow her to sit inside the Death Row area, door with the food flap open and talk to some within hearing distance. The sound echoes so that it is extremely difficult to hear anyone. One has to learn the art of lip-reading. When the newspaper was gotten by her with my story she allowed the others to read *but* not me. I could see them reading and pointing, and I must admit that I got somewhat abusive with my tongue toward her. If you write to her, tell her I beg her forgiveness and, if possible, correspond with her through you as I, from experience, know — and I simply can feel "it" in my bones and heart — that it was utter extreme fear for her children's welfare that brought the crime to a head, as with me. Jenny: beware of fear, as it is written — whatsoever ye fear most occurs eventually — many years for me as Sabrina was 17, Richard 14 and Jess 11. I don't know exactly how, why or where for, but fear is anyone's greatest enemy as the devil feeds on fear and eventually uses it, for I know how great my fear was.

It is also written about forgetting the past and pressing on — I think this is why I found difficulty in replying, so I came to the conclusion to answer you and I really don't know why but perhaps, inadvertently, this will aid someone else in avoiding fear so great that one kills to protect those they love the most in this world, even to the extreme that they will risk Hell's eternal torment to keep them safe.

I just want you to know, Jenny, that now God has given to me peace and this peace I offer to you, Christina and all I come in contact with or write to, even pertaining to legal aspects. I sign off peace, or peace to you. I do this with no fear because it is written about "if not worthy, your peace will return to you." So I shall say bye to you for now, as this peace is being sorta kinda disturbed, so I withdraw until later.

God bless, keep, guide, protect you and yours — give you strength, power, me, too. . .

Peace and love and prayers to you and all,

Shirley

Remind me of where is it written "enough for now" as to where I quit. . .

Dear Shirley,

I'm glad you wrote again. Your letter was open. I feel like I learned more about you, your fear, your thought that you were "protecting" and your consideration of God's wrath and finally, His peace. Whew! That's a lot of thinking, Shirley. It makes me quite sure that you have been considering this horrible thing clearly and for a very long time. I suppose time doesn't take away the conscience. I felt like your story was familiar — perhaps because your hell is similar to the one so many women speak about. I hope that we will talk more. I'm learning something, and I think others might, too. The rules were so strict, you were probably so trapped by your ex, even after you left him and he was still telling you how you had to raise your children. That would make a woman mad! The south is notorious for being tough on women. I don't know how much credence to give gossip, but the culture does seem a bit. . . old-fashioned. I suppose if you saw that that might be harmful, you would try to detach, and in a state that forbids straying from the societal norm, you probably had very little support.

You mention the laws in Arkansas as being "against women." Women do more time for same crimes, and so forth. I realize that's true. I have researched the stats, and it's unfair. It's true about our society expecting women to behave much more. . . "appropriately" than men: Men commit a sex crime, ruin a woman's life, and we blame it on access to pornography. 7 years, they are free.

A woman spends her life trapped in an abusive situation, commits a singular act, as awful as it may be it's not a serial "pattern," and she and all she loves suffer at the hands of our laws for the rest of her life. This sickens me. I have never known a woman like yourself to be a "repeat offender" like so many men who don't receive the harsh sentences. *And,* women like you, as your letters describe, are at a point of so much pain when things finally happen. When the courts allowed your husband to take your children, why didn't they take action to help you with the obvious grief a mother would experience over such trauma? It is cruel and inhumane. A state that allows such separation should provide counseling. If a court could take my children, I'd need admittance!

You speak of your children by name, you talk so openly about that night when you felt so lost, or so it sounded to me. I could imagine trying to get free — getting on the freeway and that last hope of running, and then the back-up on the freeway, finally just running from the car, screaming. I empathized with you and your petrified (I'm sure) kids.

Will you explain to me what your life was like, before you finally killed? You may think it's bizarre but I would like to know how you learned to cope with your life, everyday, without losing it sooner? Not that "losing it" is all right but why that night? And are you okay with yourself now? I don't mean, are you crazy or not, I mean, emotionally, how are you now, years later? I would ask you what you would have done differently, and of course, the answer is a given, but given the *exact* circumstances I wonder if you would have felt like you had any place to go, to talk to someone? It seems you were so isolated from sharing what must have felt like Hell.

And, yes, you said if I wanted to hear more about the "Hill," you would tell me in segments. I would if you are up to it. And then I might understand better what made you want to spend the remainder of your time before the trial in a jail?

I will write to Ms. Riggs and share what you asked me to with her. I'm sure you will offer her peace, as you seem to work hard toward remembering that that is God's gift to you. Forgiveness, therefore, peace. You can rest from your pain, through the grace God blesses you with.

I hope to hear from you soon, and I'll let you know if Ms. Riggs replies with a message for you. . .

Take care,

Jenny

Dear Jenny,

I trust God that this letter find you all well, healthy and in very, very good spirit. I am fine and dandy — well, healthy and in great spirits.

The reason I didn't want to go back to the "hill" but preferred to sit in jail was putting up with being quizzed, etc. . . .was done and had I remained in jail I would have been able to visit with my family — mother, brothers, sisters, kin-folk and perhaps a few friends might have come. Prison is not "healthy" as it is an institution but it was closer. Don't know all seemed to disappear. My sister had to hire a lawyer to see me in 1974. The jail was in her city — the hospital over 4 hours one way. Also, would have been able to see the Public Defender more than once. That Judge was angry because he had yelled prior to the "hill" that he would give me the electric chair. Mistrial under him. OK, yes, the judge who actually sentenced me died this year and I don't think he was all that old. The way I found out was my letter I had written him was returned with "deceased" written on it.

My dear, Jenny, my children are fine. It would be best if you and I both pray that yours would be fine, if ever you felt such torment. All women. I won't even attempt to explain how I know what these feelings are, but I know. How come you never speak of your husband, or are you separated? You don't have to tell me but perhaps I could help clarify some matters, you never know.

As for the "enough for now" while I was writing my remembering began to get next to tears — yes, still after 25 years as of July I do come to tears if recalling in detail so tell me where I left off, so I could resume as you did about the "hill." I don't keep copies of letters. Hardly enough room for legal crap to store for future reference, more later. To much going on in here — noise, TV, talking at table. . . not conducive for writing right now. God bless you all, give you protection, health energy and excellent spirits.

Me, too. Peace,

Love, Shirley

— thanks for saying you'd write to Ms. Riggs

Dear Shirley,

Just a quick note:

I talked to Christy Riggs. She was nice — desperately haunted by her crime. She said that yes, you had been "rude" on just one occasion, but that was the past, and she didn't have any bad feelings whatsoever. She was going to communicate through me anything she wanted to let you know, as she talked about the restrictions of writing to you from DR. She has it pretty tough, but she can relate to your tragedy. She hopes for change in the way people view her "crime" and your "crime," because, like me, she feels that these tragedies happen for different reasons than other crimes like rape or serial murder, etc. . . ..she called it Maternal Filicide, and was going to share more about her story with me.

You have my prayers. . .

Jenny

Dearest Jenny,

I think if I could have hidden away two things would have happened. I would have calmed (if that's possible, if you could see me then) and gone home and faced them leaving or I would have done what I did anyway. I can't say now they are "better" in Heaven, but I know they are okay. They never got to grow. I just have to pray. Else I'll keep out of my head. I think my family had to leave me. They see me and they think of the kids. They couldn't forget. I wish different, of course, but don't blame. If I could stay on the "hill" Doctors could cure me. Here I just stay in trouble even though I know rages are wrong there is little here to help. Have I helped you? That would feel good.

Blessings,
Shirley

P.S. As far as the past, I can hardly speak of it, my ex. He was strict, kept me like a little girl but worked me like a horse. It was humiliating. My daddy was the same. There's still no excuse, so I wanted to protect my kids. You get whacked for doing things wrong, like a dog. I wanted better. It turned against me. He married Sandy and they were tradition. I was divorced. I had moods, I admit that, but there were no drugs and people down South don't talk. They gossip, though, about divorces and things like that. I guess I embarrassed my kids, where I thought I'd make them proud. I hated them for leaving me. Would you believe they were everything to me? Men, I can take or leave, the divorce was fine — I didn't care what he left me or didn't — except my kids. Then he got them. I went crazy. I suppose I am still. My attorney wanted me in an institution to get help, but I'm here because the state said I should be. To punish me more, my attorney says. It's true. The meds don't work, I have a hard time, but the gals get me, and try and get along. Me too. That's all we can ask for, right?

Shirley

SUZAN CARSON

Susan Barnes (later Suzan Carson) was born into a life of ease on September 14, 1941. No one, not even Susan herself, could have guessed the violent turn her life would later take. Currently serving three consecutive sentences of 25 years-to-life in California, Suzan Carson links her crimes to her intimate relationship with her husband and the social movements of earlier decades.

On the surface, Susan's crime seems simple: three murders committed in rage and passion. Yet her story is most frightening because of the seeming "normalness" of Susan's childhood and early adulthood. Nothing in her story suggests that Susan was a "born killer," and nothing suggests, either, that her crimes carry such powerful mitigating circumstances as many of the others in this book. Susan's letters reveal a woman who, in her efforts to change the world, went violently astray.

Susan's childhood was one that most little girls only dream about. With a wealthy and respected Arizona newspaper executive for a father, Susan was exposed to the good life: culture, comforts, and freedom. She was also attractive, athletic and bright. Though some reports dubbed her intellectually illiterate due to early problems with dyslexia, in truth Susan's only real "suffering" was from an under-stimulated mind. Easily bored, she waited eagerly for something challenging to enter her life.

Stimulation would come her way when she dropped out of high school and married Arizona businessman Leland Hamilton. Leland offered her a lifestyle similar to the one her father had provided. Not even early marriage or pregnancy could disrupt the ease that defined Susan's life.

At 17, Susan became pregnant with her first child, and the second child was born only a couple of years later. Young and vivacious, she enjoyed her role as an active mother more than her role as wife. Though personally unfulfilling, Susan's marriage provided her with many comforts: with few worries, Susan spent her days relaxing and socializing at the local country club. Underneath, however, Susan felt the same restlessness that had plagued her adolescence. Parties, society and money were appreciated, but superficial. As she matured, Susan intensified her search for deeper fulfillment.

During the 1960s Susan began to participate in the "culture." She threw herself passionately into pursuits of new experiences, experimenting with hallucinogenic drugs, lovers, alternative "art vandalism," and the occult. Susan wanted to mark her newfound lifestyle as more than just a passing phase. She changed her name from Susan to Suzan; the unique spelling complemented her unique life and sealed her changed identity.

Wary of the choices Suzan was making choices, Leland divorced her in 1970. At first, Suzan stayed in the couple's Scottsdale home with their two children, but soon even the youngsters decided her partying was too far-out and they went to live with their dad.

By 1977, Suzan had toned down her half-decade of experimentation. Introduced to the Islamic religion (to which she still adheres), she immediately began to educate herself about Islam. She threw herself into her newly adopted spirituality, reading the Koran and attending Islamic lectures and religious gatherings.

On Thanksgiving Day of the same year, Suzan met James Carson, who was recently divorced and nine years younger. The couple's mutual attraction was not dampened by their age difference, and they soon became lovers. When James moved in with Suzan, he also became involved in her religious practices. Suzan requested that he change his name to Michael, his "true name," because in the Bible it referred to an angel.

The couple shared more than a spiritual connection; Michael and Suzan also agreed on radical politics. Michael's radicalism could be traced back to his childhood when he had been ill and his bones had become brittle because of a rare disease. As a fragile child for whom physical activity was a health risk, he became a bookworm. Political subjects and Marxist tracts fascinated Michael, who went as far as to start a small SDS chapter — the Students for a Democratic Society (a quasi-Marxist revolutionary party) — in his hometown of Tulsa, Oklahoma. Generally, he was a disappointment to his father, a successful oil company executive and a man who had once served as an advisor to President Nixon. Both Michael and Suzan saw themselves as the "black sheep" in their families, and their rejection of familial expectations united them in their future pursuits.

Suzan and Michael fed off each other, their religious and political ideologies becoming more radical. In an act of rebellion against consumerism and mainstream society, they sold all of their belongings and flew to London to marry. Their flight also reflected their belief that anything meaningful could not occur in the U.S. Though eccentric, their lifestyle was, as yet, harmless.

After Suzan and Michael returned to Scottsdale, following their wedding, however, their radicalism took an ominous turn. An elderly neighbor caught Suzan roaming her condo naked, and called the police without waiting for an explanation. In what appears to be an act of incredible overkill, a squad landed in front of the home and several officers forced their way inside, without a warrant. During the search, police found marijuana in the couple's home, and promptly arrested both Suzan and Michael. The trauma of the incident multiplied when officers refused to allow Suzan to dress herself before being taken in for booking. Ignoring her protests, police claimed that Suzan's naked body was "evidence." Unfortunately, such idiocy validated the couple's disdain for the police and authority.

Months later, a verdict was finally reached regarding the drug charge: Suzan was convicted of a felony misdemeanor and received six months' probation. After her run-in with the law, Suzan was a changed person. A negative yet harmless perspective was transformed into a war against Government. Michael shared Suzan's embitterment, and for the couple the only true question was how to react to their mistreatment.

Their first response was to move, and in 1981 the couple headed to San Francisco's Haight-Ashbury District. Changing their living space and starting life over in a new city seemed like a reasonable, though temporary, solution. While pondering their next political step, they hopped from house to house, boarding with several different people. Their last known residence in the city was with Karen Barnes, a 23-year-old topless dancer with a drug problem. The couple left the flat suddenly, after committing their first murder.

On March 7, 1981, Karen Barnes's landlord came by to check on the threesome and found Karen lying dead on the basement-flat's floor. Stabbed thirteen times in the face and throat area, her skull crushed with a heavy instrument, she had been cared for tenderly after the brutal attack. A pillow had been placed underneath her head and a blanket covered her bloodied body. Suzan's name had been written across the refrigerator in crayon. Neighbors recalled having seen the "Moslem couple", but they were now nowhere to be found.

Suzan and Michael fled to Oregon, and the month of March found them atop a mountain, living in a shack. They named their new residence "Allah's Mountain". Within a month, they moved again. Suzan was "called" to Los Angeles, and sent Michael ahead to scope out California. Returning to Oregon, Michael found Suzan half-starved and screaming about being harassed by witches — indicating that Suzan was becoming increasingly delusional.

Though the Carsons left immediately, they never made it to LA. Instead, they found work on a pot farm in northern California's Humboldt County. There, they started to actually earn an income; and Michael dedicated much of his time to working on his manuscript, *A Cry For War*. The manifesto called for a revolution and included a hit list targeting President Ronald Reagan, Prime Minister Margaret Thatcher, California Governor Jerry Brown, and cult leader Charles Manson.

In 1982, the Carsons moved again, calling a treehouse in Big Sur, California, their home. Soon, however, the landlord decided he did not like the pair and violently evicted them. As revenge, the Carsons concocted Molotov cocktails and torched the tree.

With few options, they returned to Humboldt County and

worked on the same farm. In their absence, Clark Stephens, a delusional junkie prone to instigating fights, had arrived on the farm. When Stephens insulted Suzan, Michael shot and killed him. Together, Suzan and Michael burned the body and buried the remains in the woods.

Once again, the couple's crimes compelled them to move. Drifting was a tiring lifestyle, and their homelessness also placed them under the scrutiny of the law. They were regularly questioned regarding crimes committed in areas they occupied. In one instance, Michael was "interviewed" after his manuscript was found during a search. At the same time, he was cited for carrying false identification. Suzan was cited for carrying ammunition in her purse. Michael was arrested as a rape suspect, although after one look the victim knew the cops had the wrong man. Unfortunately, Michael had kept his .38 with him during his arrest and officers later found it stashed in the back of their patrol car.

Warrants were immediately issued for their arrest. When Clark Stephens' body was found on May 17, the Carsons' names appeared on a list of acquaintances and suspects. Michael was worried, but he was not considered a murder suspect. He told the police he thought Leland Hamilton might have been involved, claiming that Leland would do anything to "sabotage" his relationship with Suzan.

A police visit to his Scottsdale home surprised Leland. Still, he cooperated in providing his testimony. Inadvertently, Michael had led investigators to the man who eventually helped clear up several unresolved crimes in various cities and counties: Leland filled in the missing details that fleshed out the story of Michael and Suzan's violence. While authorities put the puzzle together, the Carsons fled.

From Bakersfield, the pair caught a ride with John Hellyer, a family man who happened to be in the wrong place at the wrong time. During the ride, he touched Suzan in what she described as an "inappropriate way". She told Michael that the "connection" felt demonic and she wanted the driver terminated. The couple murdered Hellyer, right in sight of the passing cars.

Michael and Suzan were quickly arrested for this latest crime, and on January 28 they were arraigned for Hellyer's murder. Eager for attention, as always, and wanting to see his name in print, Michael wrote an article from his cell drawing attention to what he saw as his "unjust" incarceration and asserting his innocence. He sent it to the *San Francisco Chronicle*. The newspaper published it. An investigator working on Karen Barnes's case happened to read it and, on a hunch, went to visit Michael in jail. Confronted with growing accusations, the Carsons confessed to everything on March 4. Suzan claimed that Karen Barnes was trying to steal her husband. As justification for her crime, she cited text from the Koran: "Thou shalt not suffer a witch to live." The insinuation was obvious, and Suzan's jealous disregard for the young woman's life appeared even more brutal.

On October 23, 1983, defense attorneys asked for a psychological evaluation. The defendants were diagnosed as sane, and both went to trial in June of 1984. Tried separately, the Carsons were both convicted of murdering Karen Barnes and sentenced on July 2, to 25 years-to-life in prison. The same sentences were pronounced in the cases of Stephens and Hellyer.

One psychologist who evaluated Suzan argued that, although intellectually superior, Suzan was under her husband's control because of her insecurities and intense feelings. The psychologist proffered that, although Suzan may have instigated specific activities in the spiritual and political realm, Michael responded with excited curiosity, encouraging her to go even further. Michael was particularly sensitive to Suzan, provoked by her social ease, sexual knowingness, and intellectual radicalism. Having been a weak child, Michael found his sense of power stimulated by Suzan's confidence. Through their relationship, he tapped into a new part of himself that suddenly made life exhilarating. He enjoyed everything radical, even if it meant murder.

Had Suzan never met Michael, she may have dabbled in similar interests without being driven to kill. Her actions were ignited by her need to possess her lover. All three murders were displays of invasion of territory: Karen Barnes wanted Michael, and Stephens and Hellyer disrespected her union with Michael. Whether their victims ignited Michael's insecurity by underscoring Suzan's attractiveness to other men, or because Suzan felt insecure about another woman being attracted to Michael, the pair used murder to permanently stop individuals from disrupting their relationship.

Ironically, it was their crimes of passion and possession that eventually separated the couple. Though today Suzan still considers Michael a "true love", Michael is less interested. In prison, he has become intimately involved with a number of men, and writes to Suzan only occasionally.

Now nearly sixty, Suzan writes with confidence, self-assurance, and a lack of tolerance for those around her. Suzan writes in the voice of a woman who has figured out her role in life, and who feels fully equipped to deal with any challenges that may come her way. She takes her mistreatment by the prison and her disciplinary punishments in stride, recognizing that her self-worth is not dependent upon gaining the prison's approval. Nevertheless, she describes herself as "practically a model prisoner." Suzan still takes her religion seriously and is engrossed in her own "spiritual reform."

Suzan identifies with those trying to change the world as well as with those who are happy to sit back and accept their lot. In prison, she has learned to deal with harsh realities, though she still seems to lack a focus for her energies — beyond survival. Her road to ruin began with a disheartened perspective on the world around her, a view to which she continues to subscribe. When she found that religion, love and spirit could not compensate for what she perceived to be an unjust society, she turned to more violent means of revolution. She explains that, "People were trying to change the *bad* with *love*, and I suppose I thought that since that was not working, obviously, maybe shocking people with a negativity would force a change for the better. This sounds like a contradiction; and I was high at the time. It probably was. I still have to think about how I ended up with these crimes. At the time, you have to see, it made sense. . ."

Dear Jennifer
(Sunday Morning)

What a trip to get your letter. I'd love to correspond. Yeah, my views haven't changed but my ways of how to change the world have. I've concluded that it can't be changed (environment, rape of earth, etc.) and that I won't participate. Too easy to lose it.

As it happens, I'm on the same wavelength as you. Conditions for women in prison are unreal. I'm in the most unreal women's prison there is. As of last Monday I was housed in AD-SEG. Reason: "Investigation!" Why? Still a mystery. Several people are under investigation. They take months to do it. It's the result of a newly formed group of cops called I.S.U. they walk around in G.I. Joe suits doing witch hunts. Meanwhile junkies run amuck, fights resulting in blood — usually over dope deals and lesbian fights. They result in occasional write-ups, but no more than that.

Meanwhile, I, who've few write-ups, all only for nonsense, am in lockdown. Do I care? No. Compared to the madness of the general population, this is heaven. My plan is to look into a civil rights suit on this once I am out. Or, if I'm here long, I'll file from back here.

I'm on mild antidepressants — a first for me. It's the result of living a zoo. The inmates are like no others I've met (uneducated, mean, junkies, loud, . . .Their ideals are non-existent. But look where they come from. Backgrounds just the same). I know this sounds shallow. I'm not judging these people. . . But try living in dormitories with them.

The cops act insane, they yell, swear, throw in new rules at will. Oddly, the best cops work where I'm housed.

I look as I've always looked — except much older. I only read part of the book. I was furious at much of it.

Thanks so much for your letter. It came at a lovely time, as I can't get to my addresses (they won't let me have them). However, as people write, I'll gather them. . .

Sincerely from my hole,

Suzan

Hi, Jenny,

I got your letter a couple of weeks ago. Forgive the delay. It's *this place*!! You have to dig that I've ended up in about the worst prison in Calif. and I'm devastated.

The fact is I'm practically a model prisoner — not do to any love of the system but because I'm not into heroin, promiscuity (both inmate's and guard's), etc., etc., etc.. The prison I'm in consists of *"the mix"* . . . chaotic, even barbaric. The guards go for it. . . it's control. What can I say? It's *"the life"* . . . dig? I myself, am under investigation *still*. I'm refusing to cooperate without a lawyer. The charge is absurd (now that they've shared that info with me), hence I know the investigation is rigged, so I'm demanding my rights. I tend to think that when prison officials get bored, my child, with its political stuff, etc., it gets tempt- ing i.e., by boosting me up as *major*, they boost themselves up. There- fore, our letters are delayed. They're supposed to Xerox, then send. However, laziness prevails and delays are endless — basically my prison life was mellow before I transferred here. I run 5 or more miles a day. I worked as a jeweler, made enough money to survive, had several kitty-cat friends (no pets, here). Had educated friends, lived in a room with the roommate of my choice, never had the door locked, played with cats, etc.. Now I'm living on the will of God exclusively. It shall be interesting to see how it turns out. I doubt that V.S.P. will accede to my demand for a lawyer, ha ha, but technically I'm within my rights.

Now, as to your letter — you *poor* thing, of course I didn't think the talk of exchanging pictures was a "move." Ha ha — *again*! Actually, at 110 lbs and 5'10 I'd love one of you, if it were me. . . wow, that is slim.

No, I meant my picture is on the front of a book. I thought that was the book you were referring to. So another hideous book is out. Well, let me assure you, I, like the infamous "Manson Girls" and others are probably the mellowest, most educated people in prison. Strange but true. One can reprioritize and accept the past with its tragic events, without dying, if still alive.

OK, talking about "earlier experiences." Via Xerox is a bit much, don't you think. Let me see off investigation first. Then I'll touch on a few things. Reading your rap about the frustration of being from a com- fortable background and then having your eyes opened about the finan- cially guided rape of the earth and of truth and justice — well, yeah. Put it this way, I was a philosophy major in college, and I believed in being true to truth. Of course I wouldn't act now as I did then, but I'll say that what I saw 20 years ago is coming to pass . . . there is such darkness. I dropped out of society as a protest — things escalated. But as I say, these raps can wait.

As to rapes and violence here — yeah. Much violence. . . but mostly mental anguish. The inmates and guards have values of garbage. But some of the inmates and guards are ok. They also despise the oth-

ers. The fact that I'm housed in isolation during investigation is a blessing really. I've had to start eating meals — I was very weak before I did.
I just figure God knows my heart. . . It's a violation of my rights, but so
be it.

Well, what do I look like? Hmmm. Curly brown-gray-white hair.
It's past my shoulder. 110 lbs, 5'4. . . muscular legs (many compliments
are paid to them) because I run. Pretty — I'm told — but older. Basically I look intelligent and I laugh as much as possible. I mean I'm basically happy and to myself. If idiots try to pick arguments I ignore them
(they act like 6th grader's). . . not quite. I was in boarding school at 6th
grade, I was a kind, nice person. . .

So you're married (mostly happy). What an honest person. I love
it. No, I get no pick-up lines. I think my look of intelligence terrorizes
people, ha ha.

Thanks so much for your letter. It brings tears because you've hit
so many nails on the head.

Your new friend,

Suzan

(Heart drawn with explanations: A Juti heart to you (I'm Moslem — not a blade Muslim — that's another trip!)

Dear Jennifer,

Finally! I couldn't find "*that perfect*" time to write. I just said,
"Screw it." Perfect, no, but passable. You see, I'm in a dorm, as in rarely
alone now. However, it's basically quiet. Everyone is sated from breakfast brunch (9000 charming Cholesterol calories. . . the food planning
here is strictly from the 1950's) I had juice and coffee. I got busted taking out toast. Pat searches. Unreal. The prison I came from, C.I.W., was
nothing like this, *nothing*!!! Not to worry. Roll and baked potato tonight,
plenty to "steal," haha. Also, I keep food at "home."

So, here I am, armed with earplugs and Walkman. Jazz. The most
"joyful" character here is a fat, old black lady, who runs around saying
"Mother Fucker" in every sentence as she comments on the incompe-
tence of staff and inmates. Many subscribe to her mentality. Some
don't. Thank God. There are 8 to a dorm. That's a Civil Rights suit that
I have to — at some time — get to. Men lifers aren't dorm housed.

Women are because women aren't outwardly violent. Only inwardly. Basically I say little and ignore mean innuendos from bored, ignorant people.

So why am I not in "*non-seg jail?*" Well, the investigation concluded. . . without my participation. I might add this. You're supposed to cooperate, dig. It seems some chick went to some cop and said I was planning to escape. On hearsay, they arrested me. Unreal. One wonders if that chick was chastised, since I was found innocent. I doubt it. Furthermore, I was charged with "conspiracy to escape". Ha Ha. Where was my co-conspirator? One does not conspire to escape — alone! What I'm saying, is they didn't even get the paperwork right.

They spring my jail release on me before I had a chance to figure out what to do, however, they were super nice about releasing me. Actually, the Warden released me. He gave me a choice of CCWF — a prison across the street that is also dormed. (Same scene) At first I was going to go. Then I found out I could go instantly to work in P.I.A. Optical. (Prison Industry Authority). Make glasses. 30 cents an hour and up. There was a 9-month waiting list. However, I go to the top of the list. It's quite hilarious how I was given the royal treatment when I was found innocent. (Frankly I thought they'd lie and find me guilty. It was almost a hope since I love the housing — no roommates.) So I await my job — probably this week. It entails moving to a different part of the prison (yard B as opposed to yard C).

Because I take antidepressants — 50 mg. Trazzadone — I do not live in the same unit with my co-workers — a plus. I'll live in a medical unit. The idea of living with whom I work with is not good. Some evil person can plague you at work and at home that way.

Also, I was unallowed in the yard at night when I went to jail. Now I go out at night. Ha Ha Ha. And dig the rumors about me, on my return: I hit a cop, I attempted suicide, I Protective-custodied myself, I told a cop I was planning to escape, I had a map of V.S.P., I ran to the fence. What did I do? I walked around with my paperwork and flashed it. I pointed out that I'd still be in jail if any of these things were so, I also found out who my enemies were (people who'd formerly informed me they were my friends and who I'd never trusted).

So now I've caught you up. I *love* your picture. You have a strong, pretty, intelligent face (Me Too!) Is that your son? He is adorable. I'm off to the yard to run and to hang out with a *real* friend — who was true to me in my absence.

I'm back. It's now afternoon. Everyone is sleeping. Not me and not my friend, we actually *do things*. Anyway, I ran 5 miles, walked with a friend, ate lunch and read a Lawrence Sanders book. I actually love his writing. I reread your letter. Thanks for the kudos on my prose ability. Actually my husband and I wrote a book called "A Cry For War." (A manifesto is what it was called by the secret service, ha). It was never published — obviously. The point of it was that those individuals in control of the world economy cared nothing for the ecology of the earth. Exactly what had the animals done to reap the effects of living in a poisonous environment? What justified it all? You know the rap. So our point was: maybe violence would get the message across, since love (60's/70's) hadn't. Naturally, it was never taken seriously. Not even by us. People will never rebel when they have enough to eat.

I basically came from a wealthy background, saw the world for what it was and rebelled. Not in the right way — obviously. Just lost it. I don't mean to undermine what happened. I feel like my intentions were on, but tragedy did not have to happen. My fault. Michael's. A dangerous, powerful combination.

My studies are a branch of Islam. Whirling Dervishes are followers of sufism. It's the mystical branch of Islam. The heart and wings. . . their color is green. I know you asked other questions . . . more later.

Suzan

Good Morning, Jen,

I'm actually in a space of relative peace and quiet (accent on relative) I'm listening to N.P.R. Weekend Edition (news). Your letter reached me by going to C1, mailroom, B4, mailroom, B1 (yes, it practically toured the prison). I started working in P.I.A., the only place you can make money as opposed to "custody" which is all jobs in the prison. The pay goes from nothing to $36.00 a month. The pay in P.I.A. starts at $45.00 a month and goes to 150.00 — you start at 30 cents an hour. Anyways, P.I.A. means I can save money for running shoes, TV Guide, a TV if mine breaks, etc. . . .when I was transferred from C.I.W. I lost all my expensive running shoes. They had colors on them. Here you can have only white, *please*!! Anyway, when I left — was removed, snarl —

from C.I.W. I'd saved $780.00. Thank God I'd chosen to save money. Now I'm at $180.00. I had to buy a different TV because my 13" one wasn't allowed. So, that was $300.00 because 9" TV's cost a fortune as there's no demand. I budgeted myself to $20.00 a month canteen — easily done. I was getting quarterly packages so basically I was comfortable in that respect. My package sender can no longer send packages, which is fine as now I'm working. The plan is to budget myself to $25.00 a month — plenty of money. . . and to save the rest. I've a friend who'll send packages next summer when she gets out. (Naturally that's at *her* insistence). The way I stretch my money is I go to "chow" ha ha and "export" (put in my sports bra) food I want for later. . . after my run or whatever. Actually, I eat in the evening while I watch an hour or two of TV in "relative" quiet. Actually, eating in the "chow" hall is ridiculous; it's loud! However, I always eat with mellow people, which brings me to my new unit. It's the mellowest unit in the prison, Thank God!! I do. From my near suicide, to bogus arrest, to anti-depressants, to vacation in Ad Seg, to practically an apology from the Warden and instant job at P.I.A. (no piggies, cops. . . are in P.I.A). *Smart* people running around working *hard* abound there. . . to a mellow unit. I view that as God's will that I not do the suicide protest trip. I really view that absurd jail trip on a *miracle* to get me out of one set of circumstances and to put me in another set of circumstance where I can survive. Why it was God's will that idiot the C.D.C. get away with the *bogus* removal of me, who was actually loved by some, from CIW to VSP (*Hell*) is only known to God. But I tell you, there I am, out on the yard telling my friend that it's time to die and 2 minutes later I'm arrested because some chick tells a cop I'm planning to leave. Do you dig that that's hearsay — only in VSP would they arrest you on hearsay. Who said it, I know not. I don't care who it was. I doubt she got written up, but she should have, do you dig that my charges were "Conspiracy to Escape?" I used to joke endlessly about "where's the co-conspirator". One can not conspire with oneself. Yes Jen, they did drop all charges. In PIA I can be funny and race around. I ended up in the one department that is dirty and fast and racing about. There's about 30 of us — mostly white or non-ghetto black and Mexicans, of course — but mostly white. My room has relatively nice people — no ghetto types thank God. I'm not a racist, but the prison breeds the gang issue, and they come in here, already having succumbed to that thinking. . . it's horrific. I'm also not a born again. I've seen them in action. *No*, I say it "sardonically" (thanks for the great word, I've not thought of in years). But anyhow, I am Christian. I say "God Willing" with a loving, exasperated look at the heavens. I'm a Moslem but nothing like prison or "Muslims" — they've done to Islam what Born Agains have done to Christianity. My opinion of the New Testament is it's great until you get to Paul.

Okay. . . . so wherever I was when I started this stream of consciousness rap was probably covered by the rap! Now that I'm mentally in a space where I can be me I'm able to do more than limp along as I write you. Your son is so cute — smart, you can tell by his bone structure and look. In fact, I was delighted at how sporty and together you look. Great. I just don't relate to stupid people. *That* sounds superior, but you lose time for fluffy explanations when you live here. It's enough that I don't go wild. I feel it's okay to be a bit critical. Live my life.

Yeah, I dig your personal thoughts that one with "eyes to look around" can drop out afraid of what they see around them. What I think is the next level of "intelligent" life then gets to rise up, and grab all the jobs with status. In their stupidity, they feel they have arrived. They call themselves "professionals" such as doctors. Unreal. Tiny lives. Life is not perfect. It's as if we are compelled to go against our best interests, by our inward moral path (idiots which are in mass in prison prove their "best interests" without a thought to goodness or fairness. "Doing the Done Thing" is an unknown concept to the overweight, beer drinking masses. Another sub-culture, another topic.

I love hearing about the dramas of your life. . . and of course, you are a wonderful writer. You get insights which is what a writer must have. OK, let me look thru this letter. Yes, you'd find me hilarious. When I'm my normal, happy self, I laugh more. I see absurdities, and somehow, I can laugh rather than become crazed. Rigidity is the rigor here. It's mindless. It can drive you mad. Naturally I don't go along with the program. I suspect that's why they think I'm escape material. It's because I'm so obviously not in lock-step. It's absolutely a "cop-out" to house long-termer women in dorms and not men. It's a violation. Yes "Bread and Circuses" (Cicero): Full stomachs, no rebellion. Yes, "quietly" run. The public should be put on notice if for no other reason than to be forced to "witness" the injustice. That way it can't be said, "Oh, we didn't know!"

Want to tell you about my husband. I love him. Next letter.

Suzan

Hi, Jen

I just got your letter and it's a special one. I love it. No, you weren't rambling — you were just tired. I mean, you were rambling, but not mindlessly, haha. I'm going to answer in increments. That is, it's Wed, 5:00 pm (classical music and earplugs block out my roommate). I'm back from work, showered, 2 grapefruits in tummy to stave off hunger and off to "chow". Normally I'd skip dinner, but I told my friend I'd go. Usually she works late — we work together, but she stays a couple hours late, so we couldn't eat together. No food is worth going for without a friend in hand. I mean you are surrounded by craziness. Anyway, I've been totally busy, Thank God. I'll answer as I get space — time to do so. Of course I love it that you consider my letters an event (me to you). I just got a letter from husband Michael. You know, it's such a long rap. I mean, our life together. Should you ever get down this way it would be so much easier to explain. Yes, I can have visitors and no I have not, or yes, I have none — whatever. Anyway, it came as a surprise, but it was a very sweet letter. So perhaps we'll start writing again. Actually I feel rather loved, what with your letters and his, now. He is almost 9 years my junior. Very smart, was going to be a diplomat, Jewish (but Moslem too. We became Moslems 20 years ago). We met, fell in love instantly (I was 35). We trekked to many countries, wanted to save the world, environmentally, became militant, and it goes on — In prison he became "gay" and I do not endorse his ideology/rationale. We've been at "war" for about 9 years. It tore me up when he turned gay. He writes now and again out of nowhere. He seems concerned and writes in a loving manner about my depression and need for meds. It's so not me but it makes sense if you know my spirit and how off this form of living throws it. I dig what you say about possessions. A friend says they "validate" you. Those colors, textures, drawings, hats, Volkswagens, dangling earrings, validate you. Yes, I've done well financially in prison. Money is the most difficult thing to obtain. So I save a lot. But give myself treats. A TV is a must, as are shoes and coffee and treats. You just have to have these things in order to put a wall between yourself and the other mentalities. It's my sense of staying alive. Bold statements are a must. They may go unheard, but they must be made. Can God say to wrongdoers that they were told, if they weren't? One must confront — especially for the earth and the animals that have no voice, but are hurt by amoral, money-loving men. Not "mankind." That implies the good people.

Islam believes in prayer to God and not to Jesus (Jesus is considered a prophet, but not God). It's a simple religion of fasting and truth and goodness (perverted by present leaders and their followers). The Koran is comprised of poetry — Juran.

There is just so much to say, but this will do for now.

I came back. Frid., 5:30 pm. . . I just reread your letter. Trust me, I don't feel your worries/problems are trivial, or your desires to create understanding for women here. . . inside or outside, choices are so difficult. I remember life outside quite well. It's no picnic — there's just space to be yourself. I mean it's possible to get that in prison, just difficult. Unfortunately depression is my result. My peers and I need a "wall". I saw my shrink today. I told him I spent my life in prison trying to remain away from everyone. I also told him it was the only place I knew where a G.E.D. was the ultimate — for inmates and the guards, haha.

OK, so dig, "NightLine" at 11:30 is going to have a series on VSPW starting Friday night. It was a trip having the crew here for a week. They were all over. I might be on. I was interviewed at my job. The subject of this place vs. CIW came up. Believe me, I articulated away, so perhaps you'll see me.

Much love, keep on keeping on — against the insanity and continue as a great mom,

Suzan

Jenny,

What a long strange trip it's been. Jail — Ad. Seg. Yes, for no rea-son. Another note dropped Investigation for escape allegations. I was busted just after I got your Nov. letter. I just got my property yesterday. I had no way of getting your address. They won't give addresses. Access to personal property they take away. Recall that I told you that if you didn't hear from me, to write. The letter comes to Ad. Seg. Then I have your address and can write. I just got your little note, wondering, of course! I was going to wait until the weekend to write but I want to get this out tonight.

No way would I be too busy to write during the holidays. I got to eat Thanksgiving, Christmas and New Year's meat there, what a treat — snarl.

Okay, prepare for a shock. You will be — shocked, I mean. I have been happy of late. I found out 6 weeks after I'd started working at Op-tical that my best friend cared for me. Well, I care for her. It's a good thing. Neither of us have ever felt that sort of thing before. However, she has a stalker. The gal went ballistic and dropped a note to ISU say-ing we were planning the awful E word. A week earlier the stalker gal had threatened my lovely, good friend. "Hell hath no fury like a woman scorned. . ." Yuck.

Lo and behold, my friend, Jennette, and I were arrested at work. We knew instantly what had happened. We knew Stalker had dropped an anonymous note. As she knew I had just been under inves-tigation for escape, she played on that.

The fact the VSP Investigations honors anonymous notes is un-real. Normally prison investigations are conducted after evidence is found. Naturally we're innocent. But it took 7 weeks for them to clear us. We were able to talk and see each other and pass letters, so it was do-able.

So the idiot warden decides to reduce my custody, meaning I can't go out at night or have my job back. Illegal. The investigation turned up nothing, hence I get everything back. Well, I've thrown a sample of the legal hoops they'll be sent to dance thru if they don't return my custody status. It looks like they'll relent. I'll find out next week. I just found out this morning that it looks like they'll reverse themselves. The warden, it appears, actually said that not guilty didn't mean innocent. I've had great fun asking where the legal documentation for "Not Guilty Not Innocent" is. . .

My room is wonderful. My TV has great reception — not always the case is VSPW as we're talking steel and cement and electric fence.

It's so fun to have a TV and Food and Radio and *clothes*!!! This is getting old. PBS is on in front of me. It's an Antique Show. I'm just glancing at the pictures.

Jennette has been doing the kidney infection trip too. You were in the hospital? Wow.

Okay, your last letter. Well, no Michael is not still the love of my life. Ha. Ha. Ha. That is so liberating. Okay, other marriage: Young, got pregnant, divorced. First had two children. Boy/girl. Lived in Scotts-dale, Arizona — money.

I'm still rehashing in my head what the right and wrong of my life (crimes) prior to prison.

Was vegetarian for 20 years. Starvation in VSPW drove me to eat cow and fish. I don't eat chicken because of their captivity. I can't eat dairy and eggs gross me out. The food in CIW enabled me to remain vegetarian.

When I started eating meat — about the time we first wrote, I devoured it. I did not get sick. I got stronger. Yeah, my normal trip is vegetarian. Not here. Of course I de-grease everything. No pig, of course. Most of the food is turkey made of fake ham, etc.. I'm surviving well eating meat which I find hilarious. I'd never thought I'd eat meat. I also never thought love would enter my life again.

Only God knows. . . Get well, God bless, Suzan (sending visiting form. Again, love your pic)

Suzan

VERONICA COMPTON

The Copycat Killer: so Veronica Compton has been dubbed. She is serving life at Gig Harbor in Washington State for assisting the Hillside Strangler, Kenneth Bianchi, in one of his murder schemes. On the surface, her crime does seem frightening — she attempted to kill a young mother, with whom she was partying in Bellingham, Washington. During her trial, the media depicted Veronica as a sort of "Valley of the Dolls" meets "Serial Killer."

In truth, Veronica never murdered anyone. Her official crime is attempted murder; her unofficial crime is having associated with Kenneth Bianchi and, in a drug-induced state of fear, having attempted to murder in his name. Veronica has also committed the crime of being unpredictable, outspoken, and unfeminine. For example, prosecutor Dave McEachran has referred to Compton as "dangerous, because she is bizarre." A member of the parole board detailed his feelings about Veronica, stating, "such actions are abnormal for a woman. . . "

Veronica's prison record, activism, and creative work reveal the passionate and thoughtful woman buried beneath her early experiences of violence and drug abuse. Since her highly-publicized trial and subsequent incarceration, her prison "resume" has defined rehabilitation. In an article about her 1999 parole hearing, at which she was denied release, *The Seattle Times* dubbed her an "angel." Veronica has spent her years in prison constructively, starting anti-violence programs, initiating mural projects, creating art work, writing her own story, earning university credits, and even marrying, and bearing a daughter, whom she misses dearly. Veronica explains her reform and well-known efforts, writing, "Believe me when I say that prison is barren, unless you instigate a world within here... Many don't survive, and you don't hear about it out there. And many of us have been drugged into submission, to tolerate our hopelessness. . . ." Even behind bars, Veronica has poured her life and her energy into creative and crucial work.

In a strange reversal of fortune, it was Veronica's passionate approach to life and her intense self-motivation that first led to her relationship with the notorious serial killer Kenneth Bianchi, and later to the crime she attempted to commit in his name. By the late 1970s, Veronica was a Hollywood star in the making. The daughter of a Mexican immigrant father and a US-born Caucasian mother, Veronica was beautiful and talented. Barely 21 years old, she had already written, directed and performed in her first play, and had received favorable reviews.

The world of Hollywood's elite had invited her into the fold. Her lover, Nathan Shapell (a man old enough to be her father) of Shapell Industries, Inc., a major construction company, was seriously debating whether or not to leave his wife and begin a legitimate life with Veronica. She had also grown close to John Sachs, an heir to the Rothschild fortune and the youngest State Economist of California (appointed by President Richard Nixon). Recognized as the protégé of the late Lawrence Merrick, the past president of the Independent Motion Pictures Producers of America Guild, Veronica had been trained in producing, directing, writing, and acting. During her two years of study with Lee Strasberg, she wrote and acted in a variety of stage plays and appeared in three movies. John Fulton, her best friend, was the president of the Philip Morris Talent Agency. Looking back, Fulton recalls that "everyone loved Veronica. What she did was a travesty; but what they've done to her is far worse... they took nothing into consideration, and we lost a truly great woman..."

Struggling to attain true stardom, Veronica decided to become the first woman to get inside the head of a serial killer. Kenneth Bianchi, part of the infamous "Hillside Strangler" duo, had killed or participated in the murders of at least a dozen women in Los Angeles, California, and Bellingham, Washington. Recently arrested, Bianchi claimed to be suffering from a dual personality disorder and described himself as a sort of "Jekyll and Hyde" — sweet, loving father and husband by day and vicious rapist and killer by night. Later, however, psychologists would prove Bianchi's claims false, and Bianchi himself would admit his guilt.

Veronica initiated her relationship with Bianchi as research for the play she planned to write, direct, and star in, entitled "The Mutilated Cutter," about a female serial killer. She thought that if only she could get into his mind, she could put it on paper. Unfortunately, Veronica underestimated both her own vulnerability and Ken's power of manipulation. They were soon interacting on a first-name basis. Veronica struggling with her career, raising a son alone while her husband was in jail on a drug-smuggling charge, attempting to convince her lover Nathan of her undying love and devotion, and fighting a drug addiction of her own that could be traced all the way back to her childhood. She felt desperate and out of control, and when Ken offered to "take control", she willingly submitted.

Ken knew exactly how to get into Veronica's head — how to prey on the part of her that had been abused and abandoned. Raped at age twelve by a neighbor, a runaway within the same year and shortly thereafter kidnapped into a prostitution ring for a brief period, Veronica had often felt that life was beyond her control. As a child, she had suffered from what would later be identified as a kidney disorder, and spent much of her time in hospitals and on various medications. Veronica learned early on that drugs were an easy way to deal with pain, and as the pain of losing herself in her relationship with Ken increased, she began self-medicating to the point that her addiction began to impair her normal functioning and to distort reality. Her drug use became so severe and critical that she suffered frequent hallucinations and convulsions.

Throughout everything, however, Veronica held herself together on the outside. As John Fulton explains, "At this point, no one knew how involved Veronica was with Bianchi, or with drugs. Someone would have helped her," but none of her friends knew just how much help Veronica truly needed. Only her husband (a marriage arranged by her father to cover for her illegitimate son) grasped the depth of her illness, and his anger towards Veronica for her lack of love and frequent affairs kept him silent.

When Ken proposed that Veronica commit a murder in his name, in order to throw the police off his tracks, she agreed. Veronica wanted only to be safe, and Ken promised to take care of her and her son when he was released — at the same time, he threatened to turn her in to the police and have her son removed from her custody if she did not comply.

The plan was for Veronica to go to Bellingham, Washington, a small town on the US-Canada border. There, she would find a woman who matched the profile of his previous victims, strangle her with a rope that Ken himself had tied and smuggled from his cell, and then send a pre-taped confession (the recorded voice of one of the actors being considered for her play) to the police. Ken figured that if the police thought that the "real" Hillside Strangler were still at large, then they would have neither the reason nor the right to continue holding him.

In September of 1980, Veronica went to Bellingham, disguised as a pregnant woman. She lured Kim Breed, a cocktail waitress at a local bar, into partying with her after work. Together the women drank, drugged, and drove around town, finally ending back up at the cheap motel where Veronica was staying. Following Ken's general plan, Veronica asked Kim if she would help her take some "joke" bondage photos, and Kim agreed. Once Kim was partly tied up on the bed, however, Veronica attempted to strangle her with the noose Ken had sent. When Kim struggled under Veronica's body, and attempted to fight back, Veronica panicked, dropping the rope and allowing Kim to escape. While Veronica lay on the floor sobbing, Kim screamed at her in fear and shock. Soon, however, Kim became more concerned with Veronica's obviously over-drugged and surprisingly fragile condition, and asked her if needed help. Veronica waved her off and, once Kim had left, wandered into the street and passed out in some bushes. Meanwhile, Kim returned to the motel with her boyfriend and had sex — in the bed where only a short time before Veronica had attempted to strangle her.

When a concerned couple walked Veronica back to her room and found Kim and her boyfriend there, Kim refused to look Veronica in the eye.

The next morning on her way back to L.A., Veronica sent the tape to police as planned, even though no murder had taken place. In fact, Kim failed to report the incident to the authorities until she heard a news story that seemed oddly familiar: police were looking for Kenneth Bianchi's accomplice in Washington State. Kim called the police, and Veronica was quickly apprehended in L.A., and held in Sybil Brand Jail. Veronica remembers: "There I was with the Manson women [a decade earlier they had etched their names in the cell wall], and Carol Bundy. All I could think was, what the hell have I done? This isn't me."

Whether it was her or not, Veronica was convicted of attempted murder and sentenced to serve natural life at the Washington Corrections Center for Women in Gig Harbor, Washington. According to the court, Veronica was so "vile" that she deserved to spend her life behind bars. Her imprisonment, however, did not signal the end of the media's focus on her case. From rising star to notorious inmate, Veronica found her life plagued with negative attention and unwanted advances. Douglas Clark, Carol Bundy's lover and co-killer, sent Veronica letters in disguise, claiming first to be a young man on the outside interested in her case, and later representing himself as a wrongly-convicted death row inmate. The "affair" became news, and even newspapers carried the story of serial killer romance.

Nevertheless, incarceration has not stopped Veronica from trying to do what she believes is right. The story of Veronica's brief 1988 escape illustrates that no matter how she may be represented, ever since getting off of drugs her priorities have remained clear: being there for those who need her in whatever capacity possible. By 1988, eight years had passed since Veronica had received a letter or a phone call from her son. Though she had mailed him packages and letters on a weekly basis, Veronica's father (who had custody of the boy) refused to allow contact — even going so far as to change the family's home phone number.

After years of silence, Veronica was shocked when one of the prison's counselors informed her that her son — now thirteen — had been running away, had been taken into state custody, and had even been housed in a juvenile facility for a period, in response to abuse at home. When Veronica was told that her son wanted to speak with her, she was stunned. On the phone, her son broke down and confessed just how much he needed his mother to be there with him. "Mom," he said, "mom, I want you to come home. I need you." Veronica told him to just "hang in there" and she would figure something out.

Three weeks later, Veronica walked out of the Washington Corrections Center for Women and headed for California. By the time she arrived in California and called her son's girlfriend, however, the FBI had already picked up her son and staked out his girlfriend's house. Veronica left a message for her son to meet her at a location in Arizona the next week. Desperate to give her son a real chance at life and happiness, Veronica planned to obtain matching false identification for both herself and her son, and then to take him to Mexico to live until he turned 21, at which point she would turn herself back in to the police. Instead, Veronica was apprehended, sentenced to an additional two years for her escape, and separated once again from her son. Veronica finds it ironic that during the efforts to recapture her, the psychologists who consulted on her case knew immediately that she had gone after her son and nowhere else.

Veronica and her son, now 26, have continued their relationship independently of the father. Though the son still struggles to overcome the confusion and fear that characterized his early years, Veronica says that they both love each other very much and are eager for a time when they can begin to make up for lost years.

While in prison, Veronica has also grown close to her mother, who speaks on behalf of incarcerated women and prison reform at conferences and activist gatherings. Veronica is now married to a retired political science professor, who listened to her presentation at a seminar in the prison and fell in love. The couple has been together for ten years and have a six-year-old daughter. Though awarded a brief parole in 1996, Veronica was returned to prison after only a couple of weeks, leaving her daughter without a mother who could be physically present. Today, Veronica's thoughts are often on her daughter, who suffers from a heart condition and spends much of her time in and out of hospitals and doctors' offices.

In an effort to meet her daughter's needs, Veronica has been seeking parole. For her most recent hearing, Veronica secured recommendations from a number of psychologists with whom she had been working for years. Their overwhelmingly positive comments read like an outstanding resume: "Based on my contact with Mrs. Compton and after consulting with staff who have known her, it is without reservation that I recommend that she be paroled and allowed to reunite with her family;" "I can see no reason at this time that Ms. Compton should not be paroled to live with her family. I believe that she will be a productive member of society and a great asset to any community in which she chooses to live;" "Veronica is more than recommended for release; there is nothing left for her to accomplish here."

Despite her impressive record and overwhelming evidence of rehabilitation, Veronica's 1999 request for parole was denied. For Veronica, who has now spent close to half her life in prison, incarceration has been a series of triumphs and unforeseen punishments. At times she has suffered from severe depression, yet her letters reveal the creative energy that is a continuous presence in her life and personality. She has written numerous chapters of an autobiography, and her skill as a dramatic actress and talented playwright show through.

Above all, Veronica has recognized, confronted, and dealt with the trauma that her act caused. Veronica admits that, in prison, she has been able to come to terms with her addictions and delusions, but her letters also chronicle the ways in which every day is a struggle for survival. Veronica has grown close to the women involved in the programs she runs, and preserves her sanity through her activist work and the friendships that have developed out of her efforts. Veronica writes that: "Rehabilitation is real. . . I needed to be here to know myself, to understand the demons driving me so close to evil — Kenneth, drugs — I had to come to understand how I could be so self-defeating, in spite of topical successes. Who I became, who many of these women become as 'criminals,' originates in early sexual and physical trauma. . . but one does heal."

Dear Jenny,

I enjoyed talking with you by phone. It is easier for me to get a feel for someone if I can intimate better. It's easier to do so when you can actually hear someone's voice, their way, before beginning a correspondence.

I couldn't believe how much more there was to share. I thought it rather odd that we were both intrigued by the same books and authors — even Frances Farmer. I didn't know people remembered her work.

I told you things about Kenneth I haven't spoken of — I'll elaborate in my tapes. Speaking of Frances Farmer, I think I relate because of the insanities she went through, under the guise of "healing." I know I needed to heal as well, but it was the craziness within the world — access to drugs, the lifestyle — that allowed me to know the freedom of such a wild and bizarre lifestyle. Not all of us can take it. Many of my friends were able to live as I describe, and go on to become Federal Court judges, actors, writers. . . I just went insane. And in prison, I spiraled further. When I refer at times to my institutional life as a time when I changed for the better, it only refers to the confinement. Believe me when I say that prison is barren, unless you instigate a world within here. Women commit suicide all around me. I think I'm only alive because I learned to be so strong. Many don't survive, and you don't hear about it out there. And many of us have been drugged into submission, to tolerate our hopelessness. I won't even touch on the rapes, the lapses of time spent in the hole; it's destructive to me, when I know it's around the corner and beyond my control.

My crime, when I acted for Kenneth and tried to murder that young woman, was utterly heinous. I have wanted to confront her since; rather, be confronted. But she has gone on with her life, which I'm happy about, for her. She needs to know how very sorry I am. Ironically, it was all of my life before that night which allowed me to become so sadistic during that time. I wonder, now and again, how she fares. If what I did lingers. I pray she is strong.

It was such a bizarre time. I picked her up, we went back to a hotel to do drugs — neither of us were virgins, but she was nevertheless an innocent, naive. I was disguised with a pillow under my shirt, a wig, glasses. Ken told me to be as "approachable" as possible. I refer to those days, in reference to Ken Bianchi, as the days of my "Master." Some call it a cop-out. He was, though — entirely. I don't know. . . but if any women out there have ever felt hostage to a man, this was another slant on an age-old crisis for a woman. Control. I felt so horrid about myself. As I deteriorated, he grew stronger. He knew he had me — someone to do his bidding.

Anyhow, Karen "drugged and drank" with me. Then I offered, as a "photographer," to take her picture. We shed our clothes, and it got a bit wild. I tied her up for bondage pictures, and that's when I tried to strangle her. It was important that I was precise in creating a pattern killing. Ken had gone over the exact way to tie the rope a hundred times with me. It had to look like a Hillside Strangler had done it, or he wouldn't go free. But instead of murdering, I passed out. She came back after I had run off, and actually made love to her boyfriend on the bed. It's strange, but she wasn't, at the time, too unraveled. It was almost two days before she decided to tell the police. Ken was the one who really pressed the issue of the manic copycat killer who was in love with him, killing to emulate him. She was less frightened, less willing to create, well, what I am now. . . cell-bound. It was Ken. At the cost of my life, my son, my sanity (which he knew damn well was all but dissipated) he let me die, alive. I am so sorry for the woman. But I still can't believe that it was me, tightening the rope. It wasn't me in every way but physically. No, that's not it, exactly; mentally, it's what I had become. Scary. That's the positive to confinement. The horrifying reality of spending enough time alone with your thoughts, your deed, to finally relent and feel everything. To give up the ideologies that made you crazy in the first place. To humble, to heal. That is the miracle for some of us here.

It's enough to say that my father was entirely dominant, until he was gone (memories are almost as impacting) — my mother couldn't take his infidelity and asked for a divorce. Myself and my brothers were mocked, half white, half Hispanic in an upscale, white community. Drugs became my life-line. Somehow, like my abuse I was able to keep my addiction a secret. By the time I met Ken, I was entirely drugged, vulnerable, distorted. . . My insecurities began so early on. The drugs were a safety net I used even as a girl. I was "susceptible."

Molestation began at five. I was raped a twelve: I was trying to "fit in" and got into a car with a teenager from my neighborhood. A slick kid, fancy car. I was twelve. He coerced me into taking drugs with him, then he raped me. That was my first introduction to "intimacy." My brother tried to become "head of household." I can't blame him for his abuse — he only had my father to model. But however it came to pass, he hurt me a great deal, physically and emotionally.

I kept my feelings to myself. I went to finishing school and then I ran off. I tried to live with my father, who had moved to Los Angeles. Hollywood Hills. It was a grand life, but incredibly dysfunctional.

I was just at that age when men begin to look at you like a woman, but you're not. I dated his friends (dad's). I was pregnant by a well-known boxer as a teen. I ended up a "Compton" to save my reputation. My father's friend worked on the Apollo missions and he had a son who agreed to "help" by marrying me. I thought his wealth was "family money." He was actually hooked up with a druglord from Mexico (more on tapes). Not long after our marriage, he was imprisoned there. In a selfish sense, it was a "good thing" for me: I never loved him. By this point, I was totally addicted to cocaine. . . hallucinating, convulsing. I recall seeing Kenneth on the 6 o'clock news — if I'd have known his power. . . My God. If I had known how powerless I was at that point. . .

I will describe in my tapes.

Take care,

Veronica

Veronica,

A quick note to let you know that I am praying for your daughter. I am so sorry that she is so ill. I thought about why I should include a letter about your child's sickness within the pages of a book. I think that it's important to know that there is so much that is out of your control. When I think how much time has gone by, how you've married and have this beautiful child, and now when she is sick, you can't get the hospital to accept your calls to check on her. She may die, and you have to live within your restraints. I listen to your voice right now, and you are hollow, quiet, barely above a whisper. It's as if you are an animal, trapped. You love her so much, you send her pictures and let her talk on the phone to our daughter; but you can't touch her when she needs you the most, and there is probably nothing more nightmarish for a mother. I know what she is to you: the reason you keep your sanity.

Thank God you have a husband and mother — when it's a time like this and you are, as you describe, "helpless to stand by watching your baby possibly die." I suppose the only thing to remember is the thousands of women who have no help. Look at how you have helped them, think what you have said to them in the tech-unit, as they've laid in your arms after a suicide attempt. A woman will try to kill herself because she can't get to her child. You have made it a "mission" at Gig Harbor to help those women get through the craziness within the confines at that place. Now you need to take those tools and help you, and thank God for a husband and mother who love her like you do.

I will keep in touch with your daughter during the next couple of days via her nurse and your family. I know now is not an appropriate time to discuss prison. I will say that the tapes are fascinating. I enjoy our calls, and have come to realize you mean a lot to my life. You have been most significant to me. No only do you offer yourself, your "insider" view allows me to understand others and I thank you for that gift.

Jen

(I'm not discounting the details of your previous marriage, Ken, or anything you wrote about. I just am leery to burden you when your child is so ill.)

Hi Jen,

Thank God, she is okay. Thank you for not making me rehash other issues while I rode that out. You are right. . . she is the most important being in my world, and it sort of took over my body. I was enraged at the constraints, yet I am conditioned to know nothing else. . . . it has been so long. No solace. People feel we deserve our punishments, and that means watching our own children suffer, helplessly, I suppose many wish for that, too. I can't blame them. It's the way things have been set up. So much hatred is planted. It's all I can do to survive, knowing that Jillian is ill and I can't touch her. I have support here, but you're right — I can't call out, not the hospital, or any place else. I have to leave it to God. Easier said, but I'm learning faith is the one thing I can have always, even as unpredictable as everything else may get.

Helping the women was good advice. I spent the weekend in a workshop. Again, people would think it is selfish to run an anti-violence program when my daughter was possibly dying. But in here, to maintain my sorts, that is how I survive. I can't be idle or it gets under my skin. The echoes and clamors and fighting and punishments. I put a barrier of "health" around me as best I can to stay alive. It sounds strange, but it's the things I'm involved in here that will keep me going.

None of what I say means I can stop thinking of my baby, it just will help me with my time, constructively. I'm so fortunate to have you and I appreciate your calls to the hospital. This is incredibly difficult for my husband to handle — and so hard for my mother.

About prison, briefly, I was denied my last parole hearing earlier this year. In spite of all the testimonials, I was told no, again. I try not to cry, but the thought of knowing I can't leave is so unbearable. I need to be with my family. My daughter needs me. I know that I did something horrible. I was barely into my twenties, I have been in prison half of my life now. I was stupid to think that I could get inside Bianchi's head. Grandiose. He ended up inside of my own (head). You know him, you know Woodfield, you know how these men operate. One minute you're there for an interview, the next you're the victim getting in their car. They charm. They manipulate. They terrorize. That's why they get away with it, again and again and again. Kenneth drew everything from me. One day I was interviewing him. One day, he seemed to know all about me. I was so drugged, I didn't see it coming — maybe I would have, sober. I know I wouldn't have acted out as some kind of hostage, robotically fulfilling his wants and needs if my mind hadn't of been drugged; let's face it, I was crazy. I wasn't deciphering reality at that point. I honestly wasn't taking responsibility for what I was doing. I was determined to continue this facade, to keep Kenneth thinking I was like him, so that he would talk to me. I wonder if he had me figured out all along — not just knowledge of my past, my vulnerabilities, but of my facade, relative to him.

I can remember letting him punish me over the phone, as if he could reach out and grab me if I didn't obey. I would self-mutilate, if that's what he wanted.

The newspapers are printing the parole denial. If there is anything good, it's that I know that while I needed to be in therapy (which I did receive here), I'm not the only one who thinks my time here has passed.

I'm so lonely. As I wrote in my journal after the decision, it's as though I can't breathe. I've tried so hard to do my best; to learn and to grow here. Not to mention, stay sane. It is endless, the work involved in detaching from this chaos, remembering to separate. I'm Veronica, I am not a part of everything wrong. I am here — but I know that I deserve to be free. Between the daily life, and my inner knowing of right from wrong, I must "work," yes, to keep myself afloat. This time one of the parole board members said that my crime was "especially heinous because I am a woman." He also said that "I had learned what to say, calculated in my responses, too much so to be trusted." I can't win. If I am honest and articulate my responses to their questions, I am acting. If I don't respond, I'm an unrehabilitatable prisoner, forever theirs. It's so frightening, I can't breathe. If I work hard here, it's in part to show my change, of course, but it's also because I want to be productive, human. It's nature. I need to feel hope, to be needed. I am punished for this. If I was rebellious or lazy, I would be unfit for society. I am in a trap, and the world cannot know. It's our secret. Mine and Gig Harbor's. It's so, so frightening. . .

I remember when I was given time for my "relationship" with Doug Clark (the Sunset Slayer). He was sending his letters from prison, to a friend's house, and then from there to me. He was posing as someone else. Someone interested in understanding my case. After responding for some months, he went public with my "love for him." The proof was the letters. They were almost academic they were so. . . loveless. But I was punished, anyhow. His lover and partner in murder, Carol Bundy, still believes that I was in love with him. We, ironically, were housed together at Sybil Brand Jail in L.A. She was terrifying. I'll never forget the way she would describe her crimes, her voice from down this dark hall. Decapitations, dressing up faces, having sex with dead bodies — Doug's favorite. I would think, I'm crazy, but I am *not* evil. What the hell has happened?!?!?

To have the Board tell me that my answers were cold and manipulative made no rhyme or reason. I have learned, admittedly in here, how to know myself. Is that calculated? It's what is sane. It took me, in honesty, fourteen years to become a healthy woman. I don't deny that. But now I speak truthfully and it's labeled cunning. I can't win. Between my daughter and these institutional standards, I feel hopeless, but I can't be that way, because of my daughter.

Veronica

Veronica,

Your life is overwhelming. When I read of your accomplishments, all from within an institution, and I look back at headlines from the late seventies, early eighties, it's as if it's two people. And to go back further, photos of you modeling, the program for your first play. . . you went from such a lovely young talent to such an addict. That's a simplification, but your harshness, your drugs, your selfishness. It wasn't you.

For one who knew such a rough start in life, you would never guess, seeing your eyes beam, in your photo with Lee Strasberg. . . did you know he was Marilyn Monroe's instructor, too? Just a bit of trivia. Anyhow, back to the subject.

You speak of your cell back in LA, after your apprehension. The word "Manson" scrawled on the wall by women from an era before you. You mention Carol Bundy whispering to you from a few cells down. A woman willing to decapitate other women for her lover, Doug Clark. You know, I met him during some previous research. He denies his "Sunset Slayings" in spite of the evidence. Carol still speaks of him affectionately, and about you with jealousy. If that were to amount to anything more than gossip, I suppose it touches clearly on issues of reformation — and lack of.

And more superficially, yet not because you were a Hollywood "starlet," there were the headlines. Obviously your career was ruined, but you could have hurt the lives of so many of your friends. Your journals. All the seedy information about who slept with whom, who was drugging, who you were sleeping with, who embezzled. Everyone trusted you. And when the courts asked for the documents, you said no. People don't realize part of the harsh penalty was a result of your unwillingness to "negotiate". I can see how good it would have been for so many investigators' careers, had you spilled the beans. A major sweep. And your silence just added more years to your incarceration. One newspaper quotes you as "rebellious". You were, in fact, totally loyal. Which is why, even now, your friends talk to me about you. Granted, they were stunned, as no one knew anything. But friends still call themselves friends, lovers still carry torches. You are not forgotten. Obviously, you were so much more than your crime.

What happened ultimately with Ken Bianchi was the end result of many other traumas. You learned to survive at all costs, but when it came down to it, you never "squealed". A child who learned to sell her body for food would later keep her mouth shut when the opportunity of time-off was available, in return for your very private journal. These people must have represented much more than "Hollywood Life," they must have represented your first true intimacies.

Jen

Jen,

Another nice call last night. Thanks. You seem to understand my. . . loyalties. I feel that way today, with you. I mean, a friendship developing. You are right, it is frightening to try to establish a friendship from "opposite ends of the world. . . " We both appear to feel "connected," but I am sure there is judgment. By now, I suppose that should be far behind me: Worries of what others think. Maybe it's my own fear of establishing a bond.

I'm glad you spoke with John (Fulton). He was an incredible friend. He was a lot more than the exec-vice of a movie studio (William Morris). You say today he is building — construction. Something like that? Regardless, it's nice to know that they all still keep tabs on me, that they all care about me. . . Now, you see why I could do nothing?

My own hands were tied. These were my first real friends. People who trusted me. I trusted. People who did not pimp me, who helped me with my career, who wished success for me. "Valley of the Dolls meets the Hillside Strangler." No one had hurt me there, in Hollywood;

only cared about me. What was I going to do? Screw everyone?

This is the first time I've ever given actual names for writing. I wanted it to happen in as positive a forum as possible. I remember John Sachs, heir to the Rothschild fortune; he was an attorney in Washington D.C. but visited "us" often in LA. He told me, when I returned from my hunt in Bellingham, I had one opportunity to get out of the country. After that, never call again. I declined. I didn't think I was in serious trouble. I was so wasted. Everyone was trying to help, to warn me. I thought what happened to Kim, what I had done, was horrific, but in my mind I never considered my actions an attempted killing. Yes, that's what I had promised Ken I would do — kill. I never felt, in my mind, I would follow through. I was acting out of submission, fear. He threatened to take my son, to tell people about the drugs, if I did not kill for him. I thought anything was worth keeping my boy. And then, up in Bellingham, I had her, straddled. I could have done it, but my heart wouldn't allow it. Some still say I was too drugged-out to go through with it — otherwise she'd be dead. Others say it was the drugs that got me there in the first place. It's like a parole board. Either way, I can't seem to find a side that will look at my actions without a bias, a hate. Probably the most honest depiction of that was after Doug Clark wrote to me, and I was under investigation. A female guard led me back to my cell, and she turned and looked at me and said, "I don't know, I just hate you." That's the way it is. Some people don't even know why they feel hate toward inmates. They can hear stories of their own suffering, of murder to self-protect. . . a million reasons besides "evil" why a woman ends up here, but people "don't know why. . . they just don't like us. . . "

I always knew I would write; women out there need to know how powerless their paths may render them. Everyone needs to at least try and understand that inmate doesn't necessarily equivalent with evil. I'm not saying we aren't here for the grief we have caused; but I will stand up for the many of us who have used our time to become well.

In a twisted way, I am the first to recognize the importance of. . . confinement. It's like the priesthood for the crooked. Nothing to do but meditate and contemplate. I have honed in on my art, my other skills, but most important, I have learned to be clear and honest about my past. With myself, that is. I feel ready to tell anyone who cares.

You ask why I've kept silent for these past two decades, regarding the media. I was approached by several studios about my story. You say John says I should go on *60 Minutes!* Well, my dear, I think it's time to talk. I'm finally ready. Many people who could have been hurt are dead. My own child can't be hurt by truth, and my old friends would respect my choices.

People find it odd a professor would marry me. It's like our friendship. Simply, we were allowed through atypical circumstances to meet. We are not monsters in cages. We think, need, feel, too. Sometimes, too much. . . Until you, I have felt that the core to any expose, book — anything — would have been my "Copycat Strangler" angle; a moniker I earned in an evening, that has never left my side. I feel I can be multilayered, better understood, within these pages, under the direction of an honest author and a respectable publisher. I know I can trust you to help me show my true self.

Veronica

The following is a letter to Veronica from her husband, written after their first visit in nearly four years.

My darling, Ver,

Wednesday afternoon. I'm just back from a 2 hr. walk, leg muscles as tight as cables. The printer is pounding out the first story which, of course, is in your hands with this. I've been thinking back on our visit like a man recalling the last oasis on his trek through the desert. What I recall with the greatest wonder is the utter normalcy of it, the sense of picking up just at where we were separated four years ago. Or rather in really a better place. I have never known you so at peace, so certain of yourself, of me; of our love and marriage. Being with you was in one way like a honeymoon, a loving encounter with all the fierce passion of a beginning. In another way it was much better, it was a homecoming like that of Ulysses to Ithaca, to the familiar and treasured after a long and terrible journey. We made of that trailer a home. I can think of nothing more hopeful than to know that after all these years, in the space of a few minutes we could do that. We've grown not just up, but wise. The ultimate wisdom is to know whom to trust, to know how to trust and to dare to do it. We did that and in it lies something more powerful than even love itself. Love so often sacrifices; trust relies. There could be no trust between us if we did not love, but a love between us without trust would be wounded. So hooray for our team, we made the cut! The prospect of more visits is beginning to seem real to me though still almost too good to be true. But the one we had was true and good; better than I could have hoped. *So* it's on cheerfully to the next and to all the others until they open the gates for you.

I have to close now. Partly I'm out of the habit of letter writing and need to start simply, partly I want to get this off today. So my beautiful wife, know that your husband is delighted with our time together, looks forward to more and meanwhile will try to keep all the plates at home well up in the air.

All my love, oh yes!
Your husband.

by Veronica Compton

Demystifying the female felon is an arduous chore. To truly under-stand a woman's crime we must first understand all that has preceded it. This means looking at the larger picture. In order to break through the mysteries and behaviors that hold us fear-struck, in contemplation of these female felons, we have to share a common premise: that women and girls are consistently abused in our society.

The women whom you have heard from in these pages are typical of women in prison. Ninety percent of incarcerated women have histo-ries of broken families, substance abuse, physical abuse, and sexual abuse. We know that for every action there is a reaction. I assert that most women in prison have committed their crimes either under the direction of and for a man, or in response to a man's behavior.

My own case is no exception. My decision to return with Jennifer Furio and revisit the most damaging and painful times of my life was one which required serious commitment and recognition of possible consequences for my mental health. I decided to go ahead with it be-cause it was a chance to strike a blow against the exploitative popular stories of women criminals. These usually rewrite the truth, to provoke further public hatred of the woman offender, in many cases piling un-deserved infamy on top of undeserved punishment.

My decision to embark on opening my personal Hell was influ-enced by Jennifer's refusal to take the standard exploitative approach.

She asked if there were mitigating factors, insights and opinions concerning the case studies of women offenders whose histories she was compiling for a book. These women had committed acts of serious violence but all had prior victimizations themselves. This was an opportunity to share information I had discovered in the works of Carol Gilligan, Lenore Walker, Judith Herman, Dusty Miller and Lenore Terri, among others. The works of these authors functioned cooperatively to help me derive a fuller truth of the female offender. I couldn't pass up the chance to work with Jennifer.

Jennifer worked to develop each woman's truth, taking care not to dismiss individual experiences because, until we can accept the particular experience of each female victim-turned-offender, we cannot discern that legally vital matter: her actual intent, or lack of criminal intent.

Our hope is to offer a perspective into the nature of the offender as she sees herself. As a society, the United States must face the formidable burden of unraveling the available materials now serving as qualitative analysis and theory on the female offender — those materials being constructed by men, from a male perspective.

Although such a woman-centered study would not have the appeal of the popular approach, Jennifer was adamant in her position as a feminist and a biographer desiring to serve the truths of these women with integrity. For myself, having directly participated in criminal behavior contrary to my own deepest desires, something that betrayed my value system, I had a great deal of confusion to sort out. To achieve this end, I've diligently pursued the "whys" of women who behave in self-undermining and destructive ways.

While mitigating factors may influence criminal behavior, they do not excuse the crime or diminish the victimization of the victim. However, they may place heavy burdens on questions of actual criminal intent. This should move society to inquire further into the basic character of the female perpetrator. I have referred Jennifer to a few specific case studies of people whom I know personally, and some of these appear in her text. The letters that form most of the case studies offer only a small window onto the full context of women's criminal violence; this book's purpose is to open up questions and inspire further study and theorization on this virtually hidden aspect of women.

As a writer, by profession — prior to my incarceration — I felt it my responsibility to offer some of my own thoughts; as a female convicted of a crime of violence, I felt it my duty to contribute the truths as I knew them.

ACKNOWLEDGEMENTS

I would like to acknowledge my family and the many activists and psychologists who supported me in preparing this work, and especially, the women who provided their stories. It took great faith, long hours, emotional exhaustion and family sacrifice on the part of many people to compile these works.

Author Dave Dun, a talented writer, provided ongoing support and encouragement.

Without Sonny Grosso's confidence in my examinations of the "dark side" of men and women that I met, I truly don't think I could have endured. While I respect his invaluable insights as a film producer and writer, I prize Mr. Grosso even more for his friendship and loyalty.

About the Author

Jennifer Furio lives in a small, bayside town on the West Coast. She is married, with two small children. She is working toward a Master's degree in women's studies and criminal psychology, and writes and lectures on the need for prison reform. She serves as a volunteer at a women's shelter, and as a Sunday School teacher and an after-school tutor.

Her first book, *The Serial Killer Letters: A Penetrating Look Inside the Minds of Murderers*, focused on why men may feel compelled to possess and violate women. It was a national success, leading to speaking engagements that have included the *Montel Williams Show* and *Inside Edition* and requests from TV talk shows such as *20/20* and *Dateline* for her "expert opinion," feature articles and interviews in magazines and newspapers as well as appearances on many regional television talk-shows and news programs.

Her third book, a biography of Veronica Compton, is scheduled for publication in late 2001.

Also from Algora Publishing:

CLAUDIU A. SECARA
THE NEW COMMONWEALTH:
FROM BUREAUCRATIC CORPORATISM TO SOCIALIST CAPITALISM

The notion of an elite-driven worldwide perestroika has gained some credibility lately. The book examines in a historical perspective the most intriguing dialectic in the Soviet Union's "collapse" — from socialism to capitalism and back to socialist capitalism — and speculates on the global implications.

DOMINIQUE FERNANDEZ
PHOTOGRAPHER: FERRANTE FERRANTI
ROMANIAN RHAPSODY — An Overlooked Corner of Europe

"Romania doesn't get very good press." And so, renowned French travel writer Dominique Fernandez and top photographer Ferrante Ferranti head out to form their own images. In four long journeys over a 6-year span, they uncover a tantalizing blend of German efficiency and Latin nonchalance, French literature and Gypsy music, Western rationalism and Oriental mysteries. Fernandez reveals the rich Romanian essence. Attentive and precise, he digs beneath the somber heritage of communism to reach the deep roots of a European country that is so little-known.

IGNACIO RAMONET
THE GEOPOLITICS OF CHAOS

The author, Director of Le Monde Diplomatique, presents an original, discriminating and lucid political matrix for understanding what he calls the "current disorder of the world" in terms of Internationalization, Cyberculture and Political Chaos.

TZVETAN TODOROV
A PASSION FOR DEMOCRACY – BENJAMIN CONSTANT

The French Revolution rang the death knell not only for a form of society, but also for a way of feeling and of living; and it is still not clear what e have gained from the changes. Todorov examines the life of Constant, one of the original thinkers who conceptualized modern democracy, and in the process gives us a richly textured portrait of a man who was fully engaged in life, both public and private.

MICHEL PINÇON & MONIQUE PINÇON-CHARLOT
GRAND FORTUNES – DYNASTIES OF WEALTH IN FRANCE

Going back for generations, the fortunes of great families consist of far more than money— they are also symbols of culture and social interaction. In a nation known for democracy and meritocracy, piercing the secrets of the grand fortunes verges on a crime of lèse-majesté . . . Grand Fortunes succeeds at that.

JEAN-MARIE ABGRALL
SOUL SNATCHERS: THE MECHANICS OF CULTS

Jean-Marie Abgrall, psychiatrist, criminologist, expert witness to the French Court of Appeals, and member of the Inter-Ministry Committee on Cults, is one of the experts most frequently consulted by the European judicial and legislative processes. The fruit of fifteen years of research, his book delivers the first methodical analysis of the sectarian phenomenon, decoding the mental manipulation on behalf of mystified observers as well as victims.

JEAN-CLAUDE GUILLEBAUD
THE TYRANNY OF PLEASURE

A Sixties' radical re-thinks liberation, taking a hard look at the question of sexual morals in a modern society. For almost a whole generation, we have lived in the illusion that this question had ceased to exist. Today the illusion is faded, but a strange and tumultuous distress replaces it. Our societies painfully seek a "third way", between unacceptable alternatives: bold-faced permissiveness or nostalgic moralism.

SOPHIE COIGNARD AND MARIE-THÉRÈSE GUICHARD
FRENCH CONNECTIONS –
The Secret History of Networks of Influence

They were born in the same region, went to the same schools, fought the same fights and made the same mistakes in youth. They share the same morals, the same fantasies of success and the same taste for money. They act behind the scenes to help each other, boosting careers, monopolizing business and information, making money, conspiring and, why not, becoming Presidents!

VLADIMIR PLOUGIN
RUSSIAN INTELLIGENCE SERVICES. Vol. I. Early Years

Mysterious episodes from Russia's past – alliances and betrayals, espionage and military feats – are unearthed and examined in this study, which is drawn from ancient chronicles and preserved documents from Russia, Greece, Byzantium and the Vatican Library. Scholarly analysis and narrative flair combine to give both the facts and the flavor of the battle scenes and the espionage milieu, including the establishment of secret services in Kievan rus, the heroes and the techniques of intelligence and counter-intelligence in the 10th-12th centuries, and the times of Vladimir.

JEAN-JACQUES ROSA
EURO ERROR

The European Superstate makes Jean-Jacques Rosa mad, for two reasons. First, actions taken to relieve unemployment have created inflation, but have not reduced unemployment. His second argument is even more intriguing: the 21st century will see the fragmentation of the U. S., not the unification of Europe.

ANDRÉ GAURON
EUROPEAN MISUNDERSTANDING

Few of the books decrying the European Monetary Union raise the level of the discussion to a higher plane. European Misunderstanding is one of these. Gauron gets it right, observing that the real problem facing Europe is its political future, not its economic future.

CLAUDIU A. SECARA
TIME & EGO – Judeo-Christian Egotheism and the Anglo-Saxon Industrial Revolution

The first question of abstract reflection that arouses controversy is the problem of Becoming. Being persists, beings constantly change; they are born and they pass away. How can Being change and yet be eternal? The quest for the logical and experimental answer has just taken off.

PHILIPPE TRÉTIACK

ARE YOU AGITÉ? Treatise on Everyday Agitation

The 'Agité,' that human species that lives in international airports, jumps into taxis while dialing the cell phone, eats while clearing the table, reads the paper while watching TV and works during vacation – has just been given a new title. "A book filled with the exuberance of a new millennium, full of humor and relevance. Philippe Trétiack, a leading reporter for Elle, takes us around the world and back at light speed." — Aujourd'hui le Parisien

PAUL LOMBARD

VICE & VIRTUE — Men of History, Great Crooks for the Greater Good

Personal passion has often guided powerful people more than the public interest. With what result? From the courtiers of Versailles to the back halls of Mitterand's government, from Danton — revealed to have been a paid agent for England — to the shady bankers of Mitterand's era, from the buddies of Mazarin to the builders of the Panama Canal, Paul Lombard unearths the secrets of the corridors of power. He reveals the vanity and the corruption, but also the grandeur and panache that characterize the great. This cavalcade over many centuries can be read as a subversive tract on how to lead.

RICHARD LABÉVIÈRE

DOLLARS FOR TERROR — The U.S. and Islam

"In this riveting, often shocking analysis, the U.S. is an accessory in the rise of Islam, because it manipulates and aids radical Moslem groups in its shortsighted pursuit of its economic interests, especially the energy resources of the Middle East and the oil- and mineral-rich former Soviet republics of Central Asia. Labévière shows how radical Islamic fundamentalism spreads its influence on two levels, above board, through investment firms, banks and shell companies, and clandestinely, though a network of drug dealing, weapons smuggling and money laundering. This important book sounds a wake-up call to U.S. policy-makers." — Publishers Weekly

JEANNINE VERDÈS-LEROUX

DECONSTRUCTING PIERRE BOURDIEU — Against Sociological Terrorism From the Left

Sociologist Pierre Bourdieu went from widely-criticized to widely-acclaimed, without adjusting his hastily constructed theories. Turning the guns of critical analysis on his own critics, he was happier jousting in the ring of (often quite undemocratic) political debate than reflecting and expanding upon his own propositions. Verdès-Leroux suggests that Bourdieu arrogated for himself the role of "total intellectual" and proved that a good offense is the best defense. A pessimistic Leninist bolstered by a ponderous scientific construct, Bourdieu stands out as the ultimate doctrinaire more concerned with self-promotion than with democratic intellectual engagements.

HENRI TROYAT

TERRIBLE TZARINAS

Who should succeed Peter the Great? Upon the death of this visionary and despotic reformer, the great families plotted to come up with a successor who would surpass everyone else — or at least, offend none. But there were only women — Catherine I, Anna Ivanovna, Anna Leopoldovna, Elizabeth I. These autocrats imposed their violent and dissolute natures upon the empire, along with their loves, their feuds, their cruelties. Born in 1911 in Moscow, Troyat is a member of the Académie française, recipient of the Prix Goncourt.

JEAN-MARIE ABGRALL

HEALING OR STEALING — Medical Charlatans in the New Age

Jean-Marie Abgrall is Europe's foremost expert on cults and forensic medicine. He asks, are fear of illness and death the only reasons why people trust their fates to the wizards of the pseudo-revolutionary and the practitioners of pseudo-magic? We live in a bazaar of the bizarre, where everyday denial of rationality has turned many patients into ecstatic fools. While not all systems of nontraditional medicine are linked to cults, this is one of the surest avenues of recruitment, and the crisis of the modern world may be leading to a new mystique of medicine where patients check their powers of judgment at the door.

DEBORAH SCHURMAN-KAUFLIN

THE NEW PREDATOR: WOMEN WHO KILL — Profiles of Female Serial Killers

This is the first book ever based on face-to-face interviews with women serial killers. Dr. Schurman-Kauflin analyzes the similarities and differences between male and female serial killers and mass murderers.

RÉMI KAUFFER

DISINFORMATION — US Multinationals at War with Europe

"Spreading rumors to damage a competitor, using 'tourists' for industrial espionage. . . Kauffer shows how the economic war is waged." — Le Monde
"A specialist in the secret services, Kauffer notes that, 'In the CNN era, with our skies full of satellites and the Internet expanding every nano-second, the techniques of mass persuasion that were developed during the Cold War are still very much in use – only their field of application has changed.' His analysis is shocking, and well-documented." — La Tribune

CARL A. DAVIS

PLANE TRUTH — A PRIVATE INVESTIGATOR'S STORY

"Raises new questions about corporate and tribal loyalties, structural engineering, and money and politics, in a credible scenario that makes my flesh creep. . . I think I'll take a train, next time. Or walk." — Western Review
"Takes us around the world and finds treasure under stones that had been left unturned After reading these 'travels with Carl,' (or is he Sherlock Holmes?), my own life seems very flat." — Book Addicts

JENNIFER FURIO

LETTERS FROM PRISON — VOICES OF WOMEN MURDERERS

Written by incarcerated women, these incredibly personal, surprisingly honest letters shed light on their lives, their crimes and the mitigating circumstances. Author Jennifer Furio, a prison reform activist, subtly reveals the biases if the criminal justice system and the media. The words of these women haunt and transfix even the most skeptical reader.

CHANTAL THOMAS

COPING WITH FREEDOM

40 million American women of marriageable age are single. This approachable essay addresses many of their concerns in a profound and delightful way. Inspired by the author's own experiences as well as by the 18th century philosophers, and literary and historical references, it offers insights and the courage to help us revel in the game of life, the delight of reading, the art of the journey, and the right to say "no" to chains of obligations and family.